The Ultimate Guide to

STRATEGIC MARKETING

Real World Methods for Developing Successful, Long-Term Marketing Plans

ROBERT J. HAMPER

New York   Chicago   San Francisco   Athens   London
Madrid   Mexico City   Milan   New Delhi
Singapore   Sydney   Toronto

1 2 3 4 5 6 7 8 9 0   DOC/DOC   1 9 8 7 6 5 4 3

ISBN   978-0-07-180909-2
MHID   0-07-180909-0

e-ISBN   978-0-07-180910-8
e-MHID   0-07-180910-4

This publication is designed to provide accurate and authoritative information in regard to the subject matter covered. It is sold with the understanding that neither the author nor the publisher is engaged in rendering legal, accounting, securities trading, or other professional services. If legal advice or other expert assistance is required, the services of a competent professional person should be sought.

—From a Declaration of Principles Jointly Adopted by a Committee of the American Bar Association and a Committee of Publishers and Associations

Library of Congress Cataloging-in-Publication Data

Hamper, Robert J.
    The ultimate guide to strategic marketing : real world methods for developing successful, long-term marketing plans / by Robert Hamper.
        pages cm
    ISBN 978-0-07-180909-2 (hardback)—ISBN 0-07-180909-0 (hardback)   1. Marketing—Management.   2. Strategic planning.   3. Business planning.   4. Marketing research.   I. Title.
    HF5415.13.H2764 2013
    658.8'02—dc23   2013023681

McGraw-Hill Education books are available at special quantity discounts to use as premiums and sales promotions or for use in corporate training programs. To contact a representative, please visit the Contact Us pages at www.mhprofessional.com.

This book is printed on acid-free paper.

To Koko and Kassie
whose support was always there

Contents

Part IV: Implementation and Control   255

9. Marketing Plan Implementation   257

10. Control and Monitoring of the Strategic Marketing Plan   273

Preface

The Ultimate Guide to Strategic Marketing illustrates and explains how to build a dynamic, future-oriented marketing plan for your company. This book provides the following:

- An overview of the marketing planning process.
- Qualitative tools to help you determine your company's vision/mission statement, goals, objectives, and environmental assessments.
- Quantitative tools to define your firm's strengths, weaknesses, and resources; to take stock of the competitive situation; and to assess your risk and opportunities.
- Questionnaires that you can use to generate the data you need if you are to create a three- to five-year dynamic marketing plan for your firm.
- A running sample case that illustrates the principles in each chapter and provides examples of completed questionnaires, forms, and matrices.
- To help you develop your marketing plans, the following topics are covered:

  Part I: The Marketing Planning Process. This section provides an overview of the entire planning process.

  Part II: Environmental Assessment. This section evaluates and develops situation analysis, environmental/competitive position, product positioning, strategic portfolio analysis, and problem and opportunity analysis. Starting with a close look at the internal and external environment of your firm, it determines your strengths and weaknesses, and formulates opportunities for you to focus on objective and strategic development.

  Part III: Developing the Marketing Plan. This section helps you to set marketing objectives for your firm, select strategies that will be in balance with

your objectives, determine your optimal market segments and the products you should develop, and choose the final marketing strategies that
will help your firm succeed.

Part IV: Implementation and Control. Many firms fail because their strategies
are poorly implemented and communicated to the people who are
responsible for carrying them out. This section indicates common pitfalls to avoid and provides guidelines to make sure that your plan gets
off to a sound start.

How to Use This Book

The Ultimate Guide to Strategic Marketing is a practical guide to the planning process. It is not intended to give you in-depth marketing theory or to discuss tactics
under a wide variety of conditions.

The emphasis is on developing a proactive marketing plan that will give your
firm a blueprint for future growth. To get the greatest benefit from strategic
marketing planning, it is recommended that you follow these steps:

1. Read through the chapter material before you fill out any questionnaires,
    checklists, or diagrams.
2. Realize that finding out what you don't know is as valuable as the informa-
    tion that you do know. Gaps in data can often reveal a company's problems
    and weaknesses. Use the questionnaires, checklists, and diagrams to dis-
    cover where you need to learn more about your company's operations, the
    competition, and the marketplace.

    Make sure that managers and staff members have a chance to review the
    completed forms and make comments. The more broad-based your data are
    within the company, the more accurate and sound they are likely to be.
3. Work through the book in sequence. A common mistake in developing
    plans is to skip steps. The data you develop for each step in the marketing
    plan will serve as a starting point for the next step.

Acknowledgments

I gratefully acknowledge the assistance of the following people in the development of this book:

Rosemary Camilleri, PhD
Diane J. Janowiak, MA
Mary J. Kipta, MBA
Richard S. Kipta

Special thanks to Casie Vogel, editor and Daina Penikas, editing supervisor for making this book possible.

Robert J. Hamper
River Forest, IL

PART I

The Marketing Planning Process

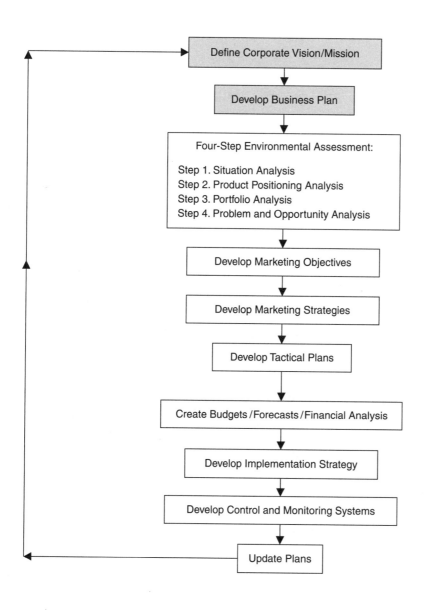

Define Corporate Vision/Mission

Develop Business Plan

Four-Step Environmental Assessment:

Step 1. Situation Analysis
Step 2. Product Positioning Analysis
Step 3. Portfolio Analysis
Step 4. Problem and Opportunity Analysis

Develop Marketing Objectives

Develop Marketing Strategies

Develop Tactical Plans

Create Budgets/Forecasts/Financial Analysis

Develop Implementation Strategy

Develop Control and Monitoring Systems

Update Plans

Starting Out

Introduction

The pace of social and economic change is accelerating in every sector, and with it, the risk of doing business is increasing. Competition is becoming stiffer as global marketing, e-commerce, and emerging markets are growing at a dizzying pace. In a world of look-alike products and services, your firm must find a way to stand out, and if it does not, it will not be competitive in the marketplace. You must hit the right target market with exactly the right product. You need only look at the cell phone market, where certain once-dominant players did not keep up with the latest technology and/or did not offer the right product. As a result, many of them lost substantial market share or are no longer in business. Brand loyalty will last for only a short while if products in the marketplace are ill conceived and poorly designed.

To succeed, your firm needs accurate marketing information to identify your target markets, determine their needs, and offer the best products and services to meet those needs. These efforts must be coordinated by developing a sound strategic marketing plan that can help your company achieve its twin goals of increased profitability and a healthy market share. Many company managers find themselves confused when it comes to developing a marketing plan. Part of the problem is that some managers do not fully understand the function of marketing and the process of active, future-oriented marketing planning.

As a result, they are merely *reactive*, trying to keep up with changing conditions or cutting costs to meet earnings objectives. Instead, they must become *proactive,* anticipating those changing conditions and developing a plan of action for the future, which is a dynamic as opposed to a stagnant plan. In return, this should increase revenues and profits, create new markets, develop new ventures, and expand existing markets.

Provided in this chapter is an overview of proven marketing techniques and a description of the marketing plan development process that is being followed by many successful companies.

Marketing Planning

Marketing planning is the development of a logically structured format for those activities that lead to the setting of marketing objectives and the plans for achieving them.

There are many external and internal conditions that will influence the development of your strategic marketing plan. Some of these issues include environmental changes, increased competition, company orientation toward risk, and management participation. These are briefly described here.

- Environmentally related problems involving your firm may show up as sales declines, increased competition, and slower revenue growth. If your competitors are not experiencing any of these problems, you may want to check your promotional results, product quality, price competitiveness, and risk assessment by management. In fact, a good control and monitoring system should define the variances from the marketing plan early on so that appropriate action can be taken and you can reach your marketing goals.
- Slower market share growth of products usually results from a mature product line, an economic slowdown, increased competition, no new ventures, or the fact that no new product regeneration is taking place.
- Increased competition is an external environmental problem that your strategic marketing plan needs to address quickly. Since the potential impact on your firm could be great, it is smart to ask yourself the following questions:
  - Why are more competitors entering your market and successfully increasing their market share while your company's performance is declining, as shown by slower growth or even a decrease in market share?

- ○ Have you kept your business plan and marketing plan up to date? Are the plans dynamic or stagnant? Are they updated continuously, or is updating them just a once-a-year academic exercise?
- ○ Are your competitors start-ups, buyouts, acquisitions, or a new division of a firm? These types of activities by competitors usually indicate that they see your market as being attractive and believe that they can surpass your firm in market share growth.
- Has management's need to stay competitive changed? Has the level of risk that management is willing to assume changed? Is management able to take on the risk associated with expanded target market selection, product modification, promotion, creativity, new distribution channels, and increased pricing flexibility?
- Does the new strategic marketing plan have the support of upper management and the necessary talent to actually implement the plan?

This is where marketing research can aid in defining problem areas. Information on the following issues will enable you to ferret out the main causes of these problems: evaluating the long-term sales potential of target market segments; monitoring competitors' activities; identifying new or regenerated products; tracking changing customer needs; evaluating the current needs and wants of your target market, product segmentation, your products' stage in the product life cycle, and growth in maturing market segments; and checking your distribution channels for efficiency. Compare the results to your current strategic marketing plan to evaluate whether it is becoming out of date.

Finding information on these issues will start you on the correct path to closing any gaps that exist in your current marketing plan.

Marketing Defined

Marketing can be defined broadly as a function within a company that seeks to generate a profit by organizing the firm's resources and activities to determine and satisfy the needs, wants, and desires of its target markets.

In the past, marketing was regarded as being synonymous with selling and advertising. Today, marketing is considered a management function. Marketing executives and other company managers decide how the company's resources should be utilized to achieve customer satisfaction and specific profit goals. Advertising and promotion usually support marketing efforts.

Notice that the emphasis is on *profits* rather than merely on *sales*. Companies are not seeking an increase in buying per se; they are more interested in the return on each item sold. As a result, they must focus their efforts on finding the target markets that are most likely to buy their products. Marketing must determine the following:

- Who the company's customers are and what they need and want
- When they want it
- Where they want it
- How they want to buy it and what price they're willing to pay

These points make up the four Ps of marketing, referred to as the *marketing mix*: product, promotion, place (distribution), and price. The four Ps are what the marketing manager considers controllable variables; that is, they can be adjusted and changed in determining strategies for the firm and for the products and services that the firm wishes to market. At this juncture you may ask, "Where are the seven Ps and the alphas and the like?" These other variables will be discussed in later chapters. However, obtaining a firm grasp of the initial four Ps, within which several scholars believe the other Ps are embedded, is critical in the development of a strategic marketing plan.

The Marketing Concept

The marketing concept reflects the current shift from production-oriented policies to a consumer- or marketing-oriented approach. Briefly defined, the *marketing concept* is a management philosophy that states that the key task of a company is to discover what various target markets want and need, and to deliver the desired products and services to those markets more effectively and efficiently than the competition does. This concept has been around for decades and is still taught in every introductory marketing class. Why, then, do many companies not use this as part of their planning process? That question will be answered in future chapters.

In the past, firms organized their resources to make and design products virtually in a vacuum. Advertising and promotion were then responsible for "pushing" products or services through the market by creating consumer demand for them. We were sold novelties, electrical gadgets, and hundreds of other items that we suddenly couldn't do without. Through the boom years of the 1950s and 1960s, companies used the push strategy to capture market share.

In the 1970s and 1980s, however, the economy experienced a series of setbacks. Two severe recessions, an energy crisis, and foreign competition brought an end to the fantasy of an ever-expanding marketplace. In the 1990s, middle managers were asked to develop a strategic marketing plan to provide a long-term strategic direction that focused on the specific needs of the market. In the late 1990s and early twenty-first century, global marketing and e-commerce have become major foci for many firms that are seeking to grow their markets. This cannot be overemphasized. Today, more and more industries are dominated by fewer and fewer large companies, while the remaining firms scramble to find and fill market segments and niches. Competition for the consumer dollar has made it vital to research what each particular customer group wants and then meet that group's needs.

As a result, corporate marketing strategies have changed from pushing products through the market to pulling them through. In a pull strategy, companies pinpoint consumer demand for a product, then manufacture the product and let consumers' demand pull it through the market. Promotion and advertising are aimed at consumers who have already been identified by market research, and they aid in creating this demand. The goals are to increase consumer awareness of the product and persuade buyers that it will fulfill their needs and wants. While it is certainly not foolproof, the pull strategy has proved successful for many companies.

The principle is clear. A firm using the marketing concept has the potential to grow at a much faster rate than a production-oriented firm, since its basic inputs for planning and product development are from the target market.

The marketing concept requires a company to adopt an integrated approach to planning and execution that includes the entire company hierarchy, from senior executives to field salespeople. Furthermore, this concept involves all the personnel and material resources of the company, with the dual end result of satisfying consumer needs and achieving the company's profit goals. With this approach in place, firms establish a central company vision and mission that serve as a focal point for management, produce the right products for each market, and achieve company sales and profit goals. The key to this process is good planning, as opposed to good luck or merely a "gut" feeling.

Global Marketing

The development of a strategic marketing plan for international firms is somewhat different from what it is for domestic firms. Since there are more environmental variables in international firms, the process becomes more complex.

More time and effort are required to identify and evaluate the external trends and events for multinational corporations than for domestic corporations. The degree of complexity is primarily driven by how many international markets you serve.

This is due in part to shareholders' or investors' expectations of sustained growth in revenue, which may be obtained only through international expansion. But if the strategic marketing plan is poorly developed, international expansion by itself is no guarantee of success.

In fact, there are both advantages and disadvantages to participating in international operations as opposed to just operating a domestic company.

Firms have numerous reasons for formulating and implementing strategies that initiate, continue, or expand international growth. One advantage of expanding internationally is that a firm can gain new customers for its products and services, which should increase the company's revenues. Growth in revenues and profits is a common organizational objective and is often an expectation of shareholders because it is a measure of an organization's success.

In addition to seeking growth, firms with international operations may have some of the following advantages:

1. International operations can spread economic risk over many different markets.
2. International operations may enable the firm to lower its production costs by using less expensive materials and less expensive labor. In addition, certain tax advantages may be obtained.
3. Competition may be limited or nonexistent.
4. International operations may enable firms to discover the new cultures and business practices of their foreign operations. Management can get better acquainted with new customers, distributors, and suppliers.
5. Most foreign governments offer incentives to encourage foreign investment.
6. Economies of scale can be achieved from operations that are global rather than limited to domestic markets. Also, larger-scale production and better efficiencies will decrease unit cost and increase pricing flexibility.

On the other hand, there are potential disadvantages of international operations:

1. International operations require an understanding of different social, cultural, demographic, environmental, governmental, legal, and economic

laws and regulations. Also, the language and value systems may differ from country to country.

2. Foreign competition is often underestimated. Your marketing research must be complete and in-depth.

3. Dealing with the country's accounting methods and operating in another currency may be beyond your firm's capabilities.

4. Obtaining external basis data may be very difficult, and the reliability of these data may be questionable.

E-commerce Marketing

E-commerce allows firms to sell products, advertise, purchase supplies, track inventory, eliminate paperwork, and perform other necessary business tasks. This function provides better customer service, increased efficiency, better products, and higher profitability. It also includes the Internet. Most individuals understand the importance of the Internet in e-commerce. It allows the target market to engage in comparative analysis of many factors of a product other than price during the buying process. The Internet needs to be included in your marketing strategy development process because of its powerful marketing potential. Entire books have been written on this topic, and an in-depth analysis of it is outside the scope of this book.

The Company Planning Process

The company planning process creates a hierarchy of plans beginning with the overall strategic business plan, moving to the strategic marketing plan, and finishing with individual product plans. Figure 1.1 summarizes the interactive nature of this process and the scope of the three plans.

Overall Strategic Business Plan

Most successful companies develop an overall strategic business plan that receives input from all functional areas. These functional areas are driven in part to meet the plan's objectives. First, senior management formulates objectives for the organization. Then, managers in various functional areas, such as marketing, contribute to the process by developing specific functional strategies and ultimately tactics to achieve the corporate objectives. Effectively, the process involves a hierarchy of plans, whereby the strategy at one level becomes the objectives at the next, and so forth.

FIGURE 1.1

The Company Planning Process and the Hierarchy of Plans

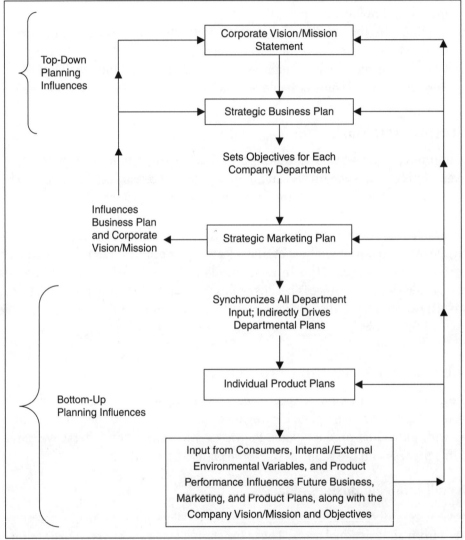

At this point, it is necessary to position marketing planning within the context of strategic planning. Strategic decisions are concerned with:

1. Defining the scope of the organization.
2. Determining the long-term direction of the organization.

3. Optimizing the activities of the organization relative to the environment in which it operates.
4. Aligning the organization's scarce resources of land, labor, and capital with its resource base. The strategic business and marketing planning process can be studied and applied using a model. Every model represents some kind of process. A widely accepted model of the overall strategic business and marketing plan is shown in Figure 1.2. This model represents a lucid and practical approach for formulating, implementing, and evaluating business and marketing strategies.

The strategic business planning process is continuous and dynamic. For example, if the competition reduces prices to gain market share, you may have to match this change by increasing promotion and decreasing costs to maintain your revenue objectives. If other competitors do the same, the firm may be in a position of not meeting the strategic business plan's objectives and strategies, which may require the firm to reevaluate its vision/mission and its key objectives and strategies. Strategy formulation and evaluation activities should be performed on a continual basis, not just at the end of the fiscal year.

Effective Business Planning Process

A good strategic business plan will contain a number of common elements. First, the plan will identify the market, its growth prospects, the target customers, and the main competitors. In addition, the plan will explain how the business will achieve its objectives in a logical manner. Then the plan will focus on the needs of the target market. It should identify the risks of doing business, including the potential disadvantages, and what contingency plans will be put into place to minimize the risks. Finally, the plan must identify the company's capital needs and how capital will be optimally used to meet investors' expected rate of return.

Once a company has established a sound planning cycle, it can revise, update, and alter its plan on a continuous basis.

Key Success Factors in a Marketing Planning Process

If a company is just beginning to realize the need for strategic planning, several key factors are essential for creating a successful planning process.

First, management must clearly see the need for change. Perhaps the company is losing key customers or experiencing a steady erosion of market share. Sales may be flat, or earnings may be declining. Whatever the metric, management must believe that the problem is serious enough to require decisive action.

FIGURE 1.2

Steps in Developing the Marketing Plan

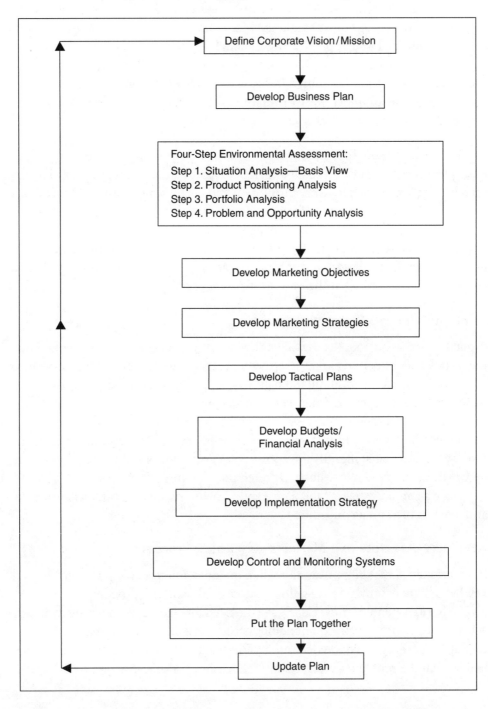

Second, someone (or, even better, some group) must champion the idea that the company needs to change through the development of a strategic marketing plan. The marketing manager, financial manager, engineering manager, and other advocates for change in the company must persuade top management that the firm needs to change and explain the benefits and advantages of accomplishing this change through developing or enhancing the strategic marketing planning process. Without a champion, and preferably more than one champion, it is doubtful that management will agree to initiate and carry through a planning process.

Third, the planning process must have high credibility with all levels of management and all users. This can best be achieved by involving middle and line managers and other users from the beginning, asking for their input, and listening to their concerns and suggestions. The planning process must involve individuals from top to bottom in an organization, and it must be melded to help the company set goals that all departments can meet.

Fourth, the finished plans must be realistic and must reflect the actual resources and capabilities of each department and of the company as a whole. Also, planners should keep managers and users abreast of changes and additions to the plans as they are made.

Fifth, managers and other users should be trained in any procedures that are essential to the planning process. These procedures include methods of data gathering, analysis and interpretation, development of budgets and forecasts, implementation, and accomplishment of other tasks that are vital to a successful planning process. Without some systematic method of gathering and assembling data, strategic planning is far more difficult. Company personnel should understand what information is needed and in what form.

Finally, written plans must be concise and well organized. Managers and users should be able to understand quickly the purpose of the plan, their assigned responsibilities, and the end results desired. The more concise and clear the plan, the more likely it is to be carried out successfully.

It is important to understand that the planning cycle in a successful firm is not a strict, linear process. Instead, as shown in Figure 1.1, it is highly interactive among all levels. It can be seen as a spiral, with constant adjustments being made to the company's vision/mission, objectives, and plans in response to changing internal and external factors. The driving force of the cycle is company goals and consumer response.

Defining the Company's Vision and Mission

Many organizations today develop a vision statement that defines what the firm wants to become. Developing a vision statement is often considered the first step in strategic planning. Many vision statements are a single sentence. The *vision statement* defines what business the organization is in and gives its very broad direction.

Once the need for planning has been established, the company must determine its mission. A company's *mission statement* defines what kind of firm its owners or managers want it to be, what business it is in, and what its broad-range goals are. As shown in Figures 1.1 and 1.2, the mission statement must be in place before you can begin to design any written plans.

Defining the company's mission takes place near or at the highest level of the planning hierarchy. Companies from small, entrepreneurial enterprises to corporate giants spend considerable time developing and refining the statement. For example, a major auto company's mission statement may read as follows:

> The fundamental purpose of our corporation is to provide products and services of such quality that our customers will receive superior value, our employees and business partners will share in our success, and our stockholders will receive a sustained superior return on their investment.

The importance of this step cannot be overstated. If the mission is defined too narrowly, it may hamper the firm's growth. Both the vision statement and the mission statement should be concise, clearly written, and enduring. Normally the vision statement is one or two sentences and the mission statement consists of no more than five sentences.

The mission statement must be updated periodically to make sure that it still defines the best course for the company. The more rapid the pace of change in a market or an industry, the more often the mission statement will need to be reexamined. All top-level managers must clearly understand the mission statement and accept its definition. No amount of planning can help your firm prosper unless you know what business you are in and what you want to accomplish. Some firms combine the vision statement and the mission statement into one statement rather than having two separate statements, since making the distinction between the two statements is time consuming and in small to medium-sized firms, both statements basically say the same thing. Throughout this book, the term *vision/ mission* will be used for both audiences; that is, those that use a single statement and those that use both.

Look over the mission statement for Techna Equipment in the sample case at the end of this chapter. It is suggested that you try your hand at writing your own company's mission statement on Form 1, "Vision/Mission Statement," found in the sample case. Even if this is only a rough draft, it will help you to clarify your thinking about your business and your overall goals. That knowledge will act as a backdrop for the work you will be doing throughout the rest of this book.

Objectives and Strategies

A strategic plan is one that covers a period beyond the next fiscal year. Usually this is for a period of between three and five years. Conversely, a tactical plan covers the actions to be taken and who is responsible in much more detail, and it is monitored closely for variances from the strategy. It is also usually very short in duration—normally for one year or less. Once the company's vision/mission is defined, management must then translate that vision/mission into a set of *objectives*, or goals, that becomes the basis for the business plan. The difference between objectives and goals is very simple and can be broadly defined: an objective is a broad statement of purpose, while a goal is very specific, with measurable results and a stated time period.

Quantitative and Qualitative Objectives

Quantitative objectives provide precise statements of performance expectations, such as sales growth, dollars per unit, percent market share, return on investment, and profit. Many managers prefer quantitative objectives, since most such objectives can be measured during the monitoring process and used for changing strategies. Consider qualitative objectives when quantitative ones are not feasible or cannot be developed. It is strongly advised that qualitative objectives be monitored very closely so that corrective action can be taken if they start moving in the wrong direction. In many instances, these objectives can eventually be quantified over time.

Suppose, for example, that Company Y's stated mission is to be a leader in the telecommunications/systems business. It must translate that statement into objectives such as these:

1. Expand into new consumer markets.
2. Develop new business communications services.
3. Explore possible overseas telecommunications linkups with foreign companies.

These objectives are more specific than the mission statement. They represent overall goals that a company wishes to achieve—goals that will shape the direction of operation for the entire business. These goals must be:

1. Reasonable—based on the realities of the market and the capabilities of the firm.
2. Obtainable—within the company's reach given its resources and personnel.
3. Measurable—yielding results that can be measured against projections or some accepted company yardstick.

However, objectives are still general. They state *what* the company wants to accomplish, but not *how* it will do so. *Strategies* explain how to meet goals. They are developed to achieve your objectives. Suppose your objective is to grow sales by 18 percent a year for the next three years. Without a strategy to get there, this objective will not be met. The strategy needs to be specifically stated, such as, "increase the advertising program by 4 percent, offer large-size purchase discounts of 9 percent, provide better product quality, and consider expanding market segments by 11 percent and international operations by 4 percent."

Strategy is a middle- to top-management activity, and it is long term–oriented. In contrast, tactics detail how strategies will be achieved. Tactics are usually developed at lower management levels, are short term in duration, are oriented toward short-term results, and are very detailed. At this point, it will be useful to help distinguish between a strategy and a tactic.

1. Importance: strategy decisions are significantly more important than tactical ones.
2. Level at which conducted: strategic decisions are usually made by middle or top management.
3. Time horizon: strategies are long term, tactics are short term.
4. Input: strategies require extra information that relates to the future. Tactical decisions depend more on internally generated data or market research information and are narrow and specific.

Again, strategies are more specific than objectives and determine the overall design or program for achieving goals, whether for a company, a division, or a product line. They are normally linked to definite periods of time—a year, three years, or five years. In the Company Y example, for instance, the strategies for the first objective might include these:

1. Segment the consumer market into categories of target markets.
2. Identify specific consumer wants and needs.
3. Develop products to meet those needs within two years.
4. Achieve a certain percentage return on shareholder equity.

As you can see, the basic strategy is to target specific consumer groups rather than to blanket the entire market with products and then determine which ones succeed.

In the planning process, strategies at a higher level become objectives for the level immediately below. For instance, strategies in the strategic business plan become objectives for the departmental level and ultimately for the strategic marketing plan. In turn, departmental-level strategies become objectives for individual product plans. As objectives and strategies move down the corporate ladder, they become more detailed and specific.

Company Planning Hierarchy

The overall strategic business, strategic marketing, and product plans make up the firm's planning hierarchy. Each of these plans will be briefly discussed, since many managers confuse their purpose and function.

The Overall Strategic Business Plan

The *strategic business plan* is a written document that spells out in detail the current status of a company's business and, more important, where the company is headed. It forces management to identify opportunities and threats, to recognize different strengths and weaknesses, to reconcile conflicting views, and to arrive at a set of agreed-upon goals and strategies for the company in a systematic and realistic way.

The business plan is prepared by top management and covers all aspects of the business: overall goals, strategies, market forecasts, pro forma financial statements, products, and any other aspects of the business. It is the master plan from which all other plans arise. However, this document is not cast in stone. In a proactive firm, the plan will be highly influenced by input from the marketing and product plans as they are developed and implemented. Thus, the firm can continually adjust to information from the marketplace and maintain a dynamic, interactive planning process from year to year.

The Strategic Marketing Plan

After the strategic business plan is developed, the strategic marketing plan must be developed, defined, and written. Marketing planning is a specialized function in the overall strategic business planning process. The importance of the marketing plan is that it serves as a major link between the business firm and its environment.

The *strategic marketing plan* can be thought of as a company's blueprint for future growth and success. In developing it, you survey the economic and competitive environment, isolate marketing opportunities, and state a course of action to take advantage of those opportunities. The plans of other departments support the marketing plan. The marketing plan, in turn, influences and modifies other departmental plans: the cost of the programs, the number of units for the production department, and the number of employees for the personnel department. All of these plans directly and indirectly influence the overall business plan of the company.

As a company's objectives and strategies are translated into marketing objectives, strategic marketing planning is developed. *Strategic planning* is a commitment on the part of management to look into the future market conditions and determine, among other things, the products and services that should be offered, dropped, maintained, or redirected to new segments. Strategic planning can be short term (one to three years) or long term (three to seven years). Tactical plans to achieve marketing strategies are usually set for less than one year and are considered to be the day-to-day marketing activities.

As a company's blueprint, the marketing plan defines the goals, procedures, and methods that will determine the company's future. It identifies the most promising business opportunities for the firm. It outlines how to penetrate, capture, and maintain its desired positions in identified target markets. The effectiveness of the marketing plan depends on two factors:

1. The level of commitment by all those who must work for its success.
2. The degree to which the plan is kept abreast of changes in the market environment. Planning is always a continuous process.

The marketing plan also serves as a communication tool that integrates and coordinates the elements of the marketing mix: product, place, price, and promotion. It specifies by product, region, and market who will do what where and when, and how to achieve the company's goals as stated in the business plan.

A successful strategic marketing plan must be:

- Simple: easy to understand and communicate
- Clear: precise and detailed

- Practical: realistic in its application and goal attainment
- Flexible: adjusting to changing conditions
- Complete: covering all significant marketing factors
- Workable: identifying responsibilities

The Product Plan

Individual *product plans* are the final and lowest level of planning related to marketing. The product plan is used to analyze product performance and establish product objectives, strategies, and tactics aimed at meeting the overall marketing plan strategies. Product plans also provide ways to determine profit and the derivation of net profit.

If a firm has a limited product line, the product plan is often incorporated into the marketing plan. Firms with many lines of business, products, or markets will develop individual product plans as separate documents, each supporting the marketing plan. The final goal is the coordination of all product plans to fulfill the objectives and strategies of the marketing plan.

Separating Marketing Plans from Product Plans

At first glance, it may seem like duplication to prepare both a marketing plan and separate product plans. This may be true at smaller companies with limited product lines, but at larger firms with many products and a variety of target markets, each product plan can be extremely complex. A single marketing plan is needed to control and guide all these plans toward achieving the company's objectives.

There are many good reasons for separating the marketing plan from the individual product plans. Having a separate product plan helps each product group clarify its action programs and encourages group involvement and commitment to the plan. It also integrates product management activity into the total planning effort. However, only those concerns and tasks that are directly related to a product should be included in the plan.

Strategic Marketing Planning Cycle

The marketing planning cycle takes place within the larger companywide planning cycle. In a marketing-oriented firm, consumer needs and wants drive the marketing planning cycle. As shown in Figure 1.3, the cycle begins by determining what goods and services consumers want. All other steps follow from this information. The feedback loop that drives the cycle is consumers' reaction to the products. Are your consumers satisfied? If not, what product changes need to be made? How can the product or service be improved?

FIGURE 1.3
Marketing Planning Cycle

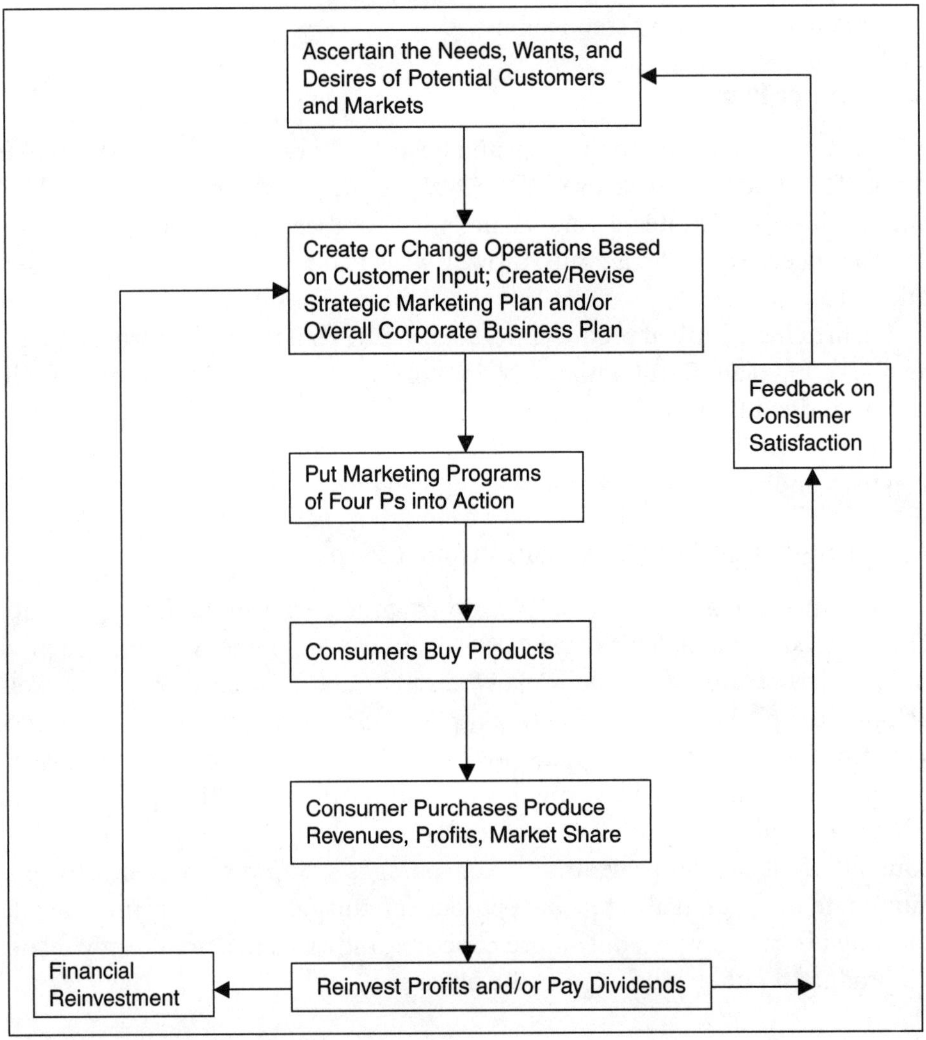

```
┌─────────────────────────────────────────────────────────────────────┐
│          ┌────────────────────────────┐                              │
│          │ Ascertain the Needs, Wants, and │◄──────────────────┐     │
│          │ Desires of Potential Customers  │                   │     │
│          │ and Markets                     │                   │     │
│          └────────────────────────────┘                        │     │
│                      │                                          │     │
│          ┌────────────────────────────┐                        │     │
│          │ Create or Change Operations Based │                 │     │
│    ┌────►│ on Customer Input; Create/Revise  │                 │     │
│    │     │ Strategic Marketing Plan and/or   │   ┌──────────┐  │     │
│    │     │ Overall Corporate Business Plan   │   │ Feedback on │ │     │
│    │     └────────────────────────────┘       │ Consumer   │ │     │
│    │                 │                         │ Satisfaction│ │     │
│    │     ┌────────────────────────────┐       └──────────┘  │     │
│    │     │ Put Marketing Programs         │           ▲        │     │
│    │     │ of Four Ps into Action         │           │        │     │
│    │     └────────────────────────────┘                        │     │
│    │                 │                                          │     │
│    │     ┌────────────────────────────┐                        │     │
│    │     │ Consumers Buy Products         │                     │     │
│    │     └────────────────────────────┘                        │     │
│    │                 │                                          │     │
│    │     ┌────────────────────────────┐                        │     │
│    │     │ Consumer Purchases Produce     │                     │     │
│    │     │ Revenues, Profits, Market Share│                     │     │
│    │     └────────────────────────────┘                        │     │
│    │                 │                                          │     │
│  ┌──────────┐  ┌────────────────────────────┐                  │     │
│  │ Financial │◄─│ Reinvest Profits and/or Pay Dividends │──────┘     │
│  │ Reinvestment│ └────────────────────────────┘                     │
│  └──────────┘                                                        │
└─────────────────────────────────────────────────────────────────────┘
```

Proactive Versus Reactive Marketing Plans

The strategic marketing plan should be a proactive document that clearly states the firm's growth objectives. Being *proactive* means that the company takes the initiative by deciding to be a leader, not a follower, in a high-potential market.

A *reactive* approach usually indicates that planning is taking place at the tactical level, too far down the planning hierarchy to affect companywide policy. The firm also is adopting a defensive position; that is, it is reacting to changes rather than determining its own future.

When planning occurs primarily at the tactical level, the company has a myopic view of the market. Planning may be based on a single product or product line. The results are potentially disastrous: growth slows, profits decrease, and market share declines. For example, suppose your competitor is constantly gathering market research information to determine consumers' current and future wants and needs. That competitor develops new products and offers them in the market. Your firm must now respond by spending considerable money to retool production lines, create promotional campaigns, and introduce new products in a short period of time.

The result is lower profit margins and smaller market share because you were late in entering the market. You are reacting to your competitor's actions and to the market rather than having a more aggressive, proactive plan. This is not to imply that you have to be first in every market, but you should not be that far behind the initial company in any market—remember, in most instances, the second mouse gets the cheese. Your company must stay abreast of market changes. This approach minimizes reactive planning by creating a proactive marketing plan that is geared to the future. Too much reactive planning has been the death of many firms.

What about the company that must be a market follower and create its own edge? The principle is the same. To be a successful niche company, you must have a future-oriented marketing plan.

If you know that opportunities exist, but you are seeing the competition seize them, you need to take stock of your planning process. It could be that you are reacting to limited, day-to-day changes in information instead of planning for the future.

Benefits of a Marketing Plan

A good strategic marketing plan explains what is to be done, where it is to be done, and who is to do each function. It eliminates confusion and makes work easier and more efficient. It increases motivation and productivity by stressing a team approach to achieving goals.

Formulating an organized and well-conceived marketing plan can have a tremendously positive impact on your firm. First, it helps the organization cope with change more rapidly and effectively, particularly through the use of contingency plans. Contingency plans offer alternative strategies should the initial strategy prove inadequate.

Second, a marketing plan helps an organization update and revise company objectives. If some unforeseen circumstances prevent the objectives from being achieved, a well-thought-out marketing plan can help a firm determine why the original goals could not be met and enable it to revise its objectives and strategies quickly.

Third, establishing a strategic marketing plan aids management decision making. The plan can serve as a point of reference for weighing alternative choices and determining which would contribute the most to meeting company objectives.

Fourth, the development of short-range and long-range marketing plans can help management evaluate its marketing efforts. Actual results can be compared against projected results. In this way, management can establish control and measurement procedures for the marketing process and determine how well it achieves its objectives.

Pitfalls in Marketing Planning

Establishing a marketing plan or detailed strategic plans is not without potential hazards. While the benefits far outweigh the drawbacks, you should be aware of some common pitfalls in your planning process.

First, defining objectives and developing a strategic marketing plan is time-consuming. The time that management invests in the planning activity can be expensive, and the results must justify that expense. Normally, the benefits of these efforts more than make up for the cost to the company.

Second, if the plan is poorly or hastily conceived or is based on erroneous assumptions or data, the outcome can be financially disastrous. In addition, such a plan cannot be adjusted to changing conditions or unexpected events effectively. Planning cannot compensate for poor research, nor can it take all the risk out of doing business. But it will give you more information for decision making, and it can control and reduce the level of uncertainty about the decisions you make.

Third, some plans fail because they are not integrated into the daily activities of the marketing function. The best plan is worthless if it sits on the shelf in a manager's office. Marketing plans should be implemented, then evaluated, revised, and implemented again. Also, the effectiveness of a plan does not depend on its length. You should create a plan that is concise and to the point. The longer the plan, the less likely it is to be read and used.

Fourth, the planners may not understand the planning process. The plan must be developed step by step, as is shown in this book. Many managers are tempted to skip steps or to draw conclusions before they have adequate data. Every member of the planning team should understand each step and contribute to completing it.

Fifth, nonmarketing managers often are not asked to provide input into the plan. The marketing plan will be implemented, in part, by managers of departments removed from the marketing function. Without their input and support, the possibility of failure increases. The final plan must be accepted by all managers and never be created in a vacuum.

Sixth, making financial projections may be mistakenly regarded as planning. Financial projections by themselves are not plans; they only forecast sales. Planning takes place when strategies for achieving the sales projections are clearly defined.

Seventh, plans can fall through when the planners fail to gather adequate data or consider the major variables that the environment may present. While it is impossible to know all the variables, having too little information is a real danger. Managers may form conclusions or decide on strategies too quickly and make serious errors in judgment. Gathering sufficient high-quality data is a critical part of good planning.

Eighth, the failure to involve key employees in all phases of the planning process does not create an environment that is supportive of change.

Finally, when too much focus is placed on short-term results, the firm can quickly outgrow the plan. The emphasis should be on developing plans that define long-term goals for company growth. Too often, companies sacrifice long-range profits for short-term results. By design, the marketing plan should be flexible enough to accommodate both short-term and long-range goals.

Take the time to work carefully through the planning steps presented in this book. The guidelines provided have been developed to help you to minimize the hazards of planning and enable you to build a sound, future-oriented marketing plan.

Marketing Plan Outline

Starting with Chapter 2, this book will take you systematically through the strategic marketing planning development process. The following chapters give the specific steps you need to take to develop a strategic marketing plan. Questionnaires, matrices, and charts to help you gather and analyze the data you need are provided.

The marketing plan outline follows the planning process discussed in this chapter. It begins with the overall company mission and business plan, which establish companywide objectives and strategies.

The next steps involve analyzing the internal and external environments as part of developing marketing objectives and strategies. You then select the best strategies and develop procedures to implement and communicate the plans. The last step is to establish control mechanisms to measure results and monitor your overall progress toward meeting the company's goals. This in turn leads back to the beginning of this cycle: making adjustments to the company's vision/mission statement.

At the end of the book, you will have a considerable body of information with which to develop your strategic marketing plan. The plan can serve as a blueprint for your company's growth and a guide for its future success.

Summary

- Marketing can be broadly defined as a function within a company that seeks to generate a profit by organizing the firm's resources and activities to determine and satisfy the needs and desires of consumers. Marketing is considered a management function and emphasizes increased profits, not merely sales.
- The marketing concept is a management philosophy that states that the company's key task is to discover what various target markets' needs, wants, and desires are and to deliver the desired products and services more effectively and efficiently than the competition does.
- Keys to a successful planning process include these steps: (1) managers must see the need for change, (2) someone or some group must champion the strategic marketing planning process, (3) the planning process must have high credibility with all levels of management, all functional areas, and all users, (4) managers and staff must be trained in procedures essential to the planning process, and (5) written plans must be concise, well written, and well organized.
- The planning process begins with the company vision/mission statement, which defines what the firm is, what business it is in, and what its broad-range goals are.
- The vision/mission statement is translated into a set of objectives that serve as the basis for the strategic business plan. Strategies then determine the overall design of programs for achieving the objectives.
- The company planning cycle includes a hierarchy of plans: the strategic business plan, the strategic marketing plan, and product plans.
- The strategic business plan spells out the current status of the company's business and the direction in which the company is headed. It is influenced by input from the marketing and product plans as they are developed and implemented.

- The strategic marketing plan can be thought of as a company's blueprint for future growth and success and serves as a major link between the firm and its environment. It defines goals, procedures, and methods that will determine the company's future.
- Product plans are used to analyze product performance and establish product objectives, strategies, and tactics aimed at meeting the overall strategic marketing plan strategies. The marketing planning cycle is driven by consumer needs and wants. It is designed to develop a proactive rather than a reactive plan.
- Benefits of a good strategic marketing plan include helping the organization cope with change more rapidly and effectively, updating and revising company objectives, aiding and managing decision making, and evaluating marketing efforts.
- Several pitfalls and hazards of market planning should be recognized: (1) the process is time-consuming, so the results must justify the cost, (2) a poorly conceived plan can produce disastrous results, (3) plans may not be integrated into the daily activities of the firm, (4) the planners may not fully understand the process, (5) nonmarketing management may be left out of the planning process, (6) financial projections may be regarded as planning, (7) planners may fail to gather adequate data or consider key variables in the environment, (8) if too much focus is placed on short-term results, the firm can quickly outgrow the plan, and (9) planners may fail to involve key employees.
- Global business and e-commerce cannot be overemphasized in today's market and future market environments. Firms are going to diversify themselves globally and through the Internet to stay competitive in the ever-changing world of economic and technological changes.

Sample Case, Phase 1: Techna Equipment*

Techna Equipment is a medium-sized firm in the Southeast specializing in computer data storage products and other smaller lines of computer peripheral equipment. The firm's product lines always have been in the forefront of technology, but in recent years, its sales and market share have declined.

---

* The company Techna Equipment, its management, its products, and all marketing data are purely hypothetical. Any resemblance to any actual firm, persons, or situations is strictly coincidental.

Techna has used marketing planning for six years, but the manager in charge of this process has not enhanced the techniques used to develop the plan since the first plan was implemented. The current marketing plan is obsolete, and the product managers are not keeping it current, since this was never deemed their responsibility. In short, Techna basically has no current strategic marketing planning system in place. This has become an issue that upper management must now address, since the lack of strategic planning has led to the decline in sales and market share and the fact that the firm's organization structure is beginning to move back toward being engineering-oriented. The newly opened position of vice president of marketing has been filled by Paul Harris, a marketing planning expert.

Techna's problem is a familiar one to Harris. It is a problem that he's seen in many companies that lack a formal, ongoing strategic marketing planning process.

Based on his experience with other companies, Harris knows that he has his work cut out for him. His first step is to research Techna's background and management history.

Techna Equipment, then the Techna Division of a major electronics company, which was going to spin it off, was bought in 1991 by three engineers—Ted Bartly, Abby Hamilton, and Will Farlin—who then formed their own company. They fit the profile of many entrepreneurs: strong in technical expertise and well connected with suppliers in the industry, but weak in financial and marketing strategy. Bartly is the only one who currently attempts any type of formal planning work; he develops the company's business plan each year. Hamilton and Farlin are more interested in engineering and product development, and Farlin is openly skeptical about the value of marketing plans and their possible influence on their engineering-oriented firm.

The three founders own 51 percent of the company's outstanding stock. Ted Bartly is the firm's president, Abby Hamilton is vice president of engineering, and Will Farlin is vice president of operations/research and development.

Techna originally offered early versions of disk drives, CRTs, and other computer equipment as its major product lines. Since 1994, however, the company has been moving into automated equipment, developing its own computer peripheral devices and software in addition to its other lines of products. The company currently has five product lines: calculators, storage software, and its three major product lines of computer storage devices. Computer peripherals have the largest impact on sales, contributing 36 percent of total revenues.

The company has been considered a high-growth firm in a high-growth industry, with several locations across the country. In the past, management has developed new products primarily through acquisitions. The company's overall capital structure is sound. Customers view Techna's products as high-quality items, and the company's excellent customer service has made it one of the most respected in the market, especially in data storage devices.

However, the computer technology supplier industry has become intensely competitive since Techna first entered the field. Major market leaders have established their company names and product lines. The field is changing so quickly that smaller companies must adapt their product offerings to the market leaders' products.

Techna has identified small to medium-sized firms as its target market, and until recently, it has done well. The company's sales have climbed from $36 million to more than $144 million in the past seven years. But over the past two years, the growth rate of sales has declined substantially, especially in the computer storage product lines.

Six months ago, Techna acquired a new line of solid-state disk drives called Storage Extreme by purchasing a small company. These drives are considered state of the art, with the product having no moving parts that could lead to breakdowns, and the competition is light, but the product is very expensive. Harris knows that competition will increase quickly as the prices drop. Techna also acquired a patent for storing all data from mainframes to the new drives used in many mini, micro, and personal computers. Harris knows that large floppy disks and 3½-inch disks, platter disks, and products like them used for storage are headed for the storage graveyard. His main mission is to phase out the old and introduce the new solid-state disk drives via a strategic marketing plan. For three months, Storage Extreme had been sold only to southeastern customers, but one month ago, Techna began offering Storage Extreme in new territories in the Midwest and Northeast.

Now the partners want to introduce Storage Extreme to the national market within the next eight months. However, only the sales and service staffs in the Southeast are trained to handle the new product. Harris can see that the acquisition, planning, and offering of Storage Extreme to date has been haphazard. The company has no real objectives, strategies, or tactics for marketing the new product in the new target market segments. This reinforces Harris's evaluation that Techna lacks any strategic marketing planning process. He wants to monitor Storage Extreme carefully, because this is the only new product the company has in the pipeline, and it has considerable sales potential.

As Harris continued his research, he pinpointed a number of other major problems.

- Although Techna has been number one in its niche for several years, its customers and competitors no longer consider it a leading-edge company. Its early successes came more from being first to the market with a high-quality product rather than as the result of a strategic plan. As the competition catches up, Techna has no detailed, forward-looking strategic business plan or strategic marketing plan for staying near the top in its industry.

    1. The primary reason for the change in position is the fact that Bartly, Hamilton, and Farlin have become increasingly reactive rather than proactive managers. Two clear indications of this shift are the following factors: Techna is milking its big revenue-producing product line dry without developing plans to regenerate products or keeping up with changing technology, and fewer new products are coming out of the R&D department.

    2. When strategic decisions about Techna's future need to be made, top management prefers to take a conservative line and follow competitors' leads—something that the firm has never done before. As a result, Techna has lost the initiatives and advantages in several product areas.

- Departments show a noticeable lack of communication and cohesiveness. Morale is low, and workers feel a lack of leadership from management.

- The marketing department, which has an effective team, has been following a push strategy rather than a pull strategy for product promotion and distribution. As a result, the marketing team is not identifying new customer groups or evaluating sales data to pinpoint the products' strengths and weaknesses in the marketplace. Management has not accepted the fact that the company needs to change its philosophy from being an engineering-oriented firm to being a marketing concept–oriented organization.

- While Bartly develops a business plan each year, it is never implemented. He creates the plan in a vacuum, without input from the functional department heads, and he has no strategy for introducing and implementing his objectives. Nevertheless, Harris feels that he can use Bartly's business plan as a starting point to make the company more marketing-oriented.

Looking over the problems he had uncovered, Harris knew that to get the company to change toward a marketing orientation in its planning process would mean making changes in the corporate culture and possibly in its organizational structure. He would need all of his diplomatic and communication skills to persuade top management that it must alter some of the company's old ways of doing business.

He began by volunteering to work with Bartly on the business plan to increase the marketing department's responsibilities in the firm. Bartly was more than willing to share what had become a thankless job.

"I've been putting this plan together for seven years, and no one has ever used it," Bartly lamented. Harris wondered why. Then he thought. "We need to get all of the department heads involved in the planning process from the start," Harris insisted. "They should be providing information and reviewing the plan at each step. Even before we begin data gathering, however, we need to establish a sound vision/mission statement. What does your current statement say?" Bartly replied that the firm's top management considered the vision and mission statements to be the same thing. Harris knew that many firms of this size felt the same way, so he was not concerned—at least the company had a statement.

Bartly sorted through the papers and found the statement. It read: "The purpose of Techna is to be a supplier of electronics and other office equipment."

Harris saw immediately that the statement's shortsighted focus was one of the obstacles to company growth and change. Techna needed a new, expanded vision/mission statement. Harris persuaded Bartly to call a top management meeting to develop one. In particular, the three partners had to answer some critical questions: Who are we as a company? What business are we in? Who are our customers? After considerable deliberation, management defined a new mission for the firm.

Form 1, Vision/Mission Statement

"The purpose of Techna Equipment is to provide the highest-quality service and electronic products to our customers through our core business and new ventures so that our market share is strengthened, our employees and business partners benefit from our success, and shareholders receive a superior return on their investment."

The statement was short and specific about the arena in which the company would compete and at what level. The previous statement, on the other hand, was much narrower and more limited. The new statement reflected not only a shift in product line, but also a goal of gaining a solid share of this market. Its open-ended expression didn't constrain or limit the company's growth.

During the process of developing the statement, the members of top management realized that they had to make changes in the company to achieve its mission. As vice president of marketing, Harris would be the one to champion the use of developing and implementing a strategic marketing planning process and raising the level of marketing expertise.

"I think it should be clear," Harris told a management group, "that for any real change to succeed, the planning process has to have top management backing and involve all levels of management from each functional area and from users. Otherwise, it will just be another plan that no one will read or implement."

The three partners agreed to give Harris their full support. Hamilton quickly saw the value of introducing a companywide planning process. "I think in the past we expected that just developing a plan would make things happen. Ted has been doing the whole job on his own, but nothing ever came of it, as it was never really implemented."

Harris said, "It's clear from the sales figures that the company can't rest on its reputation, and you do not want to become just an order-taking firm. Too many other companies are entering this market, and fast. On top of that, technology in this field is changing so rapidly that unless we take the initiative, your customers are going to see us as lagging behind the competition."

Farlin, the most skeptical about the entire marketing approach, spoke up. "Just exactly how are you going to get this whole planning process going? The way you talk, we don't have much time, especially since we are planning to launch Storage Extreme nationally in eight months."

Harris agreed. "The first step is to find out where we stand right now and get some idea of where the firm's current policies will take us in three years. That means collecting a lot of data, both internal and external. That's why it's crucial that we have the cooperation of all departments."

Harris held up the completed vision/mission statement. "We've already taken the first step. The vision/mission statement is the foundation for the strategic business plan. Ted Bartly and I have reviewed the current strategic business plan, and we have identified some missing pieces."

Harris explained that Techna's strategic business plan objectives failed to include all departments and were generally too narrow, focusing on specific products, for example, rather than on product lines. Second, the objectives often were blue-sky items—not reasonable, obtainable, or measurable. Third, the plan included elements at the tactical level but should have stayed at the strategic level.

Finally, the business plan was more than 300 pages long. No one around the management table had ever read through the document or had any intention of following it. Because Bartly had worked on the plan by himself, it was only as good as his knowledge of the company's internal and external environment. In some areas, Bartly admitted, he had rather sketchy information.

Harris outlined the planning process: The strategic business plan objectives must provide direction for the company. What product lines do we want to develop? What markets do we want to enter? What markets do we want to exit?

"These business strategies, in turn, become the objectives for each department. And each department works out its own strategies and the tactics to achieve them. The marketing plan coordinates all of these departmental strategies and acts as the major link between the firm and its internal and external environment."

But Harris made it clear that the success of a new strategic marketing plan depended on two key factors:

- The level of commitment from all those involved in the planning process—especially all of top management
- The degree to which the plans keep up with the changes in the market environment—a strategic marketing plan is always a continuous process

"I realize we've talked about a lot of work at the beginning, but believe me, the results will be worth it," Harris emphasized. "We'll have a strategic marketing plan that explains what's to be done, where it's to be done, and who is to do each job. The plan will stress a team approach to achieve our goals, and it will be a plan that can boost morale and make working together easier and more productive.

"Techna will be able to respond faster to competitive challenges and marketplace changes, and in this field, that can make all the difference," Harris added. "You'll have more reliable data at your fingertips and contingency plans to choose from. And we'll have some yardsticks for evaluating our marketing efforts, rather than using a hit-or-miss method to evaluate our marketing strategies. The strategic marketing plan will also include a comprehensive implementation plan."

Hamilton and Bartly were enthusiastic about the process, and even Farlin seemed resigned to it. "I guess it's either learn this strategic marketing approach," Farlin said, "or lose our company." Bartly added, "We need this approach for our new product as soon as possible to get it produced and to the market so that our buyers will stock it and distribute it. This will also apply to our other current product lines."

Vision/Mission Statement

After reading the vision/mission statement for Storage Extreme, try your hand at writing your own company's mission statement on Form 1. Even if the statement is only in rough form, it will help you to clarify your thinking about your business and overall goals.

PART II

Environmental Assessment

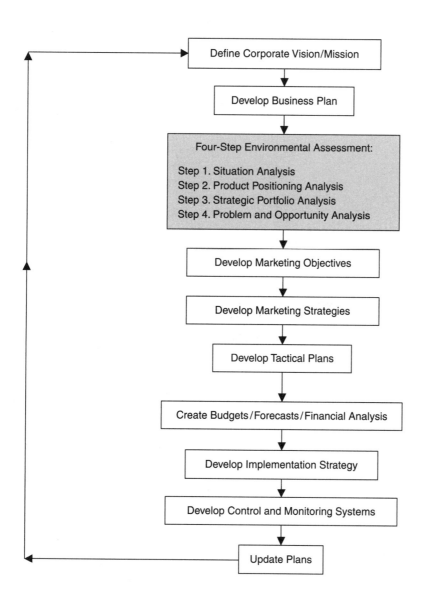

2

Step 1: Basis View—Situation Analysis

Introduction

A solid marketing plan is no better than the basic data on which you build it. This chapter begins the first step, gathering the data on which you will construct a strategic marketing plan.

This first step is called the basis view, in which you will assess your internal and external environments. Its purpose is to stimulate your thinking about various internal and external factors that affect your firm and the products and services that it offers. If you understand these factors, you can spot emerging threats and opportunities arising from changes in your business environment.

Keep in mind that in this step, you are focusing on the broad picture rather than gathering detailed information about each environmental factor. That type of detailed analysis begins in Chapters 3 to 5. For now, you need to understand the general strengths and voids in your *knowledge base* regarding your organization and its operating environment. This approach gives you some idea of what research you need to do to fill in those voids.

Importance of the Analysis

If you have never undertaken an environmental assessment (which is much like a marketing audit, SWOT, ETOP, or something similar), the basis view may seem unnecessary or rudimentary. Some managers believe that because they have years of tenure with their firm, they know where it stands and where it should go. To them, an internal and external analysis is superfluous.

Nothing could be further from the truth. Although this assessment takes time to conduct, it is essential to generate valuable marketing data on which to base strategic decisions. If the analysis is incomplete or inadequate, the entire plan will suffer.

As you work through the first step of the environmental analysis (the basis view), you will find that not all the factors discussed can be quantified on some type of objective scale. You may have to rely on your experience and on the experience of other managers and staff members to evaluate certain factors.

For example, if you manufacture computer game consoles, what types of computerized or programmable consoles will attract consumers next year? Although you can conduct market research on consumer preferences, needs, and past buying patterns, the answer may still be difficult to pin down. In the final analysis, marketing managers may have to make decisions based on their own intuition regarding which way the consumer is likely to jump in the coming season.

Emphasizing Qualitative Data

We will not focus on *quantitative* data at this point, but will concentrate on *qualitative* data regarding demand, competition, and cost structure. The questions asked in this chapter are not meant to be answered in detail right away; they are meant to prepare you for more quantitative work in later chapters. However, these questions *will* need to be answered in depth as you work through the book.

Remember, the purpose of this step is *discovery*: to discover what you do and don't know about your company and the environment in which you do business. Form 2, "Assessing the Environment/Competition—A Qualitative Approach," provided in the sample case, will help you to evaluate your situation. Use this questionnaire as a research tool. It is not a way to judge anyone's ability or knowledge, but simply a means of discovering what is known and what is not known about the company's overall situation. Successful companies spend considerable time and money discovering their weak points as well as defining and developing their strengths.

Basis View

Understanding the total business environment in which a firm competes is basic to marketing planning. The environment determines not only what a firm must do if it is to thrive and grow, but what the firm could accomplish in the future.

This basis view covers three sections:

1. *External factors.* These are the general market conditions in which the organization operates and over which it has little control. Three critical areas are focused upon demand, competition, and economic climate.
2. *Internal factors.* These are general conditions within the organization over which it has control. This section concentrates primarily on key areas: marketing, personnel skills, manufacturing and services, and financial resources.
3. *Internal/external factors.* These include influences from both within and outside your firm that affect its performance and success. Some of them can be controlled by management, while others cannot. This section focuses on a life-cycle analysis for the industry, your company, and your products; cost structure; legal constraints; and distribution channels.

The variables of each type that are listed here and discussed in the following section are the minimum number that should be considered either quantitatively or qualitatively in developing a marketing plan. If there are other variables that are important to your firm, add them to the list. If some of the variables do not fit your company, delete them and add those factors that do fit your organization and its environment.

After each variable, a series of questions is asked for your response. Note any questions that you and other managers in the firm cannot answer. Briefly assess how the lack of data will increase the level of uncertainty and risk in developing strategies. You will also realize at this point how much research is needed to fill in the data voids that these questions reveal.

Assessing the Environment/Competition— A Qualitative Approach

Form 2, "Assessing the Environment/Competition—A Qualitative Approach," will help you to gather data about the major advantages and disadvantages that you and your competition may have over the other. This form provides a basic first view of what you know and do not know about your environment and your competitors. Since this is a qualitative approach, it is limited in its use, but it can provide you with needed ideas for additional research and will clarify your product position against your competition's.

The Environmental Advantages-Disadvantages Matrix has four quadrants. A market in Quadrant A is one that has few advantages and few disadvantages. If your analysis puts you in this particular quadrant, you should minimize the amount of resources that you expend, since the market may be very small. On the other hand, if you are introducing a product, you would check to see whether the market has high potential for future growth. If it does, then it would be appropriate for you to start obtaining resources to grow your product in that target market. A market in Quadrant B has many advantages and few disadvantages. If you are in this quadrant, you should expend resources to grow the product in its target market. A market in Quadrant C has both many advantages and many disadvantages. You need to expend enough resources to maintain your current position, but stay alert for any market changes, since the product is in its mature stage. If the product starts to lose its advantages and keeps or increases its disadvantages, then you will need to consider cutting the resources used to support the product, taking action to regenerate the product, or just letting it fall out of your product portfolio, since its revenues will start to decrease. If your market is in Quadrant D, consider exit strategies, as there are many disadvantages and limited advantages. If the market is shrinking or the product is becoming obsolete, look to conserve the firm's scarce resources and consider eliminating the product. You may want to look over Form 2 in the sample case at this point to become familiar with the questions prior to reading further.

In answering questions about your products and those of your competition, you'll also be generating valuable data to be analyzed and used later. In particular, these data will help you fill out the forms in the following two chapters. In those chapters, you will be shown how to draw conclusions from the data you develop, what the data mean in relation to your company's situation, and how you can use this information to develop your strategic marketing plan. Also, one of the main purposes of this form is to start you thinking about what strengths your firm commands and what elements it does not excel at. By doing the proper research and analyses, you will make the changes that will help your firm succeed.

External Factors

External factors are those from the outside that affect the firm and over which you have little control: demand, competition, economic climate, growth rate, and technological and political factors. The terms used are defined because they may have different meanings for different individuals, and clarity is essential as the analysis progresses.

You need to develop as complete an understanding as possible of these variables and their effects on your organization. The success of your marketing plan hinges largely on how well you estimate their influence.

Demand

Demand is the single most significant situational variable because it has the greatest impact on what your firm can or cannot do. At the same time, it is one of the more difficult factors to determine and predict.

Demand is usually defined as the number of units of a particular product or service that customers wish to purchase over a specific time period and under a particular set of conditions. Demand for a product can be affected by several factors:

- Consumers' income levels
- The price and availability of competitors' goods
- The appearance of superior substitute products
- Advertising efforts
- Economic trends
- The size of the market
- Accessibility of the market and product availability

To survive in the marketplace, a firm must gauge the demand for its products and services. This demand estimate drives the revenue forecast that underlies the advertising program, production schedules, product enhancements, inventories, capital expenditures, and even optimum staff levels.

When you are analyzing the demand for your products, you will need to answer the following questions:

- What is the current size of the market in units or dollars, and what will it be in the future?
- How do consumers purchase existing products or services?
- What are consumers' basic behavior patterns and attitudes?
- Is it best to analyze the market as a whole or in various segments?
- Can the market be segmented into homogeneous groups on the basis of types of products or services bought and consumer behavior?
- Should a separate marketing program be developed for each target market? If so, what does success in each such market require?
- What is the extent of demand for the firm's products or services?
- What is the nature of that demand: seasonal or year-round; fluctuating, weak, or strong?

You can obtain information on the nature of the demand for your products, the size of the market, and consumer behavior by conducting market research yourself, by hiring a marketing firm to do parts of the research for you, and/or by collecting the information from available sources. These sources include industry surveys, reports of private market research firms, Internet searches, government studies, and association surveys and studies.

Competition

After demand, the second most critical element in your environmental assessment is understanding your competition. If you do not, you will fail to develop a successful marketing plan. Intense competition calls for a different marketing program from moderate competition.

Competition among firms can be either *direct* (another company is in the same market area) or *indirect* (a mail-order firm offers a line of products similar to yours), and competition is based only partly on price. Nonprice factors can be just as important to customers. Such factors include service, product differentiation, quality, and support services.

While they are aware of their direct and indirect competition, most firms fail to consider the potential threat from new entrants into the market or the expansion strategies of current or future competitors—especially global and e-commerce entrants. You should be aware that newcomers can enter your market from one of several starting points:

- The new firm plans to enter through diversification.
- The new firm offers products and services identical to yours and is planning to expand into your market from other customer markets in which it operates.
- The new firm currently offers a limited product line to customers in your area, but it is planning to expand its offerings to include products or services that you now offer.
- The new firm decides to use forward integration to gain entry into your market.

Analyzing possible threats from newcomers and the expansion threats of others in your area is one part of understanding your competitive situation.

To analyze direct and indirect competition, consider the following questions:

1. What is the current strategy of your competition? Although this information is elusive, you can make some educated estimates of your competitors' strategies by observing their marketing programs, through secondary research, and by looking at their product history. Gaining market intelligence should be a top priority of the company. Consider these questions about your competitors:

- How do they define their mission?
- Are their companies being managed for sales, growth, market share, net income, return on investment, or cash flow?
- What are their marketing mix, manufacturing policy, purchasing policy, and physical distribution policy?
- What size are their budgets, and how are they allocated?
- How vertically integrated are they?
- How have they defined their business in terms of customer groups, customer functions, and technology?
- To what extent are they affecting your company's growth rate, market share, and profitability?

2. How are your competitors performing? The answer to this question will help you determine whether they are reaching their goals and whether they have the resources and capabilities to carry out their strategies.

   Actual performance should be determined as closely as possible in terms of sales, growth, market share, profit margins, net income, and return on investment (ROI).

3. What are your competitors' strengths and weaknesses? An analysis of competitors' strengths and weaknesses should include a comparative assessment of factors such as the following:
   - Product and product quality
   - Dealers and distribution channels
   - Marketing and selling capabilities
   - Operations and physical distribution
   - Financial capabilities: resources and outlays
   - Costs and how they are changing
   - Margins
   - Pricing flexibility
   - Resources to expand market share
   - Sufficient personnel to implement their strategies
   - Size of your competitors in terms of market share and coverage
   - The effectiveness of their distribution policies
   - Their international and e-commerce links

4. What action can be expected from them in the future? You need to have some idea of how your competitors are likely to respond in the near

future to changes in the industry. You will need to answer the following questions:

- How are they likely to respond to ongoing changes in the external environment?
- How are they likely to respond to specific competitor moves?
- When and where are they most vulnerable?
- When and where are they strongest?
- In what markets are they most vulnerable to your competitive programs?
- Do they have the resources to move into international markets and e-commerce?
- How can you best compete with them in these and other markets?
- How fast can they regenerate their product lines as they mature?
- Can they enter new segments with modifications of their current product line?
- Can your firm keep pace with their regeneration and their new target markets?

The more complete your understanding of the competitive picture, the more successful you will be in designing marketing strategies.

Environmental and Economic Climate

In addition to demand and the competitive situation, you must also gain some perspective on the overall economic climate in which you do business. Marketing programs can easily be disrupted by changing economic conditions. For example, many firms were caught by surprise when OPEC initiated an oil embargo in the 1970s. Likewise, the high interest rates of the late 1970s and early 1980s hurt the profitability and cost structure of many firms, while declines in consumer disposable income hurt such leisure businesses as travel and entertainment.

Since economic conditions are constantly changing, you will need to consider how your firm can adapt to change for long-term success. You should answer some of these questions:

- What are the social, political, economic, and technological trends that are occurring now and those that are likely to occur in the next one to three years?
- How should you evaluate these trends in terms of their impact on your industry and your firm?

- Do these trends represent opportunities or threats to your firm?
- How are basic economic conditions affecting sales and other functions of your firm? How are they likely to affect your firm in the next one to three years?

Information on economic conditions can be obtained from a variety of sources, including government studies and surveys, Federal Reserve Bank bulletins, industry reports and seminars, the Internet, industry publications, and private forecasting and researching firms.

Growth Rate

Understanding the potential growth rate in any industry or marketplace is of the utmost importance. You will need to define your total potential market, and, within that market, you will need to identify your products' current stage in the industry life cycle. Many people look at the growth rate as the number of units sold in a particular market and what future rate is possible. But measuring the growth rate means pinpointing your products' position in the industry life cycle and projecting the likelihood of their advancing into its next phase.

For example, if most of the products in a market are in the mature phase of the industry life cycle and the outlook for the product mix in that market is that it will become not just dated, but obsolete, the future growth rate may be very low or negative. Those firms that want to survive will have to develop new products or services and find new target markets. On the other hand, if the market is in the mature phase because of some correctable factor, the products can possibly be regenerated with whatever new features are needed, and the industry and the products will return to their growth phase. For example, not long ago, the computer industry was in the mature phase because of the current products' slow processors, but the industry could be regenerated with faster processors. The growth rate should increase if the demand is in place. If you do not understand the growth rate in your industry, it will be very difficult for you to develop financial projections, segment projections, allocation of scarce resources to the firm, and other projections that require a market growth rate.

Technology

One of the most important items to understand with regard to technology is how fast it is changing in your target market. In certain markets, technological change is very slow. In other markets, a product can be available on January 1 and be out of date literally in six months because of a technologically superior new product. It will be very important for your team to understand any new technological developments that might affect present and future products or equipment that your firm produces and sells. The technology of your particular market will put you at a serious disadvantage against the competition if you do not understand its pace of change.

Political Factors

The political arena can include lobbyists, consumer-affairs groups, the Securities and Exchange Commission, and politicians. These groups typically try to protect consumers, regulate markets, and prevent potential monopolies from forming. They often implement changes in laws and regulations that might affect your particular products, equipment design, and marketing. This topic is discussed in more detail in later chapters.

Internal Factors

Internal factors are those that affect the company from the inside and can be controlled more directly by the firm. The principal internal factors to consider are your firm's marketing, personnel skills, manufacturing and services, and financial resources. Other internal factors include management leadership, company image, and organizational structure.

Marketing

Evaluating the marketing function in your organization is critical for developing a successful strategic marketing plan. You can evaluate these items in terms of weak to superior strength. If you find that your firm has many elements that are in the weak category, then it is time to look at how these can be shored up. At the opposite end of the spectrum, you will want to determine how to keep your strengths and improve them. A partial list of elements to consider includes:

- Does your firm have a vision/mission statement and an overall strategic business plan that is successful in its function?
- Are you gaining or losing market share?
- How effective are your distribution channels?
- How good is your promotional effectiveness?
- How do consumers see your product quality and service reputation?

- Is your market share growing or shrinking?
- How effective are your research, development, and new product innovations?
- What has been your effectiveness in defining your target markets, entering them, and achieving your growth-rate objective?
- Have you effectively differentiated your products from those of your competitors?

It is imperative that you look at your marketing operations very thoroughly so that you can correct any major—and sometimes minor—deficiencies.

Personnel Skills

Part of the marketing planning process involves evaluating the skills and experience of your company's employees. You want to make sure that you have adequate staff to carry out the goals you set for your firm. Employees must also have the level of skills necessary to perform the work.

For example, you may plan to increase sales by 22 percent over the next two years. Do you have enough staff members with the skills required to explore new markets, increase the size of your sales territory, and service accounts without losing quality?

Your evaluation should gather the following information:

- What types of skills and experience will you need to accomplish your corporate goals and vision/mission in the next three to five years?
- Do you have the number of skilled staff members required to accomplish your projected goals?
- How do your staff's skills compare with those of your competitors?
- What training programs will you need to upgrade the skills of your current staff?
- What are the cost differentials of hiring skilled people versus upgrading the skills of your present staff?
- Is your firm static or dynamic in its leadership?
- Is management at all levels able to respond to competitors' moves?
- Is management flexible in response to competition and market changes?

A careful audit of personnel is essential to any marketing plan.

Manufacturing and Services
The manufacturing and services process that you will be investigating is very important, especially when it comes to technology and financial performance. The following questions will aid you in starting an initial evaluation of your manufacturing and services abilities:

- At what capacity level is your firm operating?
- If your firm is near 90 percent of capacity, do you have the financial resources to increase its capacity?
- If you increase capacity, will the market growth rate justify that strategy?
- Does your workforce possess the knowledge base needed for your manufacturing and services process?
- Does your firm have economies of scale, and does it use modern facilities management techniques?
- Is your inventory management technique up-to-date to minimize stockouts?
- Are your facilities able to deliver a service or product by the contract date?

These questions alone can tell you that, if your manufacturing and services are not up to speed relative to those of your competitors, you will begin losing market share very quickly. For example, if you are not delivering on time as a result of capacity restraints, your customers will become dissatisfied and may move to a competitor. If your customers depend on your product or service as a key input for their output, every time you miss a contract date for delivery, you may cause that customer to miss a key delivery date and potentially lose current and future customers. If you are that customer, ask yourself this very simple question: "Why am I dealing with a firm that cannot meet its delivery dates, which is costing me business, just because it cannot run its operations correctly?" This customer is just using common sense by finding a new supplier because of your firm's inadequate planning. This analysis also reveals that certain functional areas of the firm should join the marketing team to avoid a communication gap.

Financial Resources
You will also need to audit your financial resources to determine whether you have sufficient capital to finance your marketing plan. Resources include cash flow from operations, real estate earnings, potential stock and bond offerings, inventory, cash, accounts receivable, available lines of credit, and any other sources you may be able to tap.

Evaluate your financial resources using the following questions as a guide:

- What will an effective marketing program cost, and can you underwrite it?
- Can you finance your growth objectives, such as new or expanded facilities, acquiring other businesses, probing new markets, and/or research and development?
- What are the sources of your funds, and when will they be available?
- Can you afford to expand internally and externally while you maintain the overall health of the corporation?
- Considering the types of financing listed previously, which ones can you afford? What is your firm's optimal capital structure?
- What rate of return on your investment can you expect? How soon?
- What profit margins do you expect or need?
- Do you have delinquent accounts?
- Is the total volume of revenue increasing or decreasing? Are revenues fluctuating, and if so, why?
- What do the pro forma statements look like under various financial scenarios?
- Can your firm access long-term and short-term capital?
- Is your firm able to obtain capital at a reasonable cost? If not, how will that change the discount rate used in your capital-budgeting techniques?
- What is your firm's financial stability?
- Is your firm meeting its targeted ROI? Is your firm meeting its targeted margins?
- Are the capital markets available to your firm in case it needs to obtain long-term debt or equity infusions?

Accurate estimates of financial resources are critical. Many marketing plans fail because firms overextend themselves financially and cannot follow through on their goals. They run out of capital before they begin to see any substantial return on their investment. On the other hand, an organization may grow too rapidly and become cash-poor, resulting in operating losses and even, in some cases, bankruptcy. Make sure your financial resources are able to support your marketing strategy.

Evaluate the other internal factors mentioned—management leadership, organizational structure, company image, and any others that you feel are important. What is the current state of these factors, what must they be one to three years out, and what must you do to bring about the required changes?

Internal/External Factors

These factors include influences from both outside and within the firm that affect its performance and success. This section will focus on a life-cycle analysis of the industry, your organization, and your firm's products; cost structure; legal constraints; and distribution channels. Life-cycle analysis provides a framework within which to develop your strategic marketing plan and to select appropriate strategies. It is one of the most useful and powerful concepts in market planning.

Life-Cycle Analysis

Like the human life cycle, the life cycle of industries, organizations, and products generally has four distinct stages: introduction, growth, maturity, and decline. Each stage of the life cycle has its own characteristics and applicable strategies. As shown in Figure 2.1, the industry life cycle exerts pressure on the organizational life cycle, which, in turn, affects individual products' life cycles. Since a change in any of these cycles has a direct influence on the others, it is important that you understand this concept and how it affects the development of your strategy.

FIGURE 2.1
Life-Cycle Analysis

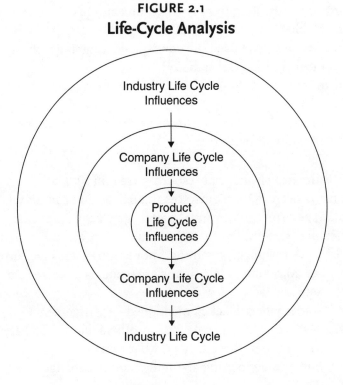

Industry Life Cycle. The industry life cycle has a direct bearing on the organizations and products that make up the industry. For example, if the industry is in a growth stage, there will be opportunities for firms to expand. If the industry is in decline, however, companies within that industry will also decline unless they are able to diversify their product lines into other growth industries or find profitable niches in the declining market.

Most industries in the United States are in their mature stage. Their growth rates are slow, and most of their markets are saturated, although they have enough new product innovations to keep the markets slowly expanding. However, if the structure of an industry changes—from regulated to deregulated, for example—the industry will move to a different stage of its life cycle.

This change happened in the trucking industry after it was deregulated in 1980. Before the change, the industry had been in a stagnant mature stage, and most carriers had clearly defined market shares. After deregulation, the industry was suddenly thrown back into a growth stage. Most firms had no real understanding of how to compete in a deregulated market and continued to run their businesses as they had been doing.

The result was that many of the firms went bankrupt or merged with others. Although many companies knew that deregulation was coming, they did little or no strategic planning to handle the new situation. Companies could react only by using crisis management tactics to try to stay in business.

An understanding of the industry life cycle and its implications is necessary to develop the proactive strategies that organizations need if they are to remain competitive and growth-oriented.

Organization Life Cycle. At the next level, the organization, firms also have life cycles marked by definitive stages. A new software company that is in the introduction stage, for example, struggles to make itself known to consumers and to establish its market position with its products and services. In the growth stage, it gains customer acceptance and experiences a period of rapid growth and expansion.

During the mature stage, it reaches its peak output and efficiency. Revenues have stabilized and started to decline. The company must evaluate its position carefully and decide on a course of action. Should it expand some products, cut back on others, diversify, redefine its vision/mission, or merge with another firm? The strategy selected can make the difference between extending the mature stage, or even going back to the growth stage, and experiencing a continued decline in revenues.

If the decrease in sales and revenues is not halted, the company will enter the decline stage and face several other problems. It may slowly lose market share

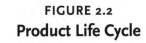

FIGURE 2.2

Product Life Cycle

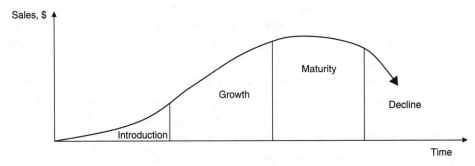

until it goes out of business, settles on a reduced market share, or sells its operation to another firm.

Product Life Cycle. Each product, too, has a definite life cycle of initial development, entry into the market, growth, maturity, and decline, as shown in Figure 2.2. Since product life cycles are discussed in more detail in Chapters 6 and 7, only a brief introduction to each phase is presented here.

It is important to know which stage in their life cycle your products have reached as you begin your planning process. This knowledge will help you determine the next stage your products are likely to enter soon, given your current strategy. It will also help you decide on any new strategies you may need if you are to maximize your market share, revenue, and profitability.

In the introduction stage, the product is placed on the market and begins to generate revenue. Competition for new products is often negligible, since this stage generally yields little or no profit. The marketing strategy is usually to gain consumer acceptance and to make the product known.

In the growth stage, consumers become increasingly aware of the product. The demand rises as sales increase. Consumers may develop brand loyalty. Competition is the most intense at this stage. The marketing strategy may include targeting more consumer groups and refining the product to satisfy customer desires.

In the mature stage, the markets have been established, sales peak and begin to decline, competition stabilizes, few—if any—new entrants are expected, and market shares are relatively stable. Market share may increase if the brand gains added value through product improvements or price restructuring. Marketing strategies usually focus on maintaining market share and considering what the organization will do when the product reaches the decline stage.

At the end of the cycle, the decline stage, revenues drop off rapidly, new technology or changed conditions in the market begin to make the product obsolete, competition declines as competitors drop out of the market, and the product is displaced or repositioned to an earlier stage. The marketing strategy is designed to minimize losses and to discontinue or reposition the product as quickly as possible.

When you analyze your products and services more closely in Chapters 3 and 4, you will answer questions such as these:

- What is the life-cycle stage of each product or product line?
- What is the organizational life-cycle stage of your company?
- What is the life-cycle stage of your industry?
- What market data support your evaluation?

Cost Structure of the Industry

Every industry has a cost structure, and knowing that cost structure is important in setting profit margins, understanding competitive vulnerability, and establishing the price of a product or service. Factors that affect the cost structure will also directly affect the company's pricing, profits, and strategies.

You need to know the current cost structure and how it is likely to change in the near future. Changes may bring the added costs of supplying more products or services, costs that in turn help to determine the marketing program that your firm should follow.

Questions you will need to answer include these:

- What is the current cost structure in the industry?
- Can you operate profitably within that structure?
- Can the current cost structure be changed? If so, how?
- If costs increase, how will your firm's pricing and profit margin be affected?
- Do your competitors have any cost advantages over your firm? What are these advantages, and how can you counteract them? Can your competitors cross-subsidize products to achieve a short-term price advantage over you?

Legal Constraints

Legal constraints can affect either the external or the internal environment of your firm. A desirable marketing plan may be hampered by antitrust laws, pricing restraints, interstate commerce restrictions, rulings on what constitutes fair competition, and deregulation of an industry.

At the federal, state, and local levels, firms face a constantly changing legal environment. Within this legal framework, you must design your marketing program. To do so means that you must monitor legal developments and assess their impact on your industry and your firm. Pertinent questions include these:

- What legal intelligence can keep you updated in order to anticipate problems or opportunities?
- How do laws and regulations constrain your marketing programs, and are your programs compliant with those laws and regulations?
- Who regulates your industry and how do current or proposed regulations affect your competitive stance, plans for acquisition or divestiture, and pricing structure?
- What legislation is pending at the city, state, or federal level that may affect your firm?
- As laws and regulations change, how should you adjust your marketing plans and programs?

You can gather information on the legal climate from a number of sources: government legislative publications, industry lobbying groups, your legislators, industry associations and seminars, the Internet, business publications and professional journals, and your own legal department if your firm is large enough to maintain this function.

Distribution Channels

Companies generally have some control over which channels will carry their products from plant to end user. You may even own part of the distribution channel in the form of trucks, airplanes, vans, ships, and other types of transportation.

For marketing planning purposes, you will need to answer the following questions:

- What distribution channels are currently available, and how can your firm access them?

- How is the structure of distribution changing, and what impact will these trends have on how your firm delivers, prices products, finances itself, and ultimately profits?
- To what extent are distributors competing, both within a channel and among channels?
- What does each channel require for promotion and for margin?
- For each channel, what are the cost-versus-revenue ratios?
- Which channels will be the most profitable for your firm to use?
- Are you using the best channels to minimize costs and maximize revenues? How might you need to change?

Instructions for Assessing the Environment/Competition— A Qualitative Approach

Form 2, "Assessing the Environment/Competition—A Qualitative Approach," will help you to gather data about your major competitors for the basis view. Look over the completed form for the sample case, which indicates the information that this questionnaire is designed to generate.

Completing Form 2

Fill out a questionnaire for each product your company markets. Make sure that department heads and other pertinent staff members look over the completed form and make comments. The broader your database, the more you are likely to learn.

The following instructions should help you complete the questionnaire.

1. Identify the market segment in which you do business and enter it at the top of the form. If you compete in more than one defined segment or market, fill out a separate form for each product offering.
2. Section A, your firm's product offering. Identify the product you offer in a particular target market. If you offer more than one product in a particular segment or market, fill out a separate form for each product. (These forms will be correlated later to identify any overlap, to develop pricing structures, and so on.)
3. Section B, competitors' products. After identifying your product, list the competitors' products that compete most directly with yours. It may be that a competitor's products are not associated with any of yours in the target market. You may want to list the competing product and assess it

anyway, since that will give you a sense of the competitor's market coverage.

On the other hand, you may know of a competitor's product that competes with yours but be unable to assess it in any detail or with any degree of confidence. This points out a void in your knowledge. In that case, simply list the competing product and note that you could not assess it at this time.

4. Section C, quantitative or qualitative judgments. Answer these questions about your product and your competitors' products in the context of your respective situations. For example, in Question C16, if your product is strictly regulated in that segment, you would rate your own regulatory climate as a disadvantage (D). In contrast, if your competitors' products are relatively free from regulation, you would rate the competitors' regulatory climate as an advantage (A) for each product. Compared with your firm, the competitors enjoy a climate that is fairly free from restrictive regulation. Add up all of the As and Ds separately. Next, add the As and Ds together to define your horizontal and vertical axis range. At this point, do not be concerned if you cannot answer the quantitative questions—but start to research them, as they will be used in the following chapters. If you find that you could not answer more than 25 percent of the qualitative questions immediately, research them and place an answer in the questionnaire. This research will also show that a knowledge gap exists and that you are starting to fill this void.

5. Section D, Environmental Advantages-Disadvantages Matrix (a qualitative view). Use the total As and Ds as plot points for the matrix. This will indicate how your product is positioned relative to your competitors in its initial environmental assessment. Underneath the matrix, write two to four paragraphs about issues that you found to be significant.

6. Section E, competitor information. Answer the questions in this section from the *competitor's viewpoint*, unless the question specifically asks you to compare the competitor's offering with your product.

Answer as many questions as you can. Wherever possible, research the questions you have trouble answering. The more complete your form, the more data you will have to develop a sound marketing plan.

Keep in mind, however, that finding out what you don't know is as critical as filling in what you do know. These voids point out where you are vulnerable to your competition or to market changes, and reveal potential problems and opportunities.

In Chapter 3, "Product Positioning Analysis," you will move on to the second step in the environmental analysis: evaluating your market positioning, life-cycle stage, and strategic gaps.

Summary

- The purpose of the basis view is to help you understand the general strengths and weaknesses in your knowledge base regarding your firm and its operating environment. This approach can help you spot emerging threats and opportunities arising from changes in a business environment.
- This step concentrates not on quantitative but on qualitative data about external, internal, and internal/external environmental factors.
- External factors include demand, competition, and economic climate.
- The key internal factors are personnel skills and financial resources, but internal factors also include management leadership, company image, and organizational structure.
- Internal/external factors include life-cycle analysis, cost structure, legal constraints, and distribution channels.
- Life-cycle analysis examines your industry, your company, and your products in terms of four stages: introduction, growth, maturity, and decline. Different marketing strategies are required for each life-cycle stage.

Sample Case, Phase 2

All members of top management gave Paul Harris approval to initiate a strategic marketing planning process. His first step was to review all the company's current marketing information. Not surprisingly, he found considerable gaps in the data. Harris called a departmental meeting to explain what the marketing team would focus on over the next few weeks.

"First of all, we need to find out where the company stands in relation to its internal and external environment—in other words, an environmental assessment needs to be completed," Paul Harris told his marketing team. "That means getting the highest-quality data from inside and outside the firm. The marketing plan will be only as sound as the underlying data supporting it. We'll focus on qualitative data first, since we can obtain it from department heads and product managers more quickly.

"I think you all understand the limitations of qualitative data, so no one is going to assign any absolute value to the information gathered. The final marketing plan will consider management experience and judgment as well as the numbers and percentages we obtain. At this point in our study, we want to find out where we have solid information and where we have gaps."

Paul Harris planned to pay particular attention to Storage Extreme, Techna's new hard disk drive product line. It was the first leading-edge product the company had procured since its last acquisition more than two years ago. Although Storage Extreme had been sold to selected southeastern customers, it would not be fully launched nationally until the new marketing plan was in place. The marketing team would also gather data for each product in the remaining five product lines.

Paul Harris explained that the marketing team would first conduct a situation analysis of the company to develop a basis set of data.

"It's vital that we get a much more thorough understanding of all marketplace variables. To begin, I developed an assessing the environment/competition questionnaire that I'll hand out to all appropriate department heads and product managers. The answers will enable us to assess their knowledge of markets, products, competitors, and the like."

"How do you get them to fill it out?" one member of the marketing team asked. "They barely returned any of the questionnaires we sent them before. In fact, only about a third of the managers even bothered to read them."

"This time top management will see to it that the forms are completed by making it part of the department heads' and managers' yearly objectives," Paul Harris replied. "That's why I insisted on having their full support before we started the planning process."

Despite his assurances, the team members remained skeptical. Harris didn't mind; he was confident that their attitude would change once the data started coming in. From then on, they'd be too busy to doubt his methods.

He asked Bartly, Hamilton, and Farlin to call a meeting of all department heads and product managers to explain the purpose of his questionnaire. He wanted to defuse any suspicions on the managers' part that the form was going to be used to weed out their ranks.

Bartly let the group know that the three partners were in agreement with the marketing vice president's approach. He then turned the meeting over to Paul Harris.

Harris stood up in front of the group. "You'll find that the questionnaire covers a lot of territory, from price structure to competitive strategy. I realize that competitor information can be hard to come by, but do the best you can with it. Internet searches will provide a lot of data for you. The whole purpose of this form is to find out what we do and don't know. I want to stress that honesty in filling out the questionnaire is important. No one is being judged by the answers; this is purely a fact-finding mission."

One of the managers interrupted, "What if we can't find any information to come up with an answer?"

"Leave the question blank. That's an indication of where you'll need to do some research later on. Right now, all you're concerned with is what you can or can't answer at this time. That's why I'm stressing honesty so much. Don't put down an answer just to look good. We don't need junk information; we need to know where everyone stands. Any questions?"

"Do we fill out one questionnaire for each product and for each of that product's competitors?"

"That's right."

A chorus of groans greeted his answer. Paul Harris held up his hands until he got silence. "I know it sounds like a lot of work, and it's something that no one does voluntarily. But the company's in trouble, and we're going to be in a lot worse trouble if we don't turn it around. We've got to have a solid understanding of the total business environment in which we're competing. That information will serve as the basis for developing our strategic marketing plan. Look at it this way: the time you invest in these forms is time invested in your jobs and in your future here at Techna."

Paul Harris could see that his words hit home. Everyone had seen the latest sales and market share statistics. "All right, take the forms with you, and let's have the completed questionnaires turned in to the marketing department one week from today."

After the managers left, Farlin shook his head gloomily. "You won't get half of those forms backs," he predicted.

A week later, to Farlin's surprise, all but two of the managers had turned in their completed questionnaires. Paul Harris saw his marketing team's morale pick up noticeably as they threw themselves into the task of analyzing the data.

For the first time, he began to feel the momentum for change building in the company.

The results of the analysis yielded a few surprises. For one thing, Farlin was concerned about the lack of detailed information that the product managers provided about the competition. As shown on the first page of Form 2, respondents judged Competitor A as the strongest threat to Storage Extreme and Competitor B as the weakest. (Section E of the sample questionnaire has been completed for Competitor A only. In practice, a form would be filled out for each competitor.)

The product managers and their staffs had the most trouble filling in questions about Competitor A's required investment, marketing strategy, price structure, profit margins, market share, growth rate, and target market segments.

The answers also showed Paul Harris that Storage Extreme's product managers were not keeping abreast of changes in the marketplace or the impact of those changes on the company. Instead, they were concerned with meeting short-term objectives, which he began to suspect were set too low. It was another sign that the company was not market-oriented.

On the other hand, Paul Harris was pleased at the managers' high level of knowledge about their own products. It was obvious that information about the internal environment was not the problem. However, the managers made it very clear from their answers that more awareness of the external environment was needed.

Paul Harris and the product managers were able to see on the matrix, for the first time, the position of their product and their competitors' products. They were very surprised to find that their product was in the most favorable position. But Harris reinforced the idea that this was an initial qualitative view only and that later results from other techniques might change this first outcome.

Paul Harris and his marketing team pinpointed all the data gaps and then assigned a special research group to fill in the voids. The group would work with management and its staff to develop the needed information. Paul Harris gave the research team three weeks to report back with its findings.

Farlin shook his head. "It'll take them six months," he said.

FORM 2
Assessing the Environment/Competition—
A Qualitative Approach

Competitor Names: A, B	Date: / /
Market Segment: DATA STORAGE	Product Manager: SMITH

	Storage Extreme			
Section A: Our product	Storage Extreme			
Section B: Competitors' products		A	B	C

Section C

1. Required investment to stay competitive	A	A	D	
2. Distribution costs	A	A	A	
3. New product innovation	D	A	D	
4. Skill level of the firm	A	D	D	
5. New product development	A	D	A	
6. Cyclicality of market segment	A	A	A	
7. Risk in market segment	D	D	D	
8. Product quality/service levels perceived	A	A	D	
9. Barriers to exit	A	A	A	
10. Price competitiveness	A	D	D	
11. Flexibility of pricing structure	A	A	D	
12. Capacity for economies of scale	A	A	D	
13. Product differentiation	A	A	A	

	A	A	D	
14. Raw materials easy to obtain	A	A	D	
15. Supplier power	A	D	D	
16. Regulatory climate	A	A	A	
17. Research and development	D	A	D	
18. Effectiveness of distribution channels	A	D	D	
19. Growth rate of total market (%)	A	A	A	
20. Barriers to entry	A	A	D	
21. Capacity utilization	A	D	D	
22. New product success	D	A	D	
23. Risk level of management	A	A	D	
24. Buyer power	A	D	A	
25. Substitution threat from competitors	A	D	D	
26. Availability of outside capital	A	A	D	
27. Financial stability	A	A	D	
28. Unit costs	A	A	D	
29. Promotional effectiveness	A	D	A	
30. Product life-cycle stage (I-G-M-D)	A	A	A	
31. Product's share of total market	A	D	D	
32. Growth rate of product's market share	A	A	D	
33. Estimated profit margin (%)	N/A	N/A	N/A	
34. Variety of applications and features	A	A	D	

Total As and Ds:

29 As	22 As	10 As
4 Ds	11 Ds	23 Ds

Section D. Environmental Advantages-Disadvantages Matrix

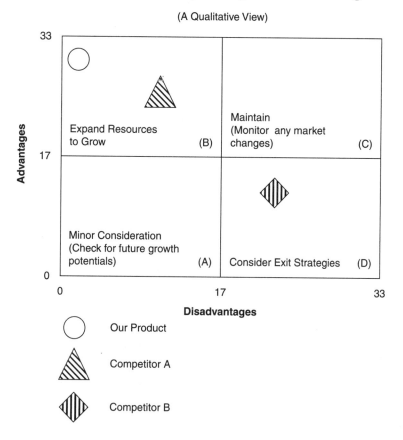

(A Qualitative View)

Summarize any significant findings:

1. Competitor A is the main threat to Storage Extreme, and Competitor B is the weakest threat.
2. Product managers had the most trouble finding firm data on Competitor A's required investment, marketing strategy, price structure, profit margins, market share, growth rate, and target market segments.
3. Product managers were able to give accurate answers for their own products but lacked certainty about the external variables affecting them.
4. The product managers' answers indicated that they were not keeping abreast of changes in the overall marketplace or the impact of those changes on the company. They were too concerned with meeting short-term objectives—another sign that the firm was becoming non-market-oriented.

Section E

Competitor: A

Product:_____

1. Does this firm differentiate its products?

Its Product Line

> No. The product is too early in development to perform that task.

Our Product Line

> Yes. Our firm is beginning to differentiate Storage Extreme by making it compatible with most connectivity devices.

2. Does this firm offer complementary products?

Its Offering

> Yes, but at a lower level of the storage drive segment.

Our Product Equivalent

> Yes, but at a lower level of the storage drive segment.

3. What stage of the product life cycle are this firm's major product lines in?

Its Offering

> Preintroduction.

Our Product Equivalent

> Introduction.

4.   Does this firm have technological advantages over our products?

Its Offering and Its Advantages

No.

Our Product Equivalent

Yes, we do. We have overcome most of the technological obstacles that Competitor A is still struggling with.

5.   Does this firm add more value than we do to any product?

Its Offering and Its Value Added

Yes—promotion, and possible price or volume discounts.

Our Product Equivalent

Yes—limited discounts and capability for add-on features as they come on line.

6.   Is it a niche company?

List Niches and Product Offering in Each

Yes—the same market segments we are currently in.

Our Product Equivalent

Storage Extreme.

7.   How does this firm's R&D compare to ours?

Describe Its R&D.

Based on Competitor A's prior products, our engineers and new venture developers firmly believe that our R&D team is superior to Competitor A's. But, since Competitor A constructs its equipment with less costly and inferior components, this can and does provide it with pricing power and discounts.

8.   Is the competitor's pricing strategy by individual product, segment, deep discounts, high end, or a market leader or follower?

Describe **Its Pricing Strategy**

Competitor A offers deep discounts to obtain large customer accounts via predatory pricing methods. This is usually based on product, but if a target segment is price sensitive, price changes are made for that segment as a whole.

9.   Does this firm have the ability for fast and flexible pricing against our firm?

Yes, it does, but our firm can respond as necessary.

10. What percent has this firm varied above or below its list price for its product to make a sale?

Product Offering and Price Variance

Plus or minus 18 percent off list price.

Our Product Equivalent

Plus or minus 15 percent off list price.

11. Is this firm decreasing prices to gain market share for the short or long term? If yes, on which products and how?

Product

Yes, data storage. Since its product is behind Storage Extreme in technology, Competitor A will resort to heavy advertising and steep price discounts. One of its strategies in the past has been to get the largest market share and sell complementary products at full price and also be able to migrate current customers to new products that will be equal to or better than Storage Extreme as they become available.

Method of Price Cutting

Decreasing prices to suppliers or retail markets. The exact amount is unknown.

12. What customer needs, wants, and desires do this firm's products fill that ours do not?

Competitor's Products

At this time, none. But it is our understanding that its data storage devices will be compatible with the top three computer makers, while ours is aimed at the small to medium markets and then at the top computer makers.

Associated Customer Voids

Any customer whose products are currently compatible with a major computer firm's product will have an easy interface.

13. Is this firm a leader or follower in new product innovations?

> Usually a follower but can catch up fast via mergers, patent buyouts, and acquisitions.

14. How does this firm's employee skill set compare to our firm's?

> Its skill set would be considered somewhat lower, since it uses contract workers and does not develop its workforce via training.

15. What distribution channels does it use?

> Any distribution channel that will give it the best price and reach its target market.

16. What are this firm's global and e-commerce strategies?

Since its products and ours are so new, it seems that both will first be sold in the United States and then sent to our overseas sales force. E-commerce strategies are still under development for both firms.

17. What is this firm's geographic coverage?

Very limited, but the products will be offered in the Northwest at first, since that is its usual marketing pattern for new products.

18. What geographic areas is this firm targeting as its major market segments?

From past experience, first the Northwest, then up the East Coast, and finally to all areas east of the Mississippi.

19. Is this firm innovative in any functional areas?

> None that we are aware of except financing.

20. Is this firm a leader or a follower in its target market segments?

> It's normally a leader, but in this situation it is playing the follower to see if our new technology is successful. We assume that is because of the cost of the equipment and materials to make Storage Extreme.

21. Does this firm grow by acquisitions, buyouts, or internal product development?

> All except internal development.

22. Do customers see this firm's products as technologically superior or inferior to ours?

> Customers rate them as above average in service and quality, but below our level.

23. What product applications does this firm have above or below our offerings?

> Because its new product is not out in full yet, we are not sure. As of now and based on what we have seen, its current product is technologically inferior to ours and has limited application.

24. Are this firm's production facilities up-to-date as compared to ours?

> Yes and no. Prior to the new technology of Storage Extreme, we would have agreed that they were. But our heavy investment in the new technology for Storage Extreme has put us ahead of all our competitors.

25. Specify this firm's target markets/segments for each of its products.

Product	Target Market/Segment
Data storage market/segments.	Not completely sure which segments will be its main focus for its new products, but once it gets to the Mississippi, it will probably follow us.

3

Step 2: Product Positioning Analysis

Introduction

The procedures in this chapter lead many successful companies to shrewd assessments of how their products are performing and where to position them. Companies must continually monitor their product positioning and how it responds to the macro and micro effects of environmental factors. These factors need to be set up categorically in a marketing information system that will follow trends and developments and use them to shape strategic positions. Of course, the marketing environment will be partly defined by the firm's vision/mission statement. Management knows (from Chapter 2) the parts of the environment that it needs to monitor if a business is to achieve its overall goals. When you have completed this chapter's Form 3, Product Evaluation Questionnaire, using the Critical Success Factors (CSF) Method, the Business Profile Matrix, and the Business Assessment Matrix, you will be able to see the current status of each product and its future based on your present marketing strategy clearly. In addition, the process will reveal any strategic gaps between your current and your expected positioning. You can then determine whether you need to change your current marketing strategy or reposition the product with a new strategic approach; for that purpose, you will use this chapter's strategic gap analysis and strategic scenario analysis.

While you do need information about each product's current position in the marketplace and its projected three-year position, the critical question is: will you meet your company's objectives in three years using your *current strategies only?* If not, then you must determine the weaknesses and voids in your current product strategies and make the needed changes that will close the strategic gaps between your projected and desired outcomes. Products must be positioned effectively so that, over a three-year horizon, you will be able to meet your marketing and company objectives. This process emphasizes the proactive nature of successful marketing plans.

However, knowing the strengths and weaknesses of each of your company's products is only the first step in recognizing each product's effect on your bottom line. In Chapter 4, based on your current marketing strategies, you will learn how to evaluate your entire product portfolio over a three-year period. Chapter 4 introduces two additional matrices that will give you foolproof strategies for strengthening that portfolio. Those evaluations will supplement the ones in this chapter and help guide you to a comprehensive strategic marketing plan.

This approach to evaluating your company's product positioning is one of several. This particular method, however, is one of the most valuable in generating product information for the development of a marketing strategy that will lead to sustained growth for your company. You may decide, as you familiarize yourself with the product positioning and portfolio analysis techniques presented in this book, that you will use more elaborate mapping approaches of your own. The purpose of this book is to ground you in basic product positioning and product portfolios; then you can tailor your own sound marketing strategies.

As you work through this chapter, you will draw on the data that you developed for the questionnaire in Chapter 2. In this chapter, you will be asked to rate various items qualitatively for Form 3, "Product Evaluation Questionnaire—CSF," but you will now assign numerical values to your responses in order to plot the position of your products on the Business Profile Matrix and the Business Assessment Matrix. (The same approach will be used in Chapter 4 for the matrices discussed there.) In this method, you will use qualitative data and convert them to quantitative data to determine the state of your company's products or strategic business units. A *strategic business unit* (SBU) is defined as one or more company divisions, a product line within a company, or even a single product. It generally has its own mission and objectives and may have its own marketing plan separate from those of other businesses within a firm. You will be introduced to scenario analysis to aid you in developing strategies and in closing strategic gaps. Scenario analysis will greatly help you in Chapter 6, which deals with strategy development.

The sample case at the end of the chapter provides a completed questionnaire and matrices for Techna's current situation and its three-year projections. To understand how these planning tools are created and used in a real-world situation, read through the sample case carefully.

Product Positioning: Micro/Macro View

Analyzing a product's position in the marketplace is crucial. Through this process, product managers can determine how a product is affected by certain factors in the environment—and, more precisely, the nature and interrelationships of those effects. Managers can also anticipate how certain trends will affect a product's future performance. This entire process allows managers to manage the product more effectively and to reduce guesswork and internal biases about the product in the marketplace.

Positioning Analysis

To analyze product positioning, marketing managers observe and research current demographic, economic, technological, political, and cultural changes.

Product positioning also includes the use of various matrices that determine a product's competitive position in the marketplace, its life-cycle stage, its attractiveness in the marketplace, its growth share, and its overall business strengths and weaknesses. These matrices reflect both controllable and uncontrollable variables. The best marketing strategy helps a company make the most of the variables that it *can* control and adapt effectively to those variables that it *cannot* control.

Starting the Analysis

To begin the analysis, you will need the following information about each product: its competitive position, the stage of the product life cycle it is in, its business strengths and weaknesses, the attractiveness of its market, its growth rate, and its market share. You should be able to obtain this information from Form 2, "Assessing the Environment/Competition—A Qualitative Approach," which you have completed for each of your firm's products.

Remember, it may seem at the outset that positioning analysis is concerned with the position of only one product or SBU. However, when you combine all your products into a company portfolio, you will discover a great deal about your firm—for example, its competitive strengths, market share, problems and opportunities, and any potential gaps in your strategies. All strategies must work together to reach the objectives set by the overall corporate business plan.

The purpose of Form 3, Product Evaluation Questionnaire—CSF, is to define key questions, attributes, or factors affecting a product so that you can then assign its initial numerical weighting. Each factor will be defined as critical, medium, or low in importance to the success of the firm (thus, the critical success method). That weighting system is implemented in the Business Profile Matrix. This system will help you minimize internal bias, expand the scope of the attributes affecting your product's future, and define strategic gaps.

Business Profile Matrix

The Business Profile Matrix, as shown in Figure 3.1, indicates the relationship between a product's *competitive position* and its *current life-cycle stage.* To complete the Business Profile Matrix, the marketing manager must determine both where the product stands in the life cycle today and where it will stand after three years.

In other words, data from Form 3 will help you determine the major weaknesses or gaps in the product's performance. Then the Business Profile Matrix suggests whether you can reposition the product during its life cycle to maintain or improve its competitive position.

The vertical axis of the matrix—the competitive position—indicates where the product stands in relation to its direct and indirect competition. The horizontal axis represents where the product is in its life cycle.

FIGURE 3.1
Business Profile Matrix

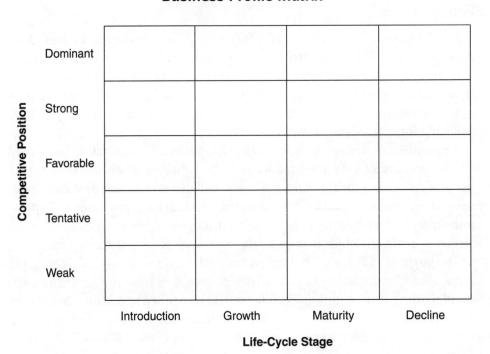

What the Business Profile Matrix shows you is critical when you are deciding how to allocate assets for product support, or even whether to keep the product in your portfolio. For example, suppose the product is in its introductory stage and falls into a strong competitive cell in the matrix. A successful marketing strategy might include moving the product into its growth stage and improving its competitive position (thus increasing revenues) by doing the following:

1. Using promotional tactics to increase buyer awareness
2. Using intensive and extensive optimal distribution channels and setting appropriate pricing

In this instance, you can see that your product is in a strong competitive position before it moves into the growth stage, where competition begins to intensify and market share is increasingly difficult to obtain.

On the other hand, suppose the Business Profile Matrix reveals that a product is in its late growth stage, it falls only into the "favorable" cell, and it is projected to fall into the "tentative" cell. Its competitive position will then decline, resulting in a lower market share and revenue.

This information is important, since in the mature stage of the product life cycle, competition is intense and profit margins correspondingly narrow. It is much more difficult to gain an increased share of the market without considerable cost to the firm. The available market is smaller, and other firms have already established brand loyalty. Considerable advertising funds may be needed to convince new customers to buy the product or to switch from their current products. In this case, the return on investment may fall to an unacceptable level, and the product will need a large cash outflow to maintain its current weak market share.

In working with the Business Profile Matrix, you will use the following process for each product:

1. Define the product's current place in its life cycle.
2. Determine where it will be, with respect to the market for all products, in three years. (The three-year projection is merely the example used in this book.)
3. Assess whether to continue or drop the product, or whether to devise corrective strategies to propel performance toward your objectives.

A completed Business Profile Matrix for the sample case is provided in Form 3 at the end of this chapter.

Business Assessment Matrix

The Business Assessment Matrix, shown in Figure 3.2, indicates the relationship between the *business strengths* supporting a product and the *attractiveness of the market* for product investment.

The vertical axis of the matrix, business strengths, shows the product's ability to compete in a particular industry. Business strengths usually involve a weighted rating of factors such as product quality, price competitiveness, relative market share, and other pertinent variables.

On the horizontal axis, market attractiveness, you numerically weight factors such as sensitivity to economic conditions, market size, competitive intensity, profitability, market growth, and other relevant variables.

As shown in Figure 3.2, the Business Assessment Matrix is divided into three sections: growth, selectivity, and harvest.

FIGURE 3.2
Business Assessment Matrix

Business Strengths	Market Attractiveness — High	Market Attractiveness — Medium	Market Attractiveness — Low
High	Growth	Growth	Selectivity
Medium	Growth	Selectivity	Harvest
Low	Selectivity	Harvest	Harvest

The *growth section* consists of three cells that indicate markets that are favorable or high in both market attractiveness and business strengths for your company's products. For those products, an appropriate marketing strategy would be to invest for growth.

The *selectivity section* indicates markets that have medium market attractiveness and business strengths. For these products, the best strategy may be simply to maintain the product's share of this market.

Matrix cells in the *harvest section* show markets with low overall market attractiveness and business strengths. A suggested strategy here may be to divest products in these markets if you cannot reposition them favorably. The main point is not to spend additional funds on products that produce low revenues or a loss.

The Business Assessment Matrix, then, presents a graphic and analytic picture of a product's investment and return possibilities, based on market conditions and on the company's capabilities. This method has been used successfully in many companies.

Like the Business Profile Matrix, the Business Assessment Matrix draws on the numerical values assigned to the questionnaire items in Form 3. Although only a few attributes in the composite are utilized in this example, you can expand or reduce the number of attributes you use. This process is a perfect application for a personal computer, which can make this matrix a dynamic planning tool.

In addition to the general strategies mentioned earlier, the Business Assessment Matrix allows marketing managers to determine which factors have the greatest or least influence on product positions. For example, one of your products may be ranked on four critical success factors as follows: high market growth, large market size, low competitive intensity, and low profitability.

At first glance, since three of the four critical factors are positive, the product seems to be in a strong position. But the fourth critical factor, low profitability, changes the picture. As a result, even though the product falls into the high-growth cell, you may discover that the return on investment is below company objectives. For this reason, it is important to look at all the critical factors. Although the initial results may look positive, only one or two negative critical success factors can alter the results considerably. In the case of our example, the firm has a high-growth product that yields little or no profit.

The next step is to determine why profit is so low. To do this, revisit the basis view (Chapter 2) and consult your original profitability analysis and the Assessing the Environment/Competition questionnaire. A careful check of that analysis should help you determine the factors that are pulling down profitability and whether the problem can be corrected.

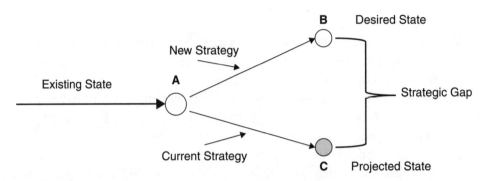

FIGURE 3.3
Strategic Gap Analysis

Strategic Gap Analysis

To illustrate how strategies are related to product planning, look at the strategic gap analysis depicted in Figure 3.3.

Point A represents the current position of a product. Point B is where the product manager (under current planning) would like to see the product within, say, three years. However, the firm's current strategies and assumptions about its environment may actually place the product at Point C in three years. The difference between Point B and Point C is known as the *strategic gap*.

If the gap seems significant and a good strategy could shrink it, the firm can change its product plans and objectives—a repositioning that shifts the product's projection closer to Point B. If the gap is negligible, or if uncontrollable circumstances prevent closing it, then the firm may opt to maintain its strategy. The company may simply allow the product to reach Point C.

Let's look at a brief example of how product managers can use this process to their advantage in developing product strategies. Look over the sample Business Profile Matrix in Figure 3.4.

Point A is the current product position, Point C is the projected position based on data from the Product Evaluation Questionnaire—CSF, and Point B is where you want your product to be in three years based on today's strategies. The area on the matrix between Points B and C is your strategic gap.

If you wish to close this gap and reach your desired position, first look at those success factors in the Product Evaluation Questionnaire—CSF that you considered *critical* to the success of your product. Determine which attributes are having a negative influence and whether you can control or change these attributes by changing your strategies. For example, if new legislation makes it

FIGURE 3.4
Business Profile Matrix—Sample Strategic Gap Analysis

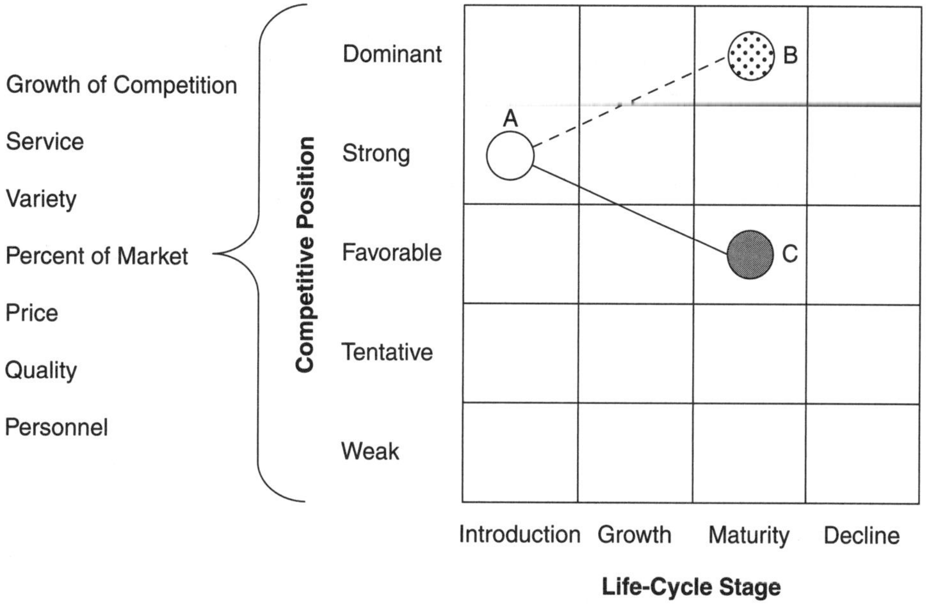

more difficult for you to sell your product across the state line, can you work to modify the legislation or to exempt your product?

If you cannot change the influence of these attributes on your product's future positioning, examine your contingency plans for new action. Perhaps you can offer more services with the product or develop a new pricing structure to undercut the competition. Follow the same steps for those factors that you consider *medium* and *low* in importance.

This process can assist you in three ways. First, it can help you to decide what strategic changes, if any, are necessary to close the gap. Second, it points out the strengths and weaknesses of your current strategies and objectives. Third, and most important, it serves as an early warning system to define problems and flag them now instead of a year or so later—when it may be too late to make changes.

It should be clear by now that a great deal depends on a sound environmental assessment. That assessment grounds successful strategies and objectives for the coming year or years. It yields strategic gap analysis, which can be a valuable tool in your strategy development and an important step in developing a strategic marketing plan.

Once you have completed the Product Evaluation Questionnaire—CSF, the Business Profile Matrix, and the Business Assessment Matrix for each product, you will need to put all the data together into a global or macro view for developing strategic plans. Such a macro view is explained in Chapter 4, "Step 3: Strategic Portfolio Analysis." Although this book is concerned only with the strategic level, the data you develop in these chapters will also help you in your tactical planning.

Product Evaluation Questionnaire—CSF

Many firms do not have adequate techniques for quantitatively assessing all the variables that the basis view considers. Therefore, this book provides Form 3, "Product Evaluation Questionnaire—CSF," which will help you analyze each product's environment. It combines both internal and external factors and provides a rating system, which is then used to plot a product's current and projected position on the Business Profile and Business Assessment Matrices. A completed Form 3 is contained at the end of the Sample Case and its results are used in associated figures.

The Product Evaluation Questionnaire—CSF, while pivotal, is flexible. You should tailor it to fit your company's needs, deleting irrelevant variables and adding those that affect your products. The questionnaire enables you to translate qualitative statements into measurable terms and results. Its objective is twofold: first, to determine whether your products are moving toward your company's goals, and second, to clarify individual product positions and signal potential problems and opportunities. If the products are not moving toward the stated objectives and strategies (desired outcomes), then a strategic gap exists, and you need to determine how to close this gap.

Defining the Terms

The Product Evaluation Questionnaire—CSF uses some special terms, which are defined here. Because these terms may have different meanings to different individuals, clarity is essential.

Section I: Competitive Position

1. *Price.* The extent to which the product enjoys a price advantage over the competition. In general, the product with a lower price has the advantage. If the item is clearly differentiated from the competition, however, the product manager has more latitude in setting the price, depending on the marketing strategy chosen.

2. *Quality.* The product's quality relative to that of competing products. Quality is the rated ability of the product to fulfill its function. It is an overall measure of the product's features, such as durability; reliability; precision; and ease of operation, maintenance, and repair.

3. *Variety.* The number of different items in a product line or the number of different features associated with a product. Variety enables a product or product line to attract customers who have different preferences and needs.

4. *Breadth of product application.* The number of different uses for the product relative to competing products.

5. *Relation to other product lines.* How closely this product is related to the firm's other products in terms of its end use. A high rating on this variable can lead to a price cross-elastic effect.

6. *Service.* The extent to which the company offers better service for its products than do competitors. Service includes the types and levels of delivery, installation, and maintenance provided by the firm and its competitors.

    Evaluating service requires an understanding of the importance of such elements to customers and knowledge of what determines customer choice. A service element may be important and yet not be a determinant of customer choice if all suppliers provide the same service level.

7. *Sales personnel.* Comparisons of the firm's salesforce with those of its competitors in terms of product knowledge, knowledge of customers and competitors, sales skills, and efficiency.

8. *Percent of market.* The product's sales expressed as a percentage of total market sales. Total market sales consist of the product's sales plus the sales of all substitute products.

9. *Growth of competition.* The entry of new competitors and products into the market and the extent to which competitive products have gained market share.

10. *Supplier power.* The extent to which a supplier can exert pressure over necessary resources and also enter your marketplace.

11. *Substitution threat.* The potential for competitors to offer substitute products that can take market share and sales away from you.

12. *Facilities management for production.* The extent to which your firm utilizes state-of-the-art facilities in its production process.

13. *Reputation of company.* The extent to which customers perceive your company as reliable.

Section II: Market Attractiveness

1. *Required investment.* An estimate of the financial resources required in all functional areas in order to compete effectively.
2. *New competitive threat.* The actual or potential loss of business to new competitors. The threat of new competition depends on the existence of barriers to entry and the risk of unexpected actions from existing competitors.
3. *Risk.* A measure of the level of uncertainty. As the rate of environmental change accelerates, the level of uncertainty increases; for example, new products and new competitors add to environmental uncertainty.
4. *Price elasticity to market demand.* An indicator of the sensitivity of demand for a product to increases or decreases in the price.
5. *Return on investment (compared to company yardstick).* The estimated return on investment that the product will generate (as a total or by SBU or product).
6. *Market size in dollars.* The total dollar value of the market.
7. *Market growth in dollars.* A measure in dollars of the expected growth level of market demand. Market demand is the total of all sales of a product and its substitutes in a defined geographic area within a defined time period. It is affected by industry marketing efforts and the environment in general. (Product units can be used here and converted to dollars.)
8. *Transactions generated.* The number of original purchases and the frequency of repeat purchases in a given time frame.
9. *Profitability—actual or estimated.* The actual or estimated profit by product after expenses and taxes.
10. *Product life expectancy.* The expected life of a product in the marketplace.
11. *Cyclicality (of demand).* The extent to which demand for the product fluctuates, seasonally or otherwise. If the fluctuations of demand are not synchronized with the pattern of supply, cyclicality can be a serious problem.
12. *Segmentation.* The division of a market into distinct subsets of customers who merit separate marketing programs and effort.
13. *Regulatory climate.* The extent to which laws and regulations affect strategic choices.
14. *Customer negotiating/buyer power.* The power of customers to negotiate changes in price or other factors when purchasing a product or service.
15. *Distribution.* Available distribution systems and their effectiveness in channeling the product to the target market.
16. *Lateral effect on sales of companion products.* The amount of cross-elasticity that exists among the firm's products.

17. *Economies of scale.* The extent to which the firm can obtain high economies of scale when production increases.
18. *Flexibility of management.* The extent to which management can adapt to changing conditions.

Section III: Business Strengths

1. *Geographic coverage.* Geographic constraints on product sales. Geographic constraints are desirable if market potentials and costs vary according to location, and if the product is available in the markets that the firm can best serve.
2. *Source structure.* Availability of appropriate sources for what is needed to produce and market products.
3. *Distribution (current system).* Evaluation of the distribution system relative to competitors' on the basis of its potential for creating sales and generating costs.
4. *Selling power.* Recognizing customer problems (needs) and providing solutions.
5. *Price competitiveness.* See *price* in Section I.
6. *Product differentiation.* The existence of distinctly different features, qualities, styles, or images that are important to the market and give products a competitive advantage.
7. *Breadth of product line.* The spectrum of products offered: a complete product line or only a specific part of a complete line.
8. *Compatibility of systems with product(s).*
   A. To what extent do your systems satisfy the needs of your product line?
   B. What relationship does this product have with other lines of business within your product group?
   C. Does the strategic direction of the product support the company's overall strategy?
9. *R&D for new products.* The likelihood of new product innovation or variations of present products.
10. *Relative market share.* The product's sales expressed as a percentage of the leading competitors' sales. A change in relative market share may be due to general environmental conditions—for example, substitute products and technological changes. Although external forces affect all competing products, they often affect them unequally. Thus relative market share is important. Measuring a product's performance against that of its competitors removes the influence of the general environment.

11. *Change in relative market share—three-year trend.* The change in relative market share over a three-year period (the current year and the two preceding years).
12. *Drawing power.* The extent to which the firm's promotion, reputation, and brand identification can draw potential customers.
13. *Financial stability.* The strength of the firm's balance sheet compared to industry norms.
14. *Profit margins.* The extent to which the target market will enable the firm to reach its profit margin objectives.

Instructions for Completing the Questionnaire

Because conditions for each company differ, you may need to adapt the Product Evaluation Questionnaire—CSF for your particular firm. To do so, follow these steps:

1. Go through the questionnaire and decide which questions you want to use. Add or delete questions to make the questionnaire more relevant to your company.
2. Decide which questions focus on factors that are *critical* to your product's success, which focus on those that are of *medium* importance, and which focus on those that are of *low* importance. Mark the questions with C, M, or L. The Cs are major critical success factors.
3. Weight each question by assigning a point spread, based on whether it is critical, medium, or low in importance. The following scale is suggested (where 1 is the least important and 10 is the most important):

 Critical: 1–10

 Medium: 1–7

 Low: 1–4

 As a C, M, or L rank is assigned to a question, fill in the appropriate range of values in the Points Assigned column on the questionnaire. (See the sample case at the end of this chapter.)

 Keep in mind that on this questionnaire, high values are not always good, and low values are not always bad. It all depends on the question and its importance to your firm. For example, if distribution channels, an asset, represent a *critical* variable for your firm's products, you will assign a value of 1 to 10 to your answers to all questions that relate to distribution channels. If an item in that category receives less than 5, you know that you are vulnerable to competition in terms of your distribution structure. In other words, a low score on distribution channels would be a negative indicator.

 On the other hand, regulatory climate, a potential liability, may be only a *low* concern. You would assign a value of 1 to 4 to your answers to all questions in this category. In this case, a low score would be a positive sign. Any item that receives a score of, say, 3 or 4 would indicate a potential problem for that product from a regulatory standpoint. Perhaps the Federal Trade Commission (FTC) is considering legislation that would make it more difficult for you to sell your product in another state.

4. Fill out your adjusted questionnaire and total the values for each of the three sections: competitive position, market attractiveness, and business strengths. These totals will be used as plot points to map your products on the matrices.

5. To determine the point values along the *horizontal* and *vertical* axes on the Business Assessment Matrix and along the *vertical axis* on the Business Profile Matrix (the life-cycle stage can be provided by the product manager), follow these steps:

   - Add up the highest values assigned to the questions in the points assigned column for each section of the questionnaire. (The highest values in the sample questionnaire are starred.)

   - Divide these totals by the number of cells along the vertical axis in each matrix. The same procedures apply to the horizontal axis in the Business Assessment Matrix. This will give you the incremental point value for each cell along each axis.

   For instance, suppose the sum of the highest values assigned to the questions in the competitive position section equals 100 points. The Business Profile Matrix has five cells along the vertical axis; therefore, $100/5 = 20$. The points along the vertical axis would be set as shown in the sample matrix that follows in Form 3A.

   If the totals of the highest points assigned are not equal for the axes on both matrices, you may want to index the totals to a base of 100. Indexing will not affect the positioning of the products.

6. For each section in the questionnaire, total the points in the column for the current year and for the projected year. (For the sample questionnaire, the current year is 201X and the three-year projection is 201Y.) These totals will enable you to plot the current and projected positions for your products on the two matrices.

7. Plot your product's current and projected positions on the Business Profile Matrix and the Business Assessment Matrix. Suppose, for example, your product is in the introduction stage and has competitive position total points of 72 for the current year. In three years, you project that your product will be in the mature stage with a competitive position

total of 59. These positions are plotted on the sample Business Profile Matrix.

8. Look over the current and projected product positions and write down any conclusions you may draw regarding product positions and any needed adjustments to current strategies.

9. Fill out a Product Evaluation Questionnaire—CSF for each of your company's products.

FORM 3A
Business Profile Matrix*

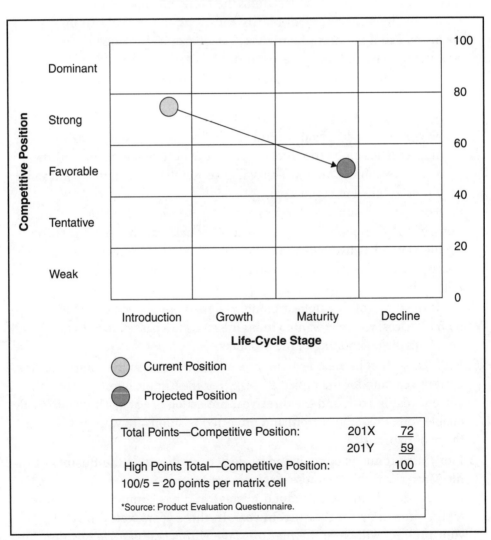

Total Points—Competitive Position: 201X   <u>72</u>
                                       201Y   <u>59</u>

 High Points Total—Competitive Position: <u>100</u>
100/5 = 20 points per matrix cell

*Source: Product Evaluation Questionnaire.

The results of the questionnaire, although not 100 percent precise, will give you a sound starting point from which to transform your qualitative data into quantitative data. This process is particularly valuable for those items where little or no quantitative information is available.

The data you generate in filling out the questionnaire will be used to complete the Portfolio Business Profile, Portfolio Business Assessment, and Growth–Share matrices presented in Chapter 4. Although many matrices have been developed to help marketing strategists position the analysis, these particular three are suggested for an important reason. Not only do they provide data for strategic planning from several perspectives, but they also act as a check-and-balance system on the results you gain from your analysis. A problem or opportunity that shows up on the Business Profile Matrix should also appear as a similar problem or opportunity on the Business Assessment Matrix and the Growth–Share Matrix. It is *very* important that you complete a questionnaire for your major competitors so that you can see where you and they are positioned in the target marketplace, and you can see the effects of changes in strategic scenarios, which in turn will help you select objectives and strategies.

Before you fill out the Product Evaluation Questionnaire—CSF, look over the completed questionnaire in the sample case at the end of this chapter. This will provide you with a better idea of the type of information the questionnaire is designed to provide. After you have finished the product evaluations, the results will guide you in formulating strategies to reposition your product from its current to its desired projected position and close any strategic gaps. You need to complete the Product Evaluation Questionnaire—CSF before you move on to the strategic scenario analysis (which draws heavily upon the questionnaire results) in the next section.

Strategic Scenario Analysis Using Weighted Averages

Now that you have completed the Product Evaluation Questionnaire using the critical success method, you can move on to a *second method* for determining a product's position: using a weighted average with strategic scenario analysis. This method uses weights and importance levels in place of the numerical values that you assigned for plotting points on the matrices: the high–medium–low critical success factors. To identify the strategic scenario factors to be weighted, you will need to think about several items that affect your industry and your company.

Each industry is likely to be somewhat different in terms of what factors are important, depending primarily on the nature of the product, customer behavior, and market type (that is, pure competition, oligopoly, or monopoly). For example, for customers whose needs include technological innovation, technological and related factors may help the products become strong business entities. The ease of new product innovations and the market environment will help you develop factors that will determine the attractiveness of the market. An analyst using this strategic scenario approach must rely heavily on management judgment, experience, and research for the selection of the few factors that will carry the most weight. For the same reason, when upper-level management's approval is needed for a project, those managers need to understand why these factors were chosen over others.

You will need to use the Product Evaluation Questionnaire—CSF to develop a list of factors that are of the utmost importance in answering questions regarding market attractiveness, competitive position, business strengths, and product life-cycle stage. These are the questions that were identified as critical. Since this is a weighted methodology, many analysts recommend having approximately four to eight factors per axis on each of the four headings: market attractiveness, competitive position, business strengths, and product life-cycle stage. After selecting the most important factors, you must *rerank* those factors as high, medium, or low. For each factor's importance level, use the ranking of low equals 0.0, medium equals 0.5, and high equals 1.00. Then determine the weight you will use for each factor. The weights must add up to 100. Simply multiply each weight by its importance level and sum up the results. The total equals the plot point for that axis. You will do a weighted table for business strengths, competitive position, and market attractiveness for today's current position and the projected three-year position. The product life-cycle stage for today and three years out will be provided by the product manager. Note: all data used in this section are from the sample case at the end of the chapter. Also, all figures, tables, charts, and interpretations are based on those data and will not be repeated in the sample case. For the sample case, the factors and importance levels used are as follows.

Competitive Position
Distribution (M)
Percent of market (H)
Service (M)
Price competitiveness (H)
Product quality (M)
Product differentiation (M)

Market Attractiveness
Required investment (M)
Price elasticity to market demand (H)
Market growth in dollars (H)

Market size in dollars (M)
Profitability (H)
ROI (H)
Distribution (M)

Business Strengths
Distribution (current system) (H)
Price competitiveness (H)
Product quality (M)
Product differentiation (M)
Relative market share (H)

Next, plot Storage Extreme's current and projected position on the Business Assessment Matrix and the Business Profile Matrix. It is strongly suggested that you develop weighted tables for your competitors as well and plot them for comparison purposes and to determine strategic gaps. Tables 3.1, 3.2, and 3.3 illustrate this procedure for Storage Extreme's plot points. To reduce redundancy, only the weights for Storage Extreme are provided in detail. The two competitors' plot points are given without the tables used to define those points.

TABLE 3.1
Market Attractiveness
(Current and Three-Year Projections)

Factor	Importance Today*	Weight Today	Rank Today	Importance Projected	Weight Projected	Rank Projected
Price elasticity to market demand	1.0	20	20	0.5	20	10
Market growth in $	0.5	15	7.5	0.5	15	7.5
Required investment	0.5	15	7.5	0.5	15	7.5
Market size in $	1.0	20	20	0.5	10	5
Profitability	0.5	15	7.5	0.5	15	7.5
Distribution	0.0	0	0	0.5	10	5
Return on investment	0.5	15	7.5	0.5	15	7.5
TOTALS		100	70		100	50

*Importance rank:
  High = 1.0
  Medium = 0.5
  Low = 0.0

TABLE 3.2

Business Strengths
(Current and Three-Year Projections)

Factor	Importance Today*	Weight Today	Rank Today	Importance Projected	Weight Projected	Rank Projected
Distribution	0.5	10	5	0.5	15	7.5
Price competitiveness	1.0	30	30	1.0	40	40
Relative market share	1.0	30	30	0.5	15	7.5
Product quality	0.5	20	10	0.5	15	7.5
Product differentiation	0.5	10	5	0.5	15	7.5
TOTALS		100	80		100	70

*Importance rank:
   High = 1.0
   Medium = 0.5
   Low = 0.0

TABLE 3.3

Competitive Position
(Current and Three-Year Projections)

Factor	Importance Today*	Weight Today	Rank Today	Importance Projected	Weight Projected	Rank Projected
Distribution	0.5	15	7.5	0.5	10	5
Price competitiveness	1.0	25	25	1.0	30	30
Percent of market	1.0	20	20	0.5	10	5
Product quality	0.5	15	7.5	0.5	10	5
Product differentiation	0.5	15	7.5	0.5	20	10
Service	0.5	10	5	0.5	20	10
TOTALS		100	72.5		100	65

*Importance rank:
   High = 1.0
   Medium = 0.5
   Low = 0.0

Competitors A and B's plot points are:

Competitor A's rank today is 72, and in three years its projected rank is 59.
Competitor B's rank today is 42, and in three years its projected rank is 29.

Compare the results with those you obtained by the first method (CSF), and if the results do not have a large variance, you are probably close in your analysis. If the position of the products has a high degree of variance, you must go back and make sure that your weights and importance levels were not overly or insufficiently aggressive. If the answer to either is yes, you will need to change the importance level(s), the associated weight(s), and, possibly, the factor(s) chosen. Figures 3.5 and 3.6 illustrate the current and projected positions of Storage Extreme using the critical success method and the weighted methodology. As expected, there is some variance, but not enough to be of concern.

FIGURE 3.5
Business Profile Matrix (Current and Projected Positions)

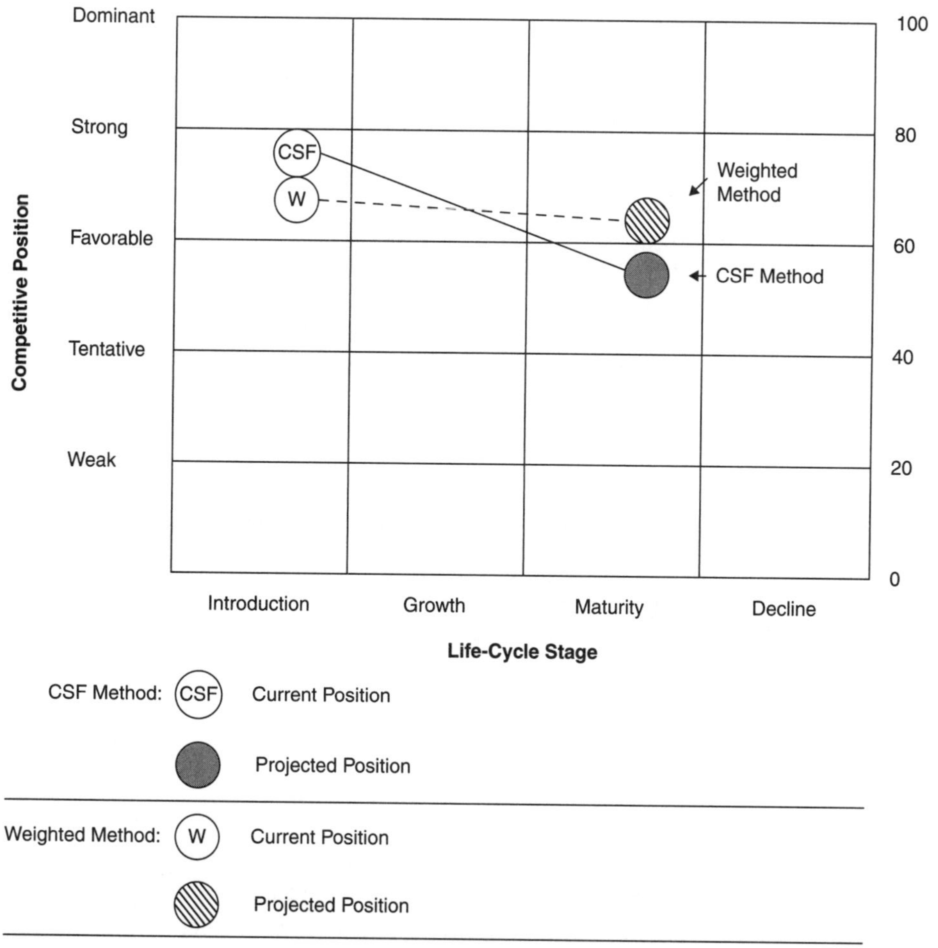

Product Life-Cycle Position: Introduction Today and Mature Projected.

FIGURE 3.6

Business Assessment Matrix (Current and Projected Positions)

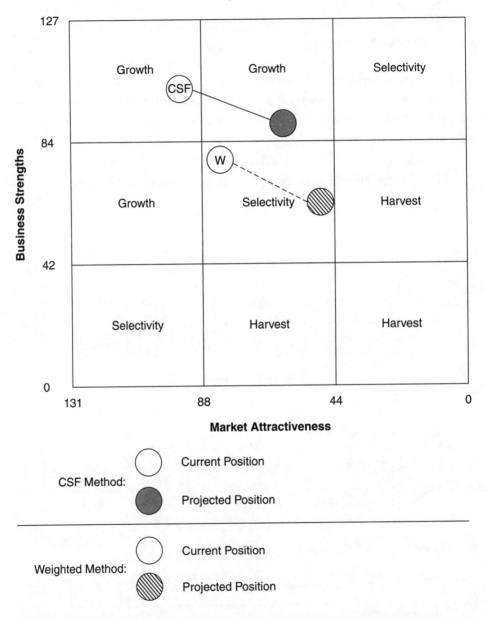

Product positions resulting from the two methods will predictably differ, but the variance should not be very large. Product managers, who have greater credibility and better product information than other executives, select the factors and develop the weights and importance levels when a weighted methodology is used, since in most cases their information is based on more established research. The critical success method is often used by firms that rely heavily on experience and less on quantitative, researched sources. Remember that the critical success method is a more in-depth approach, and, as a result, you will gain increased knowledge of your competition. It will also allow you to locate the factors that are most critical for you and your competitors. The choice is yours. It is recommended that you try using both methods and then draw conclusions. Also, remember to use both approaches for your competition, so that you can do strategic scenario analysis as well.

Strategic Scenario Analysis—Detailed

You are now at a point where you can examine, in detail, the output developed from the input information in Chapters 2 and 3. You should also examine the matrices in detail and make necessary changes in the questionnaire with respect to:

1. Your potential new strategies for the future.
2. The effect of your new strategies on your product's position in the marketplace and the effect of those strategies if your competitors do nothing in response to them.
3. Your competitors' probable strategic responses, if they are dynamic, to the changes in your strategies. Think about what steps your competitors may take and how they will affect your product's position.

Thus, you can look at your own and your competitors' product positions as they stand today and also see how you and they will be positioned in the future. This prediction results from changing the inputs on the Product Evaluation Questionnaire—CSF for you and your competitors and observing those strategic changes in your products and your competitors' products in the future. Naturally, such predictions will help you as you try to optimize your strategic selection.

For example, suppose one of your product managers decides to simulate a change in strategies to see the effect. Your product is in the early growth stage, and he decides to increase advertising, dramatically decrease price per unit, and begin to rely on increased unit volume to drive sales to your profit objectives. He then changes the factor(s), weight(s), and/or importance level(s) on the questionnaire to mirror this new strategy and show the results of the product's new three-year position. At the same time, he also changes the relevant elements for your competitors' products to how he believes, based on past experience and research, that they will change their strategies in response to your changed strategies. Now you are able to see the product dynamics of your target market environment in relation to changes in strategies. In this example, your competitors may have deeper financial pockets and can outspend you on advertising and undercut your price. That scenario would appear on the matrices and show that your strategy might not be a very attractive one.

Figures 3.7 and 3.8 illustrate how this strategy succumbs to analysis: as your product moves inevitably toward the decline stage, Competitor A is moving to a strong, mature position. Hence, your new strategies cause Competitor A to respond in such a way that your market share and revenues will drop. Competitor B is probably doing nothing in response to your strategies and will be eliminated. This result with regard to your product's position and the response by Competitor A warns you to avoid this strategy. Since scenarios are only simulations, you need to understand how the competition will react. This is where all your research comes into play.

You may have to perform several iterations of strategy scenarios and observe what works and what does not work until you find your competitors' vulnerabilities. Then you will concentrate on exploiting their vulnerabilities with new strategies. Again, map out what you believe will happen over the three-year span—just to be on the safe side.

Summary

- Product positioning analysis helps managers to determine the nature, interrelationships, and impact of environmental factors for each product and to anticipate trends and competitive moves so as to optimize strategies.
- This process allows companies to manage their products more effectively and to assess each product in its market, minimizing guesswork and internal biases.
- Marketing managers must make reasonable assumptions about demographic, economic, technological, political, and cultural changes. They should test their assumptions against what can be observed in the environment.
- Product positioning analysis includes the development of certain matrices to determine competitive position, life-cycle stage, market attractiveness, growth share, and business strengths and weaknesses. The matrices reflect both controllable and uncontrollable variables.
- The Business Profile Matrix predicts how a product's passage through its life cycle will gradually reposition it competitively unless you use the matrix to help determine the appropriate marketing strategy.

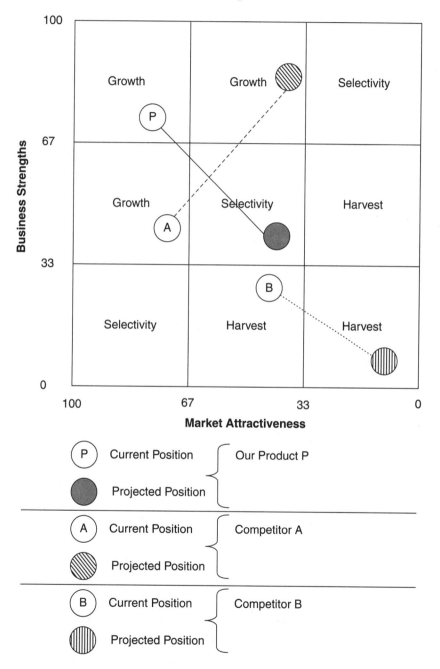

FIGURE 3.7
Business Assessment Matrix (Current and Projected Positions)—
Scenario 1 Strategies in Place

FIGURE 3.8
Business Profile Matrix (Current and Projected Positions)— Scenario, 1 Strategies in Place

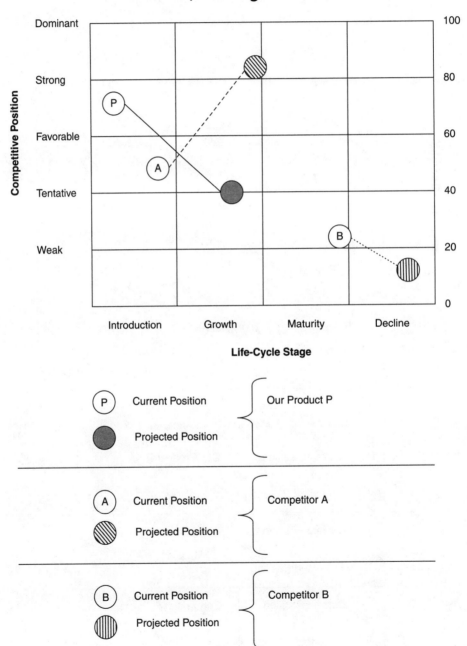

- The Business Assessment Matrix shows how to balance the business strengths supporting a product and the attractiveness of the market in determining product investment. The matrix is divided into three sections: growth, selectivity, and harvest. It gives a graphic and analytic picture of a product's investment and return possibilities, a picture that is based on market conditions and on the company's capabilities.
- Strategic gap analysis shows you the difference between your product's desired position and its projected position. The process can help you to (1) decide what changes in strategy, if any, are necessary to close the gap, (2) detect strengths and weaknesses in your current strategies and objectives, and (3) identify problems early on while there's still time to make changes.
- Strategic scenario analysis allows you to make changes within the questionnaires and observe the results on the product map. That analysis may go through many iterations before it reveals your competitors' weak points. You will then be able to exploit those weak points fully by designing sound strategies within a strategic marketing plan.

Sample Case, Phase 3

At the end of three weeks, Paul Harris received the results of his staff's efforts to fill in the data gaps revealed by the Assessing the Environment/Competition questionnaire. Although his staff was able to fill in some of the information, there was still some data missing.

"What's the next step?" one of his marketing team members asked.

"We need to do a comprehensive product evaluation. I've developed a Product Evaluation Questionnaire that I want to use. It will give us more quantitative data, but we may still have to rely on managers' gut feelings for the answers to some of the questions."

The staff members looked dubious. "How can you be sure that the 'gut feeling' data have any validity?"

"I'll have the managers present their completed forms to me in person so that I can ask questions about their answers. You'd be surprised how that improves the data I get."

Harris and the three partners called a product management meeting to explain the Product Evaluation Questionnaire. Harris first expressed his appreciation for the managers' cooperation so far, emphasizing in particular the honesty of the answers he had received.

"Now we need to gather information on each product and analyze both its current position and its projected three-year position based on today's strategies.

"In the case of Storage Extreme, for example, we can map its current and projected position based on data developed by market research and forecasting groups. This could include a policy of collecting information on current customers for the new solid-state disk drive and expanding market share by finding new users nationwide.

"We can then put together a portfolio of all the products and determine whether we like the direction in which they're going. If we don't, we'll need to develop new strategies and objectives to improve their projected positions."

One of the managers raised her hand. "Does this mean that we have to fill out another form? How many of these things are there?"

Bartly interjected strongly, "This planning process is a high priority for the company. However many forms there are, that's how many everyone will fill out."

Harris heard the subdued murmurs, which could mean rebellion if he did not change the tone of the meeting. "I understand your feelings. No one I've ever worked with has wanted to fill out these questionnaires, but they've always appreciated what they learned from them. It may be a chore to fill out these forms, but I can guarantee that you will get something out of it for yourselves."

Harris handed out copies of the Product Evaluation Questionnaire—CSF and explained the ranking and point systems. The marketing department had already assigned preliminary point values to the critical, medium, and low rankings, but the product managers could change the point values at their discretion. It would be up to the individual product managers to assign a C, M, or L rank to each question and to use the point values associated with each rank.

"You'll have to make some assumptions in answering certain questions, but our marketing group is here to help you. If some assumptions have a wide variance—for instance, the growth rate of the GDP over the next three years—calculate a baseline that everyone can use. Let's say the growth will be 3.9 percent over the next three years. You can use that figure in answering all questions that involve GDP projections."

"Some of these answers will be based on your judgment as much as on objective facts or figures. Use the comment section to explain and support your answers. Don't worry about having to explain anything in any great detail. Remember, this is not a test of your knowledge but part of a data-gathering process that is fundamental to any good plan. I must emphasize that we will be completing the form not only for our products but for our top two or three competitors as well." The product managers hung their heads, but they did not object too much, since they already had a lot of new competitive information from the prior studies.

"Turn in the completed forms to me personally, so we'll have a chance to discuss your answers. We have a tight schedule to keep, so I'd like the questionnaire returned two weeks from tomorrow."

Harris was particularly interested in which items the product managers would consider to be of critical, medium, and low importance. To make sure that none of them exaggerated or understated their responses, he would compare their answers with the market-share data, sales figures, and other information his staff had developed independently. The managers, in turn, would be gaining valuable experience in gathering data and analyzing their products from a marketing perspective. Harris felt confident that this would make them feel more invested in the planning process, which would be a valuable asset when it came time to implement the final plan.

Within two weeks, Harris had received the questionnaires from every manager, complete with comments, rankings, and mappings. He was pleased with the thoroughness of the responses, particularly for Storage Extreme. (The completed Product Evaluation Questionnaire for Storage Extreme can be found after the matrices at the end of this case.) Harris explained how and when they would use strategic scenario analysis to test objectives and strategies and select the ones that would meet the overall business plan. The managers were excited about this opportunity, which also gave them a greater incentive to obtain richer data in their research. Harris was also very pleased with the results of the weighted-average method, since its results correlated well with all prior research and matrices. (Tables 3.1, 3.2, and 3.3 are identical to the ones utilized in the sample case and will not be repeated here.)

Harris analyzed the results for each product. Because Storage Extreme has a three- to four-year life span in a high-growth, fast-paced industry, he was not surprised to find that in three years, Storage Extreme would move to the early mature stage. If the projected life span had been longer, the downward trend would have indicated a problem. To be sure that the projections were correct, Harris needed to determine whether the current strategies for Storage Extreme were still applicable after portfolio analysis was completed. The next step would be to see how the entire product portfolio looked before developing strategic objectives and selecting marketing strategies. The CSF Method was used for both forms as the Weighted Method was shown in the text.

FORM 3A
Business Profile Matrix*

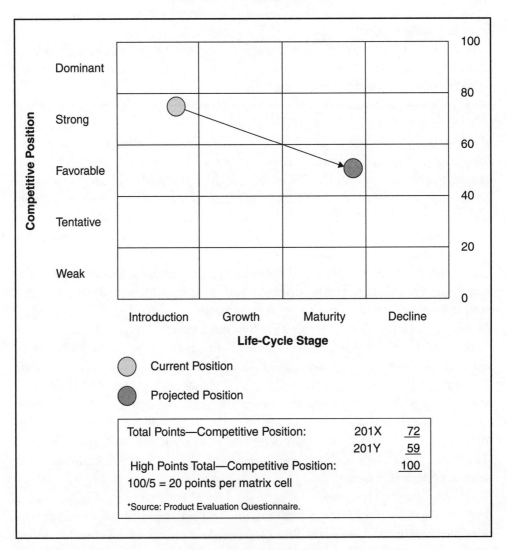

Current Position

Projected Position

Total Points—Competitive Position:	201X	72
	201Y	59
High Points Total—Competitive Position:		100
100/5 = 20 points per matrix cell		

*Source: Product Evaluation Questionnaire.

Conclusions Drawn from Business Profile Matrix (Overview)

1. Storage Extreme is in the higher section of the strong cell of its introductory stage. This will drop as the product reaches the mature stage of its life cycle, but by how much cannot be determined at this time, since there are virtually no competitors and the product is a brand-new technology.

2. Storage Extreme should gain significant market share and realize a low positive profit margin at first, but the cash flow and profit margins in the future will increase. Funds should be allocated now to capture the large market share with possible price flexibility, and the funds should be tapered off as the product reaches the mature stage and substitute products begin entering the market.

3. No major voids exist. Those that do exist and allow the product to fall in competitive position are largely outside of management's control, unless profit margins are also allowed to drop.

4. The marketing manager should determine specific plans to migrate current customers for the old products to Storage Extreme—especially the early adopters.

5. No strategic gaps exist; the product is following the success sequence.

Conclusions Drawn from Business Assessment Matrix (Overview)

1. Storage Extreme has very high business strengths, market strengths, and competitive position—including no major voids.

2. The market is large, has very high potential, and is very attractive to investment; market attractiveness is high, and the business strengths required to ensure a successful product exist. No strategic gaps currently occur.

3. In three years, Storage Extreme is expected to decline in business strength and market attractiveness because of an expected increase in the number of competitors, and the product will enter its mature stage. Prices and profit margins will also decrease by definition as a result of the highly competitive market.

4. Once Storage Extreme reaches the mature stage, the firm should invest only enough to maintain its market share. A new substitute prototype product will be out in three years to fill Storage Extreme's technological voids. Again, the new product should be out first, capture a large part of the market, and become the potential market leader.

5. The timing for phasing out Storage Extreme and migrating its customers to a new substitute product will be crucial in three years so as to maintain and/or increase market share for the firm as a whole.

FORM 3B
Business Assessment Matrix*

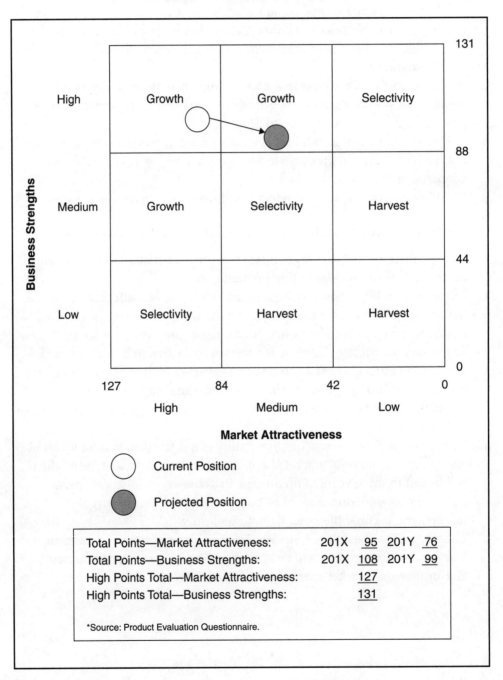

Market Attractiveness

○ Current Position

● Projected Position

Total Points—Market Attractiveness:	201X <u>95</u>	201Y <u>76</u>
Total Points—Business Strengths:	201X <u>108</u>	201Y <u>99</u>
High Points Total—Market Attractiveness:	<u>127</u>	
High Points Total—Business Strengths:	<u>131</u>	

*Source: Product Evaluation Questionnaire.

FORM 3
Product Evaluation Questionnaire— Critical Success Method

Our Product: Storage Extreme   Date: XX/XX/XX

Product Manager: Smith   Product: Storage Extreme

Section I: Competitive Position

Critical Success Factors Ranking: C, M, L

Points Assigned: Critical, 1–10; Medium, 1–7; Low, 1–4

Remember, you must select the factors, rank them (C, M, or L) and assign values to each so that the questions from the environmental analysis fit your environment—the following are only examples for the sample case. * Indicates high points used to calculate High Points Total for each section.

1.   **C**   Price

To what extent does our firm have a price advantage over competitors?

Current Year (201X)	Three-Year Projected (201Y)	Points Assigned
Low	3	3
Moderate 7		7
High		10*

Comments:

> Currently, as we have few competitors and economies of scale, we can charge a premium price to increase target market share and profit margins. In three years, the target market will become fully saturated and will offer a technologically superior product. The product and target market will be in the mature stage, and competitive pricing will force profit margins down.

2.   __M__   Quality

To what extent does our firm have better quality than our competitors?

Current Year (201X)	Three-Year Projected (201Y)	Points Assigned
Low		I
Moderate	5	5
High 7		7*

Comments:

> Currently, end users view our products as higher in quality than our competitors', but this will change slightly as our competitors increase their quality standards.

3.   __C__   Percent of market

Current Year (201X)	Three-Year Projected (201Y)	Points Assigned
Low		3
Moderate	6	6
High 10		10*

Comments:

> Our product is projected to have 14 percent of the southwestern market in eight months. In three years, market size will greatly expand. Our initial projections are that we will have 36 percent of that market; however, this is likely to be 29 percent because of an increase in foreign competition, e-commerce, and rapid changes in technology.

4. __L__   Variety

To what extent does our firm have a broader assortment associated with this product than our competitors?

Current Year (201X)	Three-Year Projected (201Y)	Points Assigned
Low	I	I
Moderate 3		3
High		5*

Comments:

> The product has limited value-added features currently; more comple-mentary features and products will be added later, but the market will be moving toward technologically superior products. Therefore, the product line is not complete at this time for all market segments. In three years, competitors will offer the same features.

5. __M__   Sales personnel

How does our sales staff compare with our major competitors'?

Current Year (201X)	Three-Year Projected (201Y)	Points Assigned
Low		2
Equal 4	4	4
Better		6*

Comments:

> The firm has extensive training and excellent compensation but requires a three-month learning curve for national coverage and possible global coverage or e-commerce.

6.   _M_   Breadth of product application

Current Year (201X)	Three-Year Projected (201Y)	Points Assigned
Low ___2___		2
Moderate _____	___4___	4
High _____	_____	6*

Comments:

> Product was placed in the market early to reach early adopters. Not all applications are available. In one year, breadth will be great enough to meet most of the needs of target market segments.

7.   _L_   Relation to other product lines

Current Year (201X)	Three-Year Projected (201Y)	Points Assigned
Little/no compatibility _____	_____	1
Moderate ___2___	_____	2
High _____	___3___	3*

Comments:

> The product is in a different product line from other offerings but is technologically superior. Several current products can be used with this product, but some will be eliminated from product lines because of obsolescence. In three years, Storage Extreme's technology will decline. Other company products will change to newer technology and will not be as adaptive to this product.

8. __M__ Services

How does our firm's service compare with major competitors'?

Current Year (201X)	Three-Year Projected (201Y)	Points Assigned
Low		3
Same 5	5	5
High		7*

Comments:

> High service is a major corporate goal. The firm has good training, high compensation, and incentives, but a three-month learning curve is still needed for Storage Extreme. The firm will have national coverage possibly in one year.

9. __C__ Growth of competition

Current Year (201X)	Three-Year Projected (201Y)	Points Assigned
Low 10		10*
Moderate		6
High	3	3

Comments:

> The product is in the introductory stage; it has few competitors today, but competition will rise substantially as high demand and large profit margins draw other firms into the market. The product also matures in about three years, and at that point, the market will be saturated and moving to the new technology.

10. __M__   Assortment

To what extent does our firm have a broader assortment than our major competitors?

Current Year (201X)	Three-Year Projected (201Y)	Points Assigned
Low		2
Same	5	5
Higher 7		7*

Comments:

> Currently we have a technological edge and complementary products. In three years, our competition will offer the same lines of products.

11. __C__   Supplier power

To what extent can suppliers exert pressure over necessary resources and possibly enter our market?

Current Year (201X)	Three-Year Projected (201Y)	Points Assigned
Low		3
Moderate 7	7	7
High		10*

Comments:

> Suppliers are many and procurement of resources is readily available. Suppliers are possibly interested in entering this highly competitive market in two years.

12. __L__ Substitution threat

To what extent can competitors produce and supply substitute products that are equal to or better than our offerings?

Current Year (201X)	Three-Year Projected (201Y)	Points Assigned
Low I	I	I
Moderate		2
High		4*

Comments:

> There are few competitors currently, and our product is complex and expensive to copy in the near future. A substantial investment will also be required, which is a barrier to entry for many smaller firms.

13. __M__ Facilities management for production

Current Year (201X)	Three-Year Projected (201Y)	Points Assigned
Low 2		2
Moderate	5	5
High		8*

Comments:

> Facilities are not yet up-to-date for full production at the present time. In less than one year, the facilities will be running at 87 percent of capacity. Competition is months behind in facilities management for this new product.

14.   **M**   Reputation of company

To what extent can competitors produce and supply substitute products that are equal to or better than our offerings?

Current Year (201X)	Three-Year Projected (201Y)	Points Assigned
Low _____	_____	2
Moderate 5	_____	5
High _____	7	7*

Comments:

> This firm is well regarded today as being on time and on budget for customers.

Total Points—Competitive Position: 72   59

Competitive Position—High Points Total: 100

Section II. Market Attractiveness

Critical Success Factors Ranking: C, M, L

Points Assigned: Critical, 1–10; Medium, 1–7; Low, 1–4

1.   **M**   Required investment

Current Year (201X)	Three-Year Projected (201Y)	Points Assigned
Low _____	_____	3
Moderate 5	_____	5
High _____	7	7*

Comments:

> Capacity expansion is needed now, but our firm has estimated that peak demand will be in one year, and new capacity will be required over the next year if we are to hit our market share goal. The product will be in the mature stage in three years; therefore, in order to remain competitive for the next three years, marketing expenditures are expected to either increase substantially during that time or decrease, if necessary, to expend funds on new, substitute products.

2.   **M**   New competitive threat

Current Year (201X)	Three-Year Projected (201Y)	Points Assigned
Low 2		2
Moderate		4
High	6	6*

Comments:

> There are few competitors today because of the high cost for new capital expenditures, advertising, and the like. As prices and materials begin to drop in price, we can expect many competitors.

3.   **M**   Risk

New products, new competitors, fashions

Current Year (201X)	Three-Year Projected (201Y)	Points Assigned
Low	2	2
Moderate 4		4
High		6*

Comments:

> High demand, new technology, and few competitors equal lower risk. In three years, many competitors and lower profits will increase the risk of lost market share and decrease future profits.

4.   __L__   Product life expectancy

Current Year (201X)	Three-Year Projected (201Y)	Points Assigned
Low		I
Moderate 2	2	2
High		3*

Comments:

> High demand, new technology, and few competitors equal lower risk. In three years, many competitors and lower profits will increase the risk of loss of market share and decrease future profits. This should cause the target markets to decrease in competitors, and most firms will be moving on to creating new technology.

5.   __L__   Price elasticity to market demand

Current Year (201X)	Three-Year Projected (201Y)	Points Assigned
Elastic	2	2
Elasticity 3		3
Unitary		4*

Comments:

> Price elasticity for this product is medium to low.

6. __C__   Market growth in dollars

Current Year (201X)	Three-Year Projected (201Y)	Points Assigned
Low _____	____3____	____3____
Moderate __6__	_____	6
High _____	_____	10*

Comments:

Fast growth now is due to high demand and few competitors. In one to two years, many competitors will be in the market. The market will begin to be saturated, and new, technologically superior products will appear.

7. __L__   Cyclicality (of demand)

Current Year (201X)	Three-Year Projected (201Y)	Points Assigned
Fluctuating_____	____I____	____I____
Moderate __2__	_____	2
Stable _____	_____	3*

Comments:

Cyclicality is moderate now. In three years, economic conditions may cause certain cycles to appear, and they will probably affect the buying patterns of customers.

8.   __C__   Market size in dollars (000)

Current Year (201X)	Three-Year Projected (201Y)	Points Assigned
To $250 _____	_____ 3 _____	_____ 3 _____
$251–$850 _____	_____	_____ 5 _____
More than $851 __ 10 __	_____	_____ 10* _____

Comments:

Market size is estimated to increase substantially over the next three years based on market and demand research, and then level off and decline rapidly as a result of new and less costly substitute products.

9.   __C__   Profitability—actual or estimated

Current Year (201X)	Three-Year Projected (201Y)	Points Assigned
Red _____	_____	_____ 3 _____
0–7% _____	_____ 7 _____	_____ 7 _____
8–12%+ __ 10 __	_____	_____ 10* _____

Comments:

Profit margins are high now because of economies of scale. When product reaches the mature stage, all firms will have equal economies. To increase market share, our firm and many competitors will lower prices to the point of considering exiting this product's market, since the profit margins are too low.

10.   **M**   Segmentation

How easily can the market for this product be segmented?

Current Year (201X)	Three-Year Projected (201Y)	Points Assigned
Difficult		3
Moderate 5	5	5
Easy		7*

Comments:

> The market is difficult to segment into discrete customer groupings. This is not expected to change within the next three years unless total U.S. coverage is obtained and global markets for this product open up.

11.   **L**   Seasonality

Current Year (201X)	Three-Year Projected (201Y)	Points Assigned
Low	1	1
Moderate 2		2
High		3*

Comments:

> Certain times of the year affect orders to a small extent, but overall, no definite seasonality pattern that significantly affects the demand for the product exists.

12. __L__   Regulatory climate

Current Year (201X)	Three-Year Projected (201Y)	Points Assigned
Little or none 1	1	1
Moderately regulated 2		2
Highly regulated		3*

Comments:

> There is no government regulation in this competitive market because of the large number of competitors.

13. __M__   Customer negotiating/buying power

Current Year (201X)	Three-Year Projected (201Y)	Points Assigned
Low	3	3
Moderate 5		5
High	7	7*

Comments:

> Currently, only large customers have negotiating power. As the number of competitors increases, all customers will have equal bargaining power through different types of pricing tactics. We will need to adjust prices to stay competitive and maintain market share.

14. __C__   Return on investment (compared to company yardstick)

Current Year (201X)	Three-Year Projected (201Y)	Points Assigned
Low	3	3
Moderate 6		6
High		10*

Comments:

> High return now is due to the low number of competitors, but in three years, competition will increase and will reduce the profit margin, as described in Question 13.

15. __C__   Distribution

Current Year (201X)	Three-Year Projected (201Y)	Points Assigned
Poor		3
Good		6
Excellent 10	10	10*

Comments:

> Compared with our competitors, our product will be national and offered through a cost-efficient distribution system. In three years, our competitors' products will be similar to ours, with equally good distribution coverage. But we do have more sophisticated global and e-commerce systems than our competitors.

16. __M__   Lateral effect on sales of companion products

Current Year (201X)	Three-Year Projected (201Y)	Points Assigned
Low _____	_____3_____	_____3_____
Moderate ___5___	_____	_____5_____
High _____	_____	_____7*_____

Comments:

> There are currently other main product lines that support Storage Extreme. Complementary products are currently in progress. The lateral effect on companion products should be minimal.

17. __M__   Transactions generated

Current Year (201X)	Three-Year Projected (201Y)	Points Assigned
One purchase every three years _____	_____3_____	_____3_____
One purchase every one to three years or longer ___5___	_____	_____5_____
One purchase every six months to one year _____	_____	_____7*_____

Comments:

> Buyers purchase this product only as needed and do not regard it as a high-repeat purchase unless the product breaks, is destroyed, or is stolen.

18. __M__   Economies of scale

Current Year (201X)	Three-Year Projected (201Y)	Points Assigned
Low	3	3
Moderate		5
High 7		7*

Comments:

> Economies of scale will increase dramatically in the first year and a half, and then, as the market becomes saturated, these economies will begin to fall.

19. __M__   Flexibility of management

Current Year (201X)	Three-Year Projected (201Y)	Points Assigned
Low	3	3
Moderate 5		5
High	7	7*

Comments:

> Upper management is semiflexible when a product is in the mature stage, is not making its ROI objective, and is clearly moving toward its decline rather rapidly with no hope of product regeneration. They will pull the budget from the failing product and immediately fund new R&D projects to replace the obsolete product with new, innovative ones.

Total Points—Market Attractiveness: 95   76

Market Attractiveness—High Points Total: 127

Section III. Business Strengths

Critical Success Factors Ranking: C, M, L

Points Assigned: Critical, 1–10; Medium, 1–7; Low, 1–4

1.　__M__　　Geographic coverage

Current Year (201X)	Three-Year Projected (201Y)	Points Assigned
Low		3
Somewhat higher	5	5
Much higher　7		7*

Comments:

Our firm has Southwest coverage available by distribution system and sales offices, but production capacity constraints limit national coverage for at least one year.

2.　__C__　　Distribution (current system)

Current Year (201X)	Three-Year Projected (201Y)	Points Assigned
Low		3
Somewhat higher		5
Much higher　10	10	10*

Comments:

Refer to Question 15 in Market Attractiveness.

3.   **M**   Quality

To what extent does our firm have better product quality than our major competitors?

Current Year (201X)	Three-Year Projected (201Y)	Points Assigned
Low _____	_____	3
Somewhat higher _____	_____	5
Much higher ___7___	7	7*

Comments:

> High service is a major corporate goal. Our firm has good service training, high compensation, incentives, and the like, but a three-month learning curve is still needed. Our firm will have national and possibly global coverage in one year. Our firm offers the best warranty in this niche.

4.   **C**   Change in relative market share—three-year trend

Current Year (201X)	Three-Year Projected (201Y)	Points Assigned
Declining _____	4	4
Moderately increasing _____	_____	7
Greatly increasing ___10___	_____	10*

Comments:

> Market share today is greatly increasing. As our product enters the mature stage, however, demand will decline, the market will become saturated, and many competitors will have entered the field. Market share growth will remain stationary or decline, with changes occurring only with major price reductions.

5. **M**   Selling power

Current Year (201X)	Three-Year Projected (201Y)	Points Assigned
Low		3
Somewhat higher	5	5
Much higher 7		7*

Comments:

Currently, we have few competitors and economies of scale, so we can change price levels to increase market share as needed. In three years, many competitors will be in the market with similar or superior products. The product and the market will be in the mature stage, and competitive pricing will force profit margins down substantially.

6. **C**   Price competitiveness

Current Year (201X)	Three-Year Projected (201Y)	Points Assigned
Low		4
Somewhat higher 7	7	7
Much higher		10*

Comments:

We can meet all of the prices of our competitors now because of our low cost structure. In the future, our competitors' cost structures will decrease. We want to keep the minimum ROI as stated in our objectives, so we will not compete on cost as vigorously as our competitors. As a result, we want a large market share now, but we also want to be in a position to move customers to our new substitute product(s) in three years. This indicates a future market decline.

7.   __L__   Breadth of product line

Current Year (201X)	Three-Year Projected (201Y)	Points Assigned
Low ____I____	_____	____I____
Somewhat higher _____	2	2
Much higher _____	_____	____3*____

Comments:

> We carry a complete product line and plan to continue this strategy to
> fill all of our defined target markets for our current products. Storage
> Extreme is still in the development stage for added breadth of its product
> line.

8.   __L__   R&D for new products

To what extent do new products or variations of present products enter our
business and stimulate customers to purchase?

Current Year (201X)	Three-Year Projected (201Y)	Points Assigned
Low _____	_____	____I____
Somewhat higher ___2___	2	2
Much higher _____	_____	____3*____

Comments:

> Updates of current products are done perpetually. Storage Extreme is the
> first in the industry and will stimulate customers in key target markets.

9.   <u>**M**</u>   Product differentiation

Current Year (201X)	Three-Year Projected (201Y)	Points Assigned
Low _____	_____ 3 _____	_____ 3 _____
Somewhat higher 5	_____	_____ 5
Much higher _____	_____	_____ 7* _____

Comments:

> We can easily differentiate our products as being technologically superior. In three years, all products will have the same features and level of technology and differentiation; therefore, advertising will cost more than the market share gained will justify.

10.   <u>**M**</u>   Relative market share

Current Year (201X)	Three-Year Projected (201Y)	Points Assigned
0–7% _____	_____	2
8–9% 4	_____	4
10–16% _____	_____	6
17+% _____	8	8*

Comments:

> We know the current relative market share, and our forecast serves as the basis for our answers regarding our predictions.

11.   __M__   Source structure

Current Year (201X)	Three-Year Projected (201Y)	Points Assigned
Low _____	_____	____3____
Somewhat higher __5__	_____	____5____
Much higher _____	____7____	____7*____

Comments:

> The source structure is good and is expected to continue.

12.   __M__   Product quality

Current Year (201X)	Three-Year Projected (201Y)	Points Assigned
Low _____	_____	____3____
Somewhat higher _____	____5____	____5____
Much higher __7__	_____	____7*____

Comments:

> Market research indicates that consumers see our products as higher in quality than those of our competitors, but this will change slightly as our competition increases and basic materials costs decline.

13.   __M__   Compatibility of systems with products

A.   To what extent do our systems satisfy the needs of our product line?

Current Year (201X)	Three-Year Projected (201Y)	Points Assigned
Low		3
Somewhat higher 5	5	5
Much higher		7*

Comments:

> The high technology of our product today enhances our current product line, but there is really no compatibility with older-technology products. But in three years, our competitors' products will equal or exceed this product's technology, and compatibility will change.

B.   __M__   Relationship with other lines within our product group

Current Year (201X)	Three-Year Projected (201Y)	Points Assigned
Low 3		3
Somewhat higher	5	5
Much higher		7*

Comments:

> As of today, the relationship to our other lines is not very good because our current products are not truly technologically compatible with this product. But in three years, many products will be compatible because of technological changes.

C. __C__   Strategic direction of the product and the company

Current Year (201X)	Three-Year Projected (201Y)	Points Assigned
Low		3
Somewhat higher 7		7
Much higher	10	10*

Comments:

> Management wants frontier products with high return and large market share to complement the firm's growth strategy. This need will decline as the product enters the mature stage in approximately three years, with large market share but reduced profit margins. Introduction of new products to replace obsolete products will continue as the product enters the decline stage.

14. __L__   Drawing power

Current Year (201X)	Three-Year Projected (201Y)	Points Assigned
Poor		1
Average	2	2
High 4		4*

Comments:

> Since we have new technology today, we are drawing new customers from competitors and other areas. In three years, all products will be similar as competition increases. Brand awareness will aid us in the early stages of product sales, but this will decline as the product matures and is replaced by technologically superior products.

15.   **M**   Financial stability

Current Year (201X)	Three-Year Projected (201Y)	Points Assigned
Low		3
Medium		5
High 7	7	7*

Comments:

> Our ability to raise short- and long-term capital and obtain lines of credit is excellent. The firm has a strong cash flow and balance sheet.

16.   **C**   Profit margins

Current Year (201X)	Three-Year Projected (201Y)	Points Assigned
Low	3	3
Medium		6
High 10		10*

Comments:

> Profit margins are high now, since this is a revolutionary product. But in three years, there will be many substitute products, and this will force the demand to drop and shrink these margins.

Total Points—Business Strengths: 108   99

Business Strengths—High Points Total: 131

4

Step 3: Strategic Portfolio Analysis

Introduction

So far, the environmental analysis has dealt with individual products. In contrast, portfolio analysis looks at the total company picture. Your firm must have a systematic approach if it is to understand how all its products fit together and how the product mix affects the overall allocations of scarce assets to each product and strategy. This portfolio analysis, in turn, will affect individual product plans, since each individual plan is a part of the total marketing plan to reach company objectives.

Portfolio analysis depicts the current and projected position of the company's entire product portfolio as dictated by its current strategy. In this chapter, the Portfolio Business Profile Matrix, the Portfolio Business Assessment Matrix, the Portfolio Modified Growth–Share Matrix, and the Product Dynamics Matrix, which map out the current and projected positions of the firm as compared to your competitors, will be utilized. This analysis will help you to select strategies to reposition or even jettison products to achieve your company's growth and market share goals.

Portfolio Analysis—Macro View

A company with several divisions and products has an important advantage over undiversified firms. It can channel its resources into the most productive units rather than allocating all funds to a single product line and hoping for the best. Successful companies often integrate their strategic planning at the corporate or division level to match scarce resources with product potential and to establish when and how they will transfer those resources.

For example, a diversified conglomerate may choose to slow the growth of its electronic games division so that it can divert the cash to expand its business software division. Such integrated planning may deliberately downplay one division's activities in the interest of increasing total corporate performance.

The product portfolio approach, which you are using in this chapter, differs in an important way from other integrated planning techniques. In the product portfolio method, strategic roles are assigned to each product on the basis of the product's market growth rate and market share relative to the competition. These individual roles must then be incorporated into a corporate strategy for the whole portfolio of products, taking into account the product portfolio's significant competitors. This analysis will show differences in growth potential, relative market share, and hence cash flow potential that are unique to each product. In turn, these differences will determine which products represent investment opportunities, which should supply investment funds, and which may be candidates for elimination from the portfolio.

The objective of this analysis is to get the best overall performance for the portfolio while at the same time keeping cash flow in balance.

If a company's products are in different industries—for example, book publishing and food service—the firm cannot compare the product lines directly. For each industry's product lines, the managers will have to develop separate portfolios.

Portfolio Business Profile and Portfolio Business Assessment Matrices

Figures 4.1 and 4.2 show the Portfolio Business Profile and the Portfolio Business Assessment matrices on which there are plotted six products of a firm whose products' average life span is less than five years. This is a very dynamic portfolio, one that is constantly changing as the firm introduces new products. These matrices show how the products move over time—that is, where they are expected to be in three years. The firm uses these matrices to identify strategic gaps and to balance the portfolio in terms of cash flow, market share, and contribution margin.

Notice the similarities between the two matrices with regard to product movements. These similarities demonstrate the check-and-balance system mentioned in Chapters 2 and 3. If your facts are correct and the matrices are correctly constructed, the results you obtained on one should be reflected in the results on the others.

But these reflections do not mean that one matrix replaces the others. Successful firms build an in-depth picture of the firm's portfolio by adding different dimensions of performance. To do so, you move from the Portfolio Business Profile Matrix and the Portfolio Business Assessment Matrix to the Portfolio Growth–Market Share Matrix (Figure 4.3). Keep in mind, however, that the profile and assessment matrices are important parts of your portfolio analysis.

FIGURE 4.1
Portfolio Business Profile Matrix

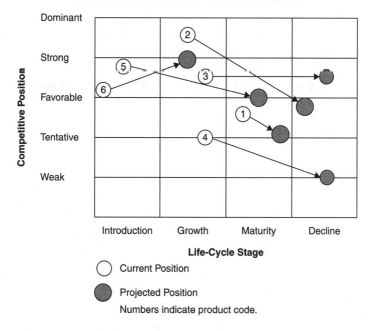

FIGURE 4.2
Portfolio Business Assessment Matrix

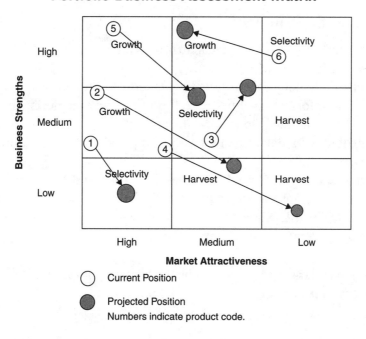

FIGURE 4.3
Portfolio Growth–Market Share Matrix

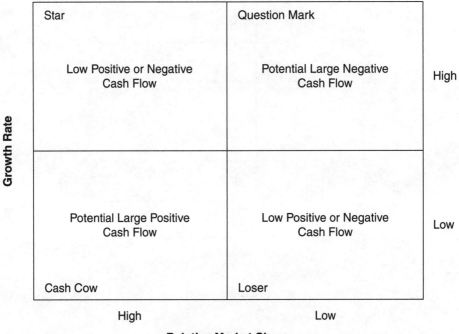

Modified Growth–Share Matrix

The Portfolio Growth–Market Share Matrix (hereafter simply called the Growth–Share Matrix) depicts your product categories. It is shown in Figure 4.3, and it provides what is usually called *portfolio analysis*. When completed, it displays the status and performance of the overall portfolio and suggests what strategy the company should adopt to ensure strong performance. The Growth–Share Matrix contributes its data directly to the company's strategy planning at the macro level.

The original Growth–Share Matrix was developed by the Boston Consulting Group, and this concept has been adapted to the approach here. Figure 4.4 shows an example of a Growth–Share Matrix using four products. The matrix indicates the following information for each product:

1. Its sales in dollars are represented by the diameter of the circle. The larger the volume, the larger the circle.

FIGURE 4.4
Growth–Share Matrix with Four Products

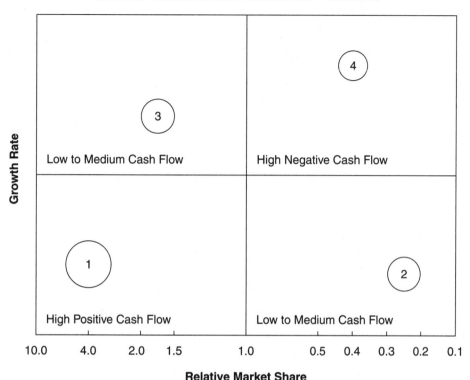

2. The vertical axis shows the growth rate of the market or industry in which the product is competing.
3. The horizontal axis shows the relative market share that the firm's product holds, compared to the share held by the competitor with the largest share.

In this matrix, growth rate simply means the percentage by which the sales volume of all firms in that particular market has changed during the most recent period for which information is available.

Relative market share is the ratio of the firm's unit sales of a product to the unit sales of the same product by the firm's largest competitor. This is the same as the ratio of the two companies' market shares. For example, if your Product A's annual sales were 3.1 million units and the market leader's annual sales were 10 million units, your firm's relative market share for this product would be 0.31 (that is, 3.1/10 = 0.31).

However, for markets in which your company is the market leader, your firm will have a relative market share of more than 1.0. Also, if you and another company both have a ratio of 1.0, that company and your firm would be tied for the lead.

Relative market share is used in this analysis instead of simply market share because it captures the relationship of your firm's share to the leader's share. For instance, your company's 15 percent market share has quite a different meaning if the market leader has a 17 percent share of the total market than if it has a 45 percent share. You are much closer to the leader if the leader has a 17 percent share than if it held a 45 percent market share to your 15 percent share.

However, you may not always know your competitors' market shares or be able to calculate the relative market share for your products. In such cases, you can change the horizontal axis from a log scale to a percentage from 1 to 100 percent, as shown in Figure 4.5, the Portfolio Modified Growth–Share Matrix. This matrix simply shows not your product's relative market share, but its market share as a percent.

As the strategic market planner, you need to think about decisions for the long-range future. You can project the Growth–Share Matrix by predicting each

FIGURE 4.5
Portfolio Modified Growth–Share Matrix

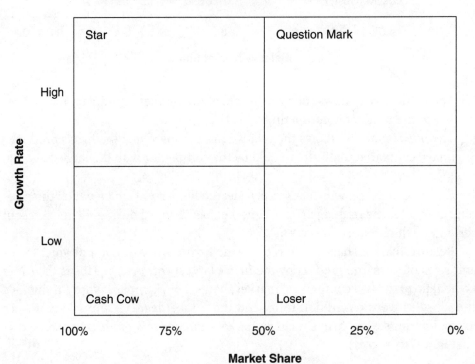

of the two elements in the figure (growth rate and market share or relative market share). Remember, even though the point from which these elements grow comes from reliable current data, the projections entail some risk.

In a Growth–Share Matrix such as the one shown in Figure 4.4, the value of the horizontal (market share) dividing line is based on a log scale. The vertical (growth rate) dividing line is based on the growth rate for sales of this product, industrywide.

Setting Growth–Share Matrix Values

It is strategically vital that you set the right values for the dividing lines in market share and growth rate, since they serve as cutoff points in your assessment of the company's portfolio. Remember, it is up to you to set the points for your particular circumstances. The example shows 1.0 as the cutoff point for the market share, but your firm may have a different point (for example, 2.0 or 0.5), depending on its objectives. You need to determine whether you like the direction in which your company is moving and, if not, what you need to do to correct it.

In this analysis, it is assumed that growth rate and cash use are correlated, as are market share and cash generation. Keep in mind two key assumptions of portfolio analysis:

1. Cash flow from products with high relative market shares will be stronger than cash flow from products with smaller shares.
2. You will need more cash for products in faster-growing markets than for those in slower-growing markets.

Interpreting the Modified Growth–Share Matrix

Once you have the matrix plotted, you will interpret its data based on the following:

- The vertical axis, growth rate, represents the level of growth in a particular product or industry.
- The horizontal axis, market share, indicates the level of your share of the market for a product. (The criteria used to set these dividing lines here are merely examples, since these criteria would probably differ in different industries.)
- Margins usually increase with market share because of the economies-of-scale effect.

- Sales growth requires cash input to finance added capacity and working capital. Thus, if you maintain your market share, then as the whole market grows, you must put in more cash.
- An increase in market share usually requires cash input to support increased advertising expenditures, lower prices, and other share-gaining tactics.
- Growth in each market will ultimately slow as the product approaches maturity. As growth slows, you are still earning cash, you can reinvest that cash in other products that are still growing faster without losing your market share position.
- The model assumes that you have chosen a unit of analysis for which market share is somewhat related to cost.

With these factors in mind, you can see in Figure 4.5 that products that are below the market share (horizontal) dividing line have modest to strong cash flows. Products that are above that line have weaker or negative cash flows.

As shown in Figure 4.5, these four product categories have been classified on the basis of their cash flow characteristics as follows:

1. *Cash cows.* These are products that generate considerable cash—more than can be profitably invested in them. Typically, they have a dominant share of a slowly growing market. These products provide the cash to pay interest on corporate debt, cover corporate overhead, pay dividends, finance R&D, and provide funds that will allow other products to grow.
2. *Stars.* These products are high-growth, high-share items. They may or may not be self-sufficient in cash flow, depending on whether their cash flow from operations is sufficient to finance their rapid growth.
3. *Question marks.* These are products with a low share of a fast-growing market. A low market share often means both low profits and weak cash flows from operations because the market is growing rapidly beyond the product. Simply to keep its market share, the company must invest large amounts of cash; increasing that share calls for even more cash. While the market is growing attractively, only substantial cash outlays will make these products strong contributors in the portfolio.
4. *Losers.* These products have a low share of a slowly growing market. They neither generate nor require significant amounts of cash. Maintaining market share usually requires reinvestment of their modest cash flow from operations, plus some additional capital. Because of their low market share, their profitability is marginal. They are unlikely ever to be a significant source of cash.

However, there is one important exception. A new product may occupy this cell for a short period during its introductory stage, before moving to the question mark or star cell during its growth or mature stage. Thus, new products that are initially placed in this cell are not treated the same way as older loser products when you choose their strategies.

By locating products on a Growth–Share Matrix, you will get a good picture of your portfolio's current health. Over time, the positions of your products will move as a result of market dynamics and your own strategic decisions. The objective of a portfolio analysis is to discover the current state of your products and use it as a basis for strategic decisions that will strengthen that portfolio in the future. This information will be of vital importance as you develop your strategic marketing plan.

Some of the movements of products and the portfolio can be predicted in general terms, depending on the strategies selected and whether the variables are controllable or uncontrollable. For example, movements on the vertical axis (that is, rate of total market growth) are largely beyond the firm's control and must be anticipated when developing your strategy.

A firm that selects only a share-maintaining strategy for its portfolio will find that eventually all its products will become either cash cows or losers, and most of them will fall into the loser category. Whether they become cash cows or losers, however, depends on the market share they hold before their market growth slows, usually before they reach their late mature stage.

Likewise, question marks ultimately become losers unless a company invests enough during the growth stage to shift them into the star category. Stars ensure the company's future because they will become cash cows as market growth slows and investment needs decline.

Future positioning and sales volume are given in Figure 4.6. The dark circles represent the data three years from now, and the lines indicate the desirable future direction. Funds are pumped from the cash cows to strengthen the competitive positions of the question marks and stars and to develop and acquire new products.

Form 4, "Portfolio Modified Growth–Share Matrix," presented in the sample case, enables you to see the current and projected positions of your product lines in a macro or portfolio view. By mapping your own product lines on the form, you can determine which products are following a "success sequence" (discussed next) and which products may need to be repositioned or eliminated from your portfolio. At this point, you have an excellent opportunity to check your financials and the cash-flow balances of your portfolio and determine what you should adjust if these are unlikely to meet your objectives.

FIGURE 4.6

Modified Growth–Share Matrix—Movement of Four Products

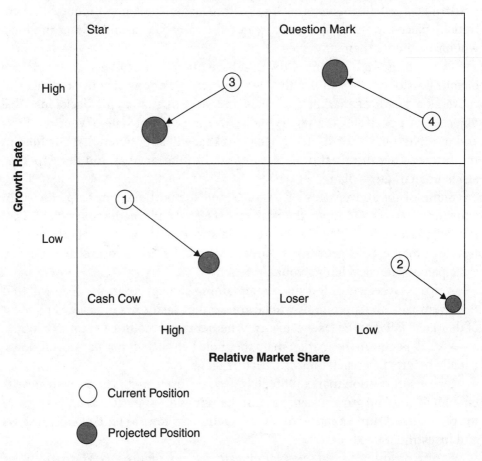

Together, the matrices in this chapter will show all of your products on an equal plane and will help you to identify which products in your portfolio need to be repositioned. You may want to develop target portfolios that will meet your firm's overall objectives and strategies. The Product Dynamics Matrix, discussed next, can be used to illustrate successful product repositioning strategies.

Product Dynamics Matrix

The Product Dynamics Matrix, illustrated in Figure 4.7, shows the optimal repositioning of a product from one cell on the matrix to another. The cells used in this matrix are equivalent to those used in the Growth–Share Matrix. The objective

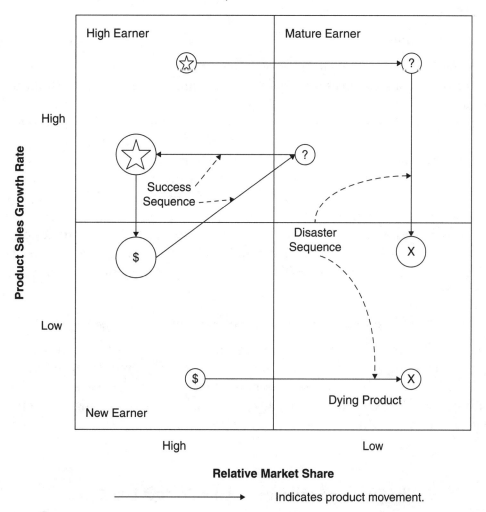

FIGURE 4.7
Product Dynamics Matrix

of this chart is to illustrate a success sequence that a product can follow to gain market share and increase cash flow. Once the product has been positioned on the Growth–Share Matrix, you can formulate specific strategies on the basis of the success sequence.

At this point, it is important to understand a key principle of the macro view. Since no firm can fully control how a target market grows, portfolio analysis becomes a way to develop a market share strategy for individual products. You are going to use all the data you have generated so far and begin to determine which strategy or strategies will help you to move your portfolio in the correct direction to achieve your overall company objectives.

Success Sequence

The basis of a sound long-term strategy is to use cash generated by cash cows to fund market share increases for question mark products in which the company has a *strong* competitive advantage. You will be able to identify such products through your competitive analysis, product evaluation, and matrices. If successful, this strategy will produce new stars that, in turn, will become the company's future cash cows. The success sequence is illustrated in Figure 4.7.

On the other hand, a question mark product with a *weak* competitive position is a liability. Such a product should remain in the portfolio only if the company has to spend little or no cash to maintain its position. This strategy will cause the product to become a loser eventually. Losers should be retained only if they contribute some cash flow and do not tie up funds that could generate profits elsewhere. At some point, the company must consider eliminating loser products from the portfolio.

The Product Life Cycle and the Success Sequence

In many respects, the success sequence is closely associated with the movement of a product along its life cycle, as shown in Figure 4.8. Product categories are closely related to product life-cycle stages—another reason that you should identify each product's position in the life cycle. Thus, life-cycle planning techniques are also useful in strategy formulation, as discussed in Chapter 7.

FIGURE 4.8
The Success Sequence and the Product Life Cycle

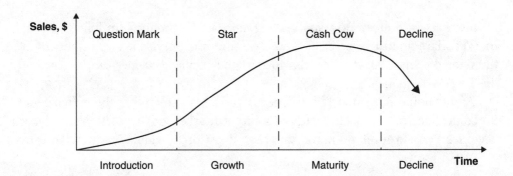

Because the Growth–Share Matrix represents performance only in the most recent period, either total category volume or a product's market share may fluctuate temporarily and cross one of the dividing lines for a moment. As a result, you may be plotting only a short-term effect for some products that fall close to the dividing lines. However, it would be wise to investigate whether even this slight movement might have some attractive strategic possibilities for your company.

Portfolio Scenario Analysis

To make it easier to understand the matrices to come, the portfolio scenario analysis presented here will use three products from your firm and three products from each of your top two competitors. In this analysis, Step 1 assumes than you make no strategic changes in any product line. This matrix will show how you and your competitors are positioned in the target marketplace, both now and three years in the future.

As shown in Figure 4.9, the Portfolio Business Profile Matrix reflects that your Product 1 is doing very well, Product 3 is stable but should have a better competitive position, and Product 2 is nosediving for some unknown reason. Competitor A's Products 1 and 3 are moving positively and gaining market share, while its Product 2 is losing ground, but at a much slower pace than your Product 2. Competitor B's products all have declining market share, and all are moving toward the decline phase faster than competing products.

Step 2 views your current and three-year projected positions and shows only the effects of strategic changes that you make that affect your product portfolio, as shown in Figure 4.10.

Step 3 determines (and Figure 4.11 illustrates) the effects of your competitors' reactions to your strategic changes. Those changes to your product portfolio may well be different from what was predicted in Step 2. (Specific strategies are left out for now and will be introduced in Chapter 7.)

Portfolio scenario analysis is similar to the strategic scenario analysis in Chapter 3, but now cash flow, advertising, and pricing strategies can be changed over the entire product line to offset gains in market share. For example, let's assume that the manager wants to increase market share for Product 3 in three years. Using this strategy indicates moving into the early mature stage, which will require, over the next three years, high business strengths, high market attractiveness, a steady growth rate, and continuous market share increases via your strategies. To accomplish this strategy, you will need to reallocate resources from the other two products. Figure 4.10 illustrates only one of our three product lines with the new strategies in place and what the analyst believes the new position will be in three years, based on the research that the firm has developed in Chapters 2 and 3.

FIGURE 4.9

Portfolio Business Profile Matrix—No Strategic Change on Our Part

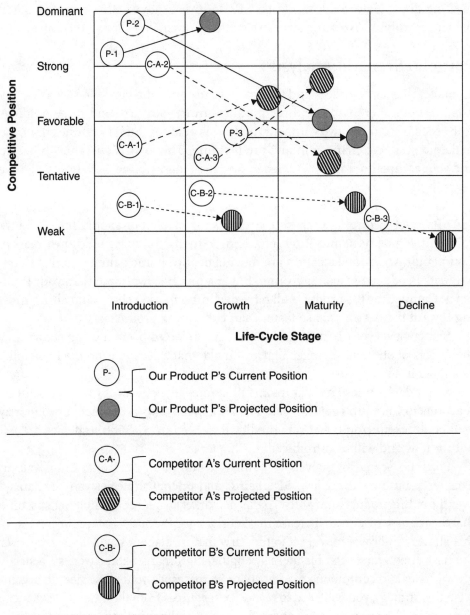

Letters and numbers indicate product code.

FIGURE 4.10

Portfolio Business Profile Matrix—Three-Year Projection for Our Product with No Strategic Changes in Competitors' Product Equivalents

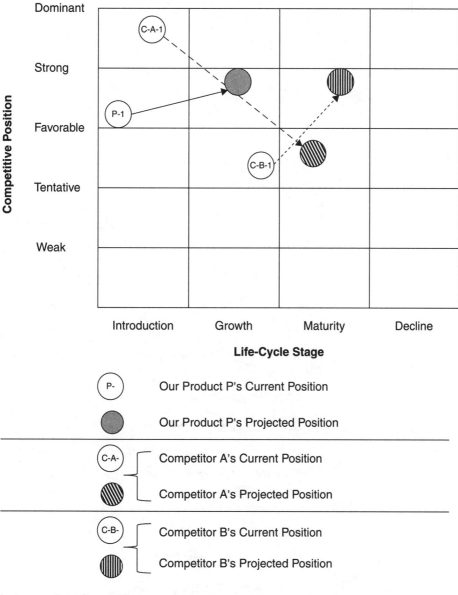

Letters and numbers indicate product code.

FIGURE 4.11

Portfolio Business Profile Matrix—with Competitors' Reaction to Our Strategic Changes

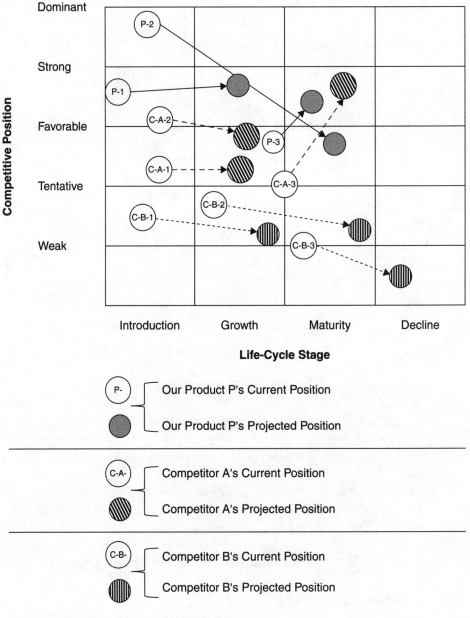

The results shown in Figure 4.11 indicate that Products 1 and 2 have lost slightly in future market share. But Product 3 will have gained enough future market share to offset both the lost market share of Products 1 and 2 and the associated decline in revenue and profits. These strategic changes look very promising, but the main question is how competitors will react to them. This reaction can pose a problem, since they can draw resources from their other product lines just as you can. This is where the product manager must rely on the questionnaires from Chapter 2 and prior research to make solid decisions and assumptions. If the research is flawed, these efforts may not work out as intended.

Competitor A used short-term outside funding to change the strategies of its Product 3 in retaliation for your strategies to gain market share. The changes in the position of its Product 1 were more dramatic than the loss of market share from its Product 2. Your analyst/product manager did not expect Competitor A to use short-term funding to outperform your firm in gaining more target market share. This strategy eroded market share projections for all three of your products' positions. Since the inflow of Competitor A's funds did not sap cash flow from its product lines, it has a major advantage. On the other hand, your Product 1 lost market share, Product 2 stayed about the same, and Product 3 lost considerable market share and relapsed nearly to its initial position, as seen in Figure 4.9. From this result, you see that this strategy may be a very poor one. In addition, with this strategy, you would have to spend money in the hopes of gaining share. Since that would never happen, that money would be lost. Also, you would be losing more dollars in the future because Products 1, 2, and 3 would all have lost market share and revenue. The total cost of this strategy makes it financially undesirable. The strategy would need to be thought through further, but this analysis might indicate that other strategies could build your net market share—possibly for all three of your products. This foresight in depth is one advantage of portfolio analysis. For example, you see that Competitor 2 lost market share for all its products. This result indicates a firm that lacks good funding, management, and formal market plan development skills.

It should be evident that the market plan developer must use the micro view first, then move toward the macro view and complete simulation studies to obtain a good understanding of what will and will not benefit the firm. Many good analysts also use probabilities in the selection of strategies to gain increased confidence in their strategic selection. The main point of the Portfolio Business Profile Matrix and the Portfolio Modified Growth–Share Matrix is this: when you develop strategies for your product in a single setting and do not take your competitors' reactions to your strategic changes into account, this can lead you into the "marketing elevator to hell."

It is imperative that you superimpose your competitors' matrices over yours to develop a sense of how they will react.

Let us follow the same approach for the Portfolio Business Assessment Matrix and the Portfolio Modified Growth–Share Matrix. First, you will look at the basis view of all three competitors' product lines. Then you will look at a view of your company only. Finally, you will look at the successes or disasters of your potential marketing-strategy change. One of the main goals is to show that the results should be very close to those of the prior matrices.

Figure 4.12 illustrates the initial view, with none of the three companies having changed its strategy. This is today's current view and where you believe your competitors' positions will be in three years. Note how this result resembles that in Figure 4.9.

Figure 4.13 shows your and your competitors' current and projected position in three years. This matrix uses the same strategic changes used in the Portfolio Business Profile Matrix. Note again that the moves are very similar.

Finally, Figure 4.14 illustrates the two competitors in conjunction with your company and shows how they will respond strategically to your new marketing strategy. As you can clearly see, the current and projected positions are very similar to those in the Portfolio Business Profile Matrix. Examining Figure 4.14, it is evident that you have a good check-and-balance system in place.

Lastly, performing the same analysis for the Portfolio Modified Growth–Share Matrix, you can see the same resemblance to the prior matrices. Start from the initial no-change strategy (Figure 4.15), then move to your own new three-year position (Figure 4.16), and end with all three companies' future projections as shown in Figure 4.17.

Next, look at Figure 4.16, which shows your firm's product lines only, and once again notice that the Portfolio Modified Growth–Share Matrix shows approximately the same results as the prior Portfolio Business Strengths and Portfolio Business Assessment matrices. This is to be expected if you have performed good research and are using very solid assumptions for your projections.

The final matrix will show the potential strategic response by your competitors to your strategies to gain more market share.

Again note how closely the three matrices—the Portfolio Business Profile Matrix, the Portfolio Business Assessment Matrix, and the Portfolio Modified Growth–Share Matrix—reflect one another's changes. This reflection indicates comprehensive research and assumptions. But all the matrices show that the strategy loses you money, as was observed previously; and that Competitor A is gaining market share. Again note that Competitor B is basically on its way out of business unless the company develops a marketing plan with new, innovative products or product regeneration.

FIGURE 4.12

Portfolio Business Assessment Matrix—No Strategic Changes

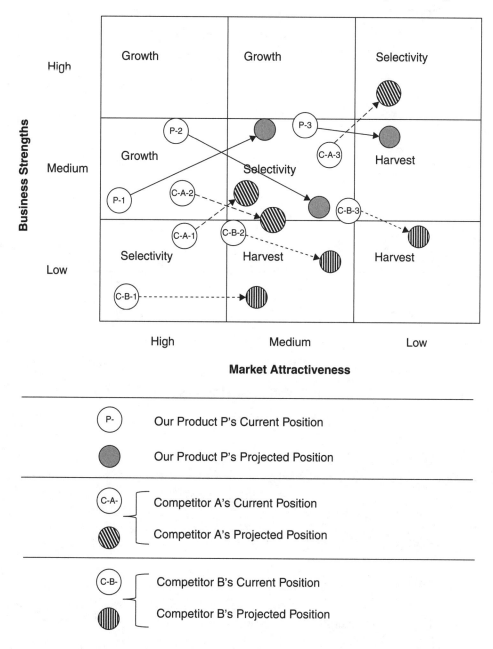

Letters and numbers indicate product code.

FIGURE 4.13

Portfolio Business Assessment Matrix—Current and Projected Positions of Competitors' Products and Ours with No Strategic Changes by Competitors

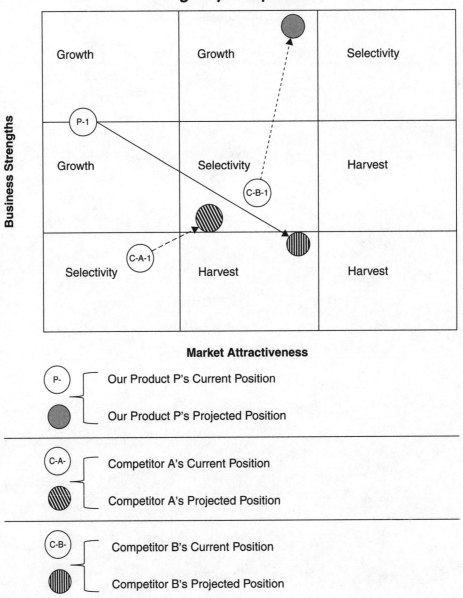

Letters and numbers indicate product code.

FIGURE 4.14

Portfolio Business Assessment Matrix—with Competitors' Reactions to Our Strategic Changes

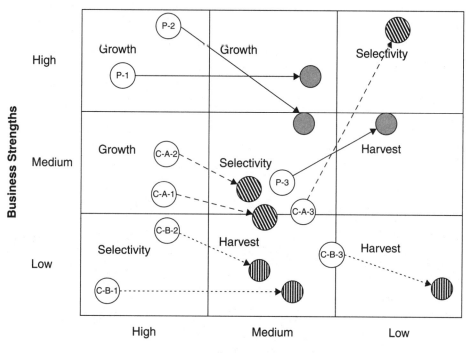

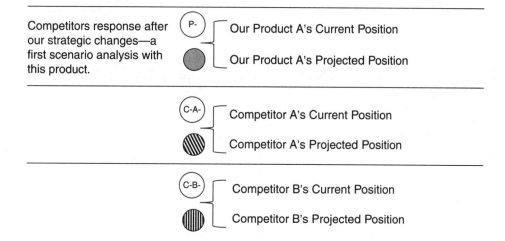

Letters and numbers indicate product code.

FIGURE 4.15

Modified Growth–Share Matrix—No Strategic Changes

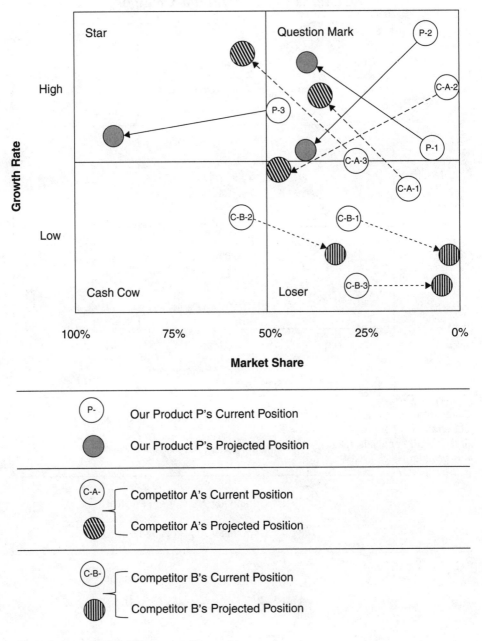

Letters and numbers indicate product code.

FIGURE 4.16

Projected Portfolio Modified Growth–Share Matrix—No Strategic Changes by Competitors

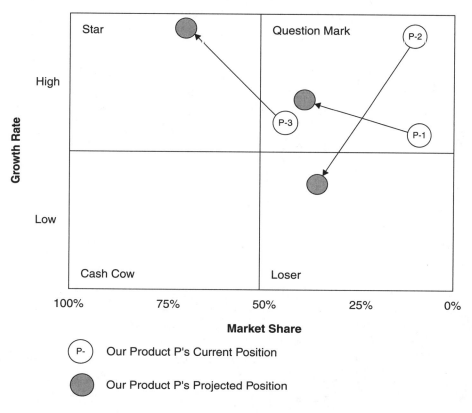

You can clearly see that all three matrices provide approximately the same results, and many product managers ask, "Why not just do one matrix and questionnaire and go with those results?" The answer is very simple: if two or all three of these matrices show large differences or variances in the three-year projected position, then a flaw in the research or assumptions has been made. You should remember that many firms have gone bankrupt or been bought as a result of using just one strategy that was based on erroneous data and/or assumptions. (Strategy development will be discussed further in Chapter 7.) The purpose up to this point has been to introduce you to two specific methods that will help you in strategy formulation: changing your strategy to achieve a more favorable market position and the selection of an optimal three-year future position as competitors change their strategies to compete with yours.

FIGURE 4.17

Modified Growth–Share Matrix—with Competitors' Reactions to Our Strategic Changes

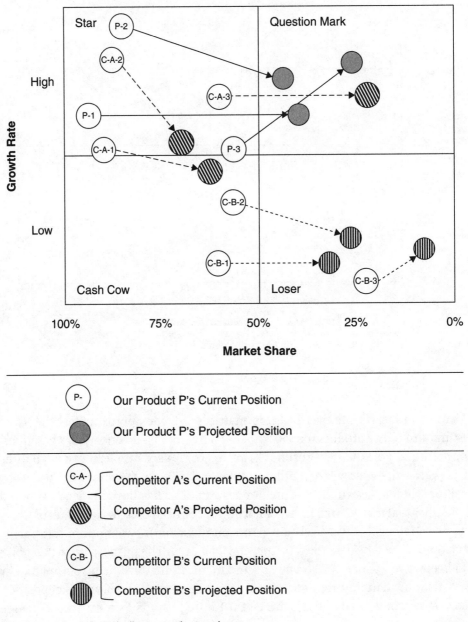

Letters and numbers indicate product code.

Common Pitfalls in Strategic Planning

Unfortunately, instead of the success sequence described here, many managers pursue "disaster sequences." For example, a company may allow a star product's market share to erode to that of a question mark. Unless this strategy is reversed or corrected, the product will ultimately become a loser.

Companies may also overinvest in cash cows, or they may try to save ailing cash cows by pumping funds into them. A better strategy would be to reposition these products according to the success sequence through such factors as product differentiation, market segmentation, and product enhancement. If firms over-invest in cash cows, they may underinvest in question marks. Instead of becoming stars, these products eventually tumble into the loser category.

Some companies spread their resources too thinly among products rather than focusing their funds to maximize performance from their strongest or most promising products. Sometimes fewer products can still provide enough diversi-fication to reduce a company's risk in the market.

Look over the disaster sequence of the portfolios presented in Figures 4.18 and 4.19 and study that firm's mistakes. What strategic errors made these portfo-lios vulnerable to loss of market share and profits?

1. Products 5 and 6 will become losers in the long run.
2. Product 1, the only new product, is a slow grower, and, as shown by the growth rate, it is the only product that will support the company's growth in the long run.
3. Products 3 and 4 will become cash cows in the future, but Product 4 will not remain a cash cow for long if it follows the path of Products 5 and 6.
4. Product 2 is losing market share rapidly.
5. Product 6, as a loser, will still be in the portfolio, but its position will rapidly worsen.

In the short run, if projections had not been made as depicted in the chart, management might believe that the portfolio looks sound, in view of its cash cows and growth rate. But the long-run view shows a firm that would decline in profit-ability, market share, and growth rate. The firm is following the success sequence in the sense that products are moving counterclockwise, but the firm's strategies are not regenerating cash cows or introducing new products. As a result, in the long run, if the firm continues its present course, it will have few cash cows or stars, no question marks, and many losers.

FIGURE 4.18
Growth–Share Matrix—Disaster Sequence in the Long Run

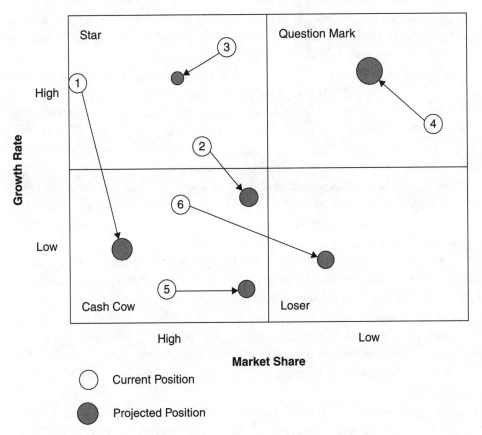

Basically, the firm has three choices: (1) regenerate cash cows to bring them back to question marks, (2) introduce new products, or (3) reexamine its company, product strategies, and company mission.

1. Product 1 is falling from introductory-stage potential directly to the loser position. Either the product is a complete failure, market research was in error, financing was not available, or strategic objectives were poorly planned.

2. Product 5 is also following a disaster sequence, moving from the star position toward the question mark, again probably through poor strategy development.

FIGURE 4.19
Growth–Share Matrix—"Lost" Portfolio

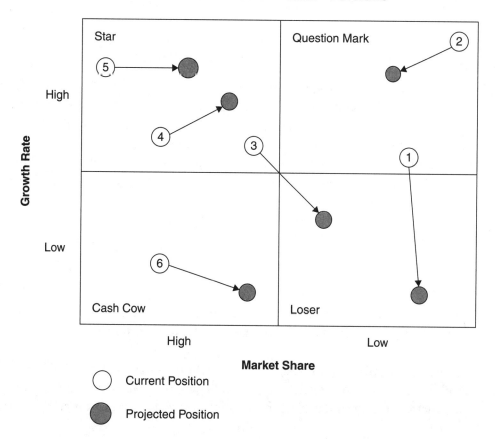

3. Product 3 is falling from high growth to the loser position.
4. Product 6 is not being regenerated. Its position as cash cow is eroding to that of loser.

The basic problem with this portfolio is that little or no planning is being done in this firm. Perhaps the firm looks at products on an individual basis without projecting their movements to see the total portfolio effect of whatever plan it has.

It's more likely that management has never mapped out the product portfolio. Management's attitude is *reactive*; that is, no future projections have been made, or they have been made in a product-by-product vacuum without considering the strategies for the other products. The firm is ignoring how products' positions develop and interact. It has an extremely shortsighted view of its products and of its future.

Product and Portfolio Analysis of Competitors

As these disaster sequences show, you will benefit from doing a product evaluation and building the matrices of your strongest competitors' products and product lines. By superimposing these competitive matrices on your own, you can spot vulnerabilities, strengths, weaknesses, and opportunities more easily.

Companies with the best product track records routinely analyze their competitors' products as well as their own. These analyses yield more accurate data on which to base their own strategic marketing plans.

In the following chapter, you will be shown how to identify problems and opportunities that turn up in your product positioning and portfolio analysis.

Summary

Since you have covered considerable ground in Chapters 3 and 4, it may be helpful to recap the main points of product positioning and portfolio analysis.

- The primary purpose of the Product Evaluation Questionnaire—CSF and the matrices up through the Product Dynamics Matrix is to assess a product's position in terms of competition, market share, and market growth.
- Each matrix, by itself, provides part of the information you need to develop strategies for the marketing plan. When you combine all the matrices, you can devise optimal product-marketing strategies across your product line.
- The flow of information from these various matrices can be summarized as follows:

Chapter 3: Product Positioning Analysis

1. The Business Profile Matrix provides data to develop marketing-mix strategies based on the position of the product in its life cycle and the attractiveness of its market.

2. The Business Assessment Matrix uses the product life-cycle data together with environmental factors to determine the attractiveness of the market and whether internal business strengths can make the product a strong competitor. This matrix also indicates whether the product should grow, be stabilized, or be harvested.

Chapter 4: Portfolio Analysis

3. The Portfolio Business Profile Matrix and the Portfolio Business Assessment Matrix are used to consolidate individual product positions and map a portfolio of the product line.
4. The Growth–Share Matrix plots a company's product line in terms of products' growth rates (cash use) and market shares (cash generation).
5. The Product Dynamics Matrix illustrates the success and disaster sequences, suggesting how to reposition products to achieve company goals.
   - The data collected from the Business Profile Matrix and the Business Assessment Matrix are used here to develop product marketing-mix strategies in order to achieve the firm's objectives.
   - The Growth–Share Matrix displays the status and performance of the overall portfolio and can suggest which strategy the company should adopt to ensure a strong performance in the near future. The information generated by the matrix is used as input into a company's strategic planning at the macro level.
   - Overall, the objective of the product portfolio analysis is to maximize return on investment on the basis of products' cash flow. All products are mapped on the Portfolio Business Profile Matrix, the Portfolio Business Assessment Matrix, and the Growth–Share Matrix. This combined view will help you to determine the overall health of the company's portfolio now and in the near future.
   - The Product Dynamics Matrix is also of major importance in strategy development, since it provides the big picture of the direction in which your company's products should be moving. By using the success sequence as a guide to repositioning products and to increasing cash flow, you can determine specific product strategies.
   - Portfolio scenario analysis can aid in determining how your portfolio's position will change based on new strategic changes, how competitors will react to those changes, how to set target portfolios, and how to check for financial balance across the portfolio.

Sample Case, Phase 4

Paul Harris now had a profile for each of Techna's products, including Storage Extreme, which had been shown to be a strong, potentially high-profit item for the firm. However, the data from the work that he and his marketing team had completed so far could not be used for strategy formulation. In the future, as the team gains more experience in refining the data and the analytic methods used, the results will become increasingly more valuable and accurate for developing the marketing plan.

At this point, Harris needed to see how the product lines were positioned and projected to move in one macro or portfolio view. This would tell him which lines were following the success sequence and which the disaster sequence. Since Techna already has a problem with declining sales and market share, the portfolio view would help pinpoint the reasons for this. This information could then be used to formulate improved objectives and strategies for the marketing plan. A portfolio view would also help managers to set capital and expense allocations at the individual product plan level.

His marketing team plotted all the products on the Modified Growth–Share Matrix and set the values for its horizontal and vertical axes. They also plotted all the products on the Portfolio Business Assessment Matrix and the Portfolio Business Profile Matrix. Harris then arranged a meeting with the three partners to show them the results of his work to date.

Harris stated at the beginning of the meeting, "The three matrices I am going to present indicate where our products are positioned today and where they are expected to be positioned in three years based on our current strategies and assumptions. We are not yet in a position to perform scenario analyses or set specific strategies. Those will be developed later, using the scenario approach to observe how we expect our competitors to react to our changed strategies."

Harris pointed to the Modified Growth–Share Matrix. "With this chart, we can assess each product line to determine which ones represent investment opportunities, which ones should supply investment funds, and which ones should be eliminated from the portfolio. This information will serve as the basis for developing our corporate marketing objectives and strategies.

"Our overall objective is to get the best performance from all product lines, while at the same time keeping the cash flow in balance. We don't want to go to the capital markets for more funds unless it's absolutely necessary. Also, the team determined that the industry growth rate on average for the six product lines is 9 percent."

FORM 4
Portfolio Modified Growth–Share Matrix

Product: Storage Extreme   **Date:** xx/xx/xx

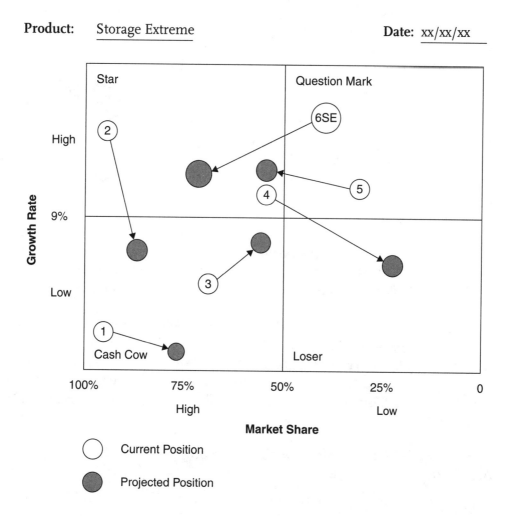

Hamilton broke in: "Why are you using a Modified Growth–Share Matrix instead of using relative market share as your basis?"

Harris replied, "The modified matrix is easier for some people to use at the beginning, when the staff is learning these new techniques. When they get more proficient and understand the internal and external environment better, we can switch to a relative market share basis for the matrix.

"The team has also completed a Portfolio Business Profile Matrix and a Portfolio Business Assessment Matrix and found that the results were consistent with what we plotted on the Modified Growth–Share Matrix." (Figures 4.1 and 4.2 shown earlier in the chapter are the same for the sample case.)

Harris continued, "The team has also developed the same portfolio matrices to include our two top competitors. We used only three of our most closely related products and our competitors' three products at this time. Note that Competitor A is of most concern to us at present. It is gaining share in markets that we are losing share in. Competitor B is not a high threat to us currently in terms of market share gain and business strengths. As I mentioned earlier, during the strategy development part, the team will use scenario analysis to aid in maximizing market share, optimizing the allocation of our scarce resources, financial balance, cash flow allocation, and so on." (Figures 4.9 through 4.14 are the exact figures that would be used here, but to avoid redundancy, they are not repeated here.)

Bartly was the most enthusiastic of the three when he saw the portfolio views of Techna's products.

"I don't know about the rest of you," he said, "but this is the first time I've seen all our products on a single graph and on an equal plane at one time. One thing I want to know: what if our products were in different industries?"

"They couldn't be compared directly; we'd have to make up separate matrices for each line of business."

Farlin waved his hand for silence. "All I want to know is, what's the bottom line on this? What is it telling us to do?"

Harris handed out copies of his summary. "I've itemized important information that the Modified Growth–Share Matrix reveals and what we need to do to correct or take advantage of each product's position." These conclusions follow closely what the other two matrices indicated.

Conclusions from the Portfolio Modified Growth–Share Matrix— All Products

The matrix shows a generally dynamic and well-managed portfolio, with Product 3 being regenerated back to a growth position and Product 5 following a success sequence. Product 6, Storage Extreme, is forecasted to follow a success sequence and so far has conformed to projected growth as forecast by the marketing team. Storage Extreme should be a high-revenue, high–market share item.

However, the matrix also shows a number of problems that pinpoint the reasons for Techna's sales and market share declines. These problems must be resolved or they will eventually result in the deterioration of the entire product portfolio.

1. Product 1 must be checked to see whether it can be stabilized or regenerated using product differentiation or a substitution strategy. If Product 1 must be replaced within three years, the vice president of marketing should contact R&D so that it can either enhance or replace this product. Until then, it can be used as a cash provider for other growing products.

2. Product 2 has a growth rate and market share that appear to be falling too fast. However, the marketing team believes that the product manager's projections for this line are too pessimistic. Revised projections indicate that these products should not decline so rapidly. They should fall only to the top of the cash cow range, generating more revenue for the firm.

3. Product 4 is following a disaster sequence. It has no planned updates to keep current with competitors, which are overtaking this item. There is not enough time to upgrade and reposition this product to catch up with the competition. The marketing team recommends that the firm drop this product.

4. Product 5 is poorly managed and has no overall marketing strategy guiding its growth, only day-to-day tactical responses. The marketing team estimates that, with sufficient funds, this product can be regenerated to give it a longer life. Repositioned properly, it can regain market share. As a cash cow, this product can make up some of its lost revenues and possibly compensate for the elimination of Product 4.

Summary of Strategic Implications

As shown on the graph, Products 1 and 4 are responsible for Techna's current decline in sales and market share. Two years ago, these products had high profit margins, good market share, and revenues equaling 36 percent of Techna's total sales. At present, they represent only 14 percent. Even Storage Extreme and other products cannot make up the 22 percent loss.

This decline is a result of Techna's lack of an overall marketing strategy and planning process. The firm had no plan to meet competitive challenges to its major product lines and consequently lost customers and market share to its main competitors.

In addition, Techna is investing too much money in Product 1 for the return being generated. Product 2, on the other hand, is underinvested. It has low revenues but very high profit margins and needs more cash investment to make it grow. These conditions also reflect the lack of adequate planning. There has been no method for determining which products should be funded and which ones should be gradually eliminated.

We need to develop objectives and strategies to get all our products on a success sequence and drop the ones that cannot be regenerated. Over the next three years, more new products and regenerated products must be located in a question mark (introduction stage) cell. This strategy will ensure that Techna continues to grow and regains its position as a leading-edge company.

After the three partners had a chance to review the summary, Harris said, "We have one more step in the environmental assessment before we're through, and that is to start plotting our main competitor's products against ours so that we can see the competition's strengths, weaknesses, strategies, and so on. Afterward, we can move on to identify Techna's key problems and opportunities that turned up in our data-gathering process. Then we'll be ready to set our marketing objectives and strategies."

"Looks like a great job so far," said Bartly.

Even Farlin had to agree.

5

Step 4: Problem and Opportunity Analysis

Introduction

The first three steps of market planning yielded an additional benefit that will be explored in this chapter: identifying problems and opportunities in their early stages. Problem and opportunity analysis does not go into great detail, but this chapter's methods will help you uncover trends that your firm should arrest and others that it should exploit.

It is not always easy to recognize problems before they become major issues. In firms of all sizes, managers frequently make the mistake of believing that minor problems will correct themselves without intervention.

On the other hand, while marketing managers are assessing their environment, they may just as easily overlook opportunities. They may lose the chance to make an early entry into a particular niche, to differentiate their product, or to edge out the competition in some way.

This chapter examines the data you developed in the questionnaires and matrices to help you pinpoint potential problems and opportunities. Some of them will be obvious; others may be hidden. The point is to identify them now so that you can design action steps and include them as part of the development of your strategic marketing plan.

Identifying Problems

A *problem* can be defined as a question or situation that presents uncertainty, perplexity, or difficulty. In practical terms, it is something that could block your company's goals and thus requires your attention and correction.

To spot a problem in its early stages, you must have some idea of what to look for and where to look. Start with the following:

1. Find any variance(s) from previous plans, such as these:

    - Your market share has dwindled.
    - Your current promotion efforts are not helping you gain market share.
    - The distributors are cutting back on order sizes.
    - Your firm is missing or delaying delivery dates.
    - You lack information about your competitors.
    - The firm has higher inventories than necessary.
    - There are increased accounts receivable that could be managed.
    - Customers are returning units more often.
    - The firm's profit margins are dropping.

2. Determine what obstacles are preventing you from reaching any of your company goals. External factors may include these:

    - There are shortages of raw materials.
    - There is increased competition in your target markets.
    - There are increased returns of products because of continuing quality control problems.
    - Price competitiveness is intensifying, and you are doing nothing about it.
    - There is a potential regulatory threat.
    - Product substitution threats are increasing.
    - The target market is changing.
    - The demographics of your target market are changing.
    - New technology and superior products are entering your target markets.
    - The firm has poor product positioning.
    - Your marketing is targeting a wrong segment of the market.
    - The firm has a poor distribution structure.

Internal factors may include these:

    - The management is becoming more risk-averse.
    - The research and development department is slow in developing new products.

- Breadth of product applications is limited.
- Product enhancements are slow to reach the target market.
- The firm has below-average marketing research.
- The firm has poor planning techniques.
- The firm has insufficient internal and external funds for expansion.
- Product servicing quality is low.
- Product quality is dropping.
- The business plan and marketing plan are not integrated.

When filling out Form 5: Problem Analysis at the end of this chapter, make sure you include *all* problems, regardless of their size. You can always eliminate some items later. Keep in mind that the obvious weak points may not do the most damage; often it's the seemingly minor problems in your environmental analysis that can create a crisis.

Analyzing Problems

After you identify the firm's problems, rank them based on their seriousness and probability. If you determine that the probability of a problem is high, you should consider developing contingency plans to help offset the problem, thus averting its threat to the firm. The figures in this chapter are blank forms for you to fill out. The sample case has a similar analysis prepared for your edification.

Using the previous suggestions, list all the problems, including both external and internal. Analyze these problems using the following five steps:

1. Use Figure 5.1 to list and rank all of the problems, based on their importance to your firm. For example, is one product's slight drop in market share critical in terms of achieving the company's objectives? Is the lack of competitor information trivial or alarming? You can use a numerical value system or a weighted system in ranking problems. First, assign a value from 1 to 10 (where 1 is the least serious to the firm and 10 is the most serious) to each problem. Next, assess the probability of a solution as being from 0 percent to 100 percent (where 0 percent is that you cannot solve the problem and 100 percent that you are certain that you will successfully solve the problem). Finally, use the assigned values for the seriousness of the problem and the probability of solving the problem to complete the matrix in Figure 5.2.

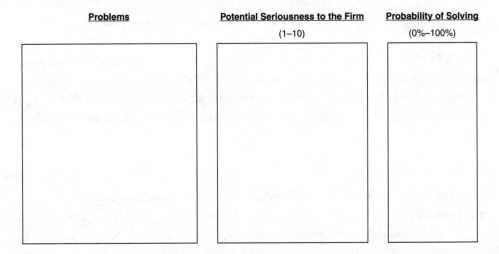

FIGURE 5.1

Problem Analysis

Assign a numerical value from 1 to 10 for each problem, where 10 is the most serious for the firm.

Assign a probability of solution to each problem (0 to 100 percent).

Note: if the probability of solution is low, consider a strategy of dropping the product or a strategy of maintaining the product without its causing increased harm to the firm.

Problems	Potential Seriousness to the Firm (1–10)	Probability of Solving (0%–100%)

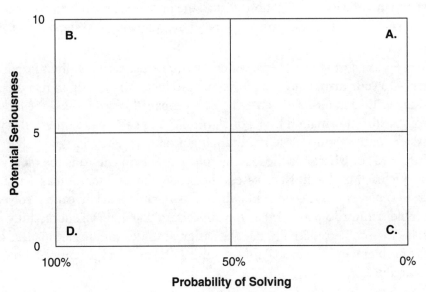

FIGURE 5.2

Problem Matrix

When a problem shows up in Cell A of the Problem Matrix, you have a very slight chance of solving it, but its threat to the firm is medium to high. This is a very poor cell in which to find a large problem. You will need to dissect this problem and try to adapt your strategies to minimize the potential damage from it. Cell B is a good position to be in, since the problem, although serious, has a very high probability of being solved. Problems in Cell C have a low seriousness to the firm, but also a low probability of solution. Monitor the problem(s) in Cell C. If the problem(s) start(s) to move toward Cell A, then make adjustments to slow this encroachment. Finally, Cell D has problems with low seriousness to the firm and a high probability of solution. Set strategies to solve these problems, since small problems can grow into large ones.

Figure 5.2, The Problem Matrix, also indicates which problems are solvable and which problems are not. Based on Figure 5.2, separate the problems into those that can be solved and those that, for various reasons, are unsolvable and place each of them in the appropriate category in Figure 5.3. Problems that can be solved usually are those over which you have some control. The control may be over price, market share, breadth of product line, or other factors that are within your power to change. A solvable problem may also reveal a hidden marketing opportunity.

Unsolvable problems are generally those over which you have little or no control. You must examine these problems closely to determine their effect on the firm. If a product is losing market share for economic reasons, it may be better to drop the product rather than pumping more cash into it in an attempt to reposition it.

Even if you have no control over a problem, make sure you write the problem down. By stating the problem in writing, you help to ensure that it won't be ignored when you are developing your marketing plan.

2. After each solvable problem, list the action(s) that your firm can take to correct it. Perhaps you can restructure your pricing system, or you may be able to target a different consumer segment to rebuild sales. The action steps you design can be incorporated into the firm's marketing plan.

3. When you contemplate actions, determine whether the problems are industry- or company-related. Do they stem from conditions in the industry, such as slowed growth, new regulations, technological changes, or global competition? Or are they primarily caused by factors within the company, such as out-of-date products, increased costs, management changes, or too narrow a product line?

FIGURE 5.3

Solvable Versus Unsolvable Problems

Solvable Problems	Action Steps	Unsolvable Problems

__List specific reason(s) for your categorization of your problems.__

4. Before you finalize your problem-solving actions, determine whether two or more problems share a single cause. For example, declining market share, slowing growth, and falling profits may all be the result of a failure to invest enough funds to maintain a product's position. By correcting the cause, you may solve several problems at once.

    On the other hand, the problems may all be caused by a shift in consumer taste that has rendered your product obsolete. There may be no way to salvage the product, since the underlying causes are beyond the firm's control. This point leads us to the fifth step.

5. Finally, determine whether solving the problem will lead to meaningful and favorable changes in your current position. This step ensures that you will focus on problems that are significant in the short term rather than

concentrating on problems that may arise in the more distant future. Also, you should consider how much the problem-solving actions will cost. For example, if the problem is not too serious to the firm, correcting it may cost the firm more money than the problem is leading it to lose. Thus, you will need to perform a financial analysis to determine which problems can and need to be solved.

The purpose of these steps is to go beyond symptoms—declining profits, decreasing market share—to the core problem, which may be a shift in consumer taste, a strategic error on the company's part, or increased competition in the market. The core problem, if solvable, is the one you want to list in your marketing plan as you develop it, along with your proposed actions to address it.

Turning Problems into Opportunities

The final stage in problem and opportunity analysis is to review your list of problems and determine whether you can turn some of them into opportunities. For example, you may discover that the slight decline in sales of a certain product is caused by a subtle change in consumer taste (such as a change in preferred style or color). If your competitors have similar products, you can probably assume that they are also experiencing the same decline. But they may not have noticed the trend. You can be sure that the moment they do, they will begin working on a solution—fast—to recover market share.

If you make the change in your product first, you can turn the problem into a short-term market window and possibly gain substantial market share.

Problems do not always signal that something is wrong; they can be opportunities in disguise. By making problem identification and analysis a regular part of developing your marketing plan, you will be able to detect the hidden opportunity in a problem and help your firm stay ahead of the competition.

Identifying Opportunities

Good problem analysis alone will not sustain a firm's growth. You must also identify and exploit opportunities. To sustain a strong pattern of growth, you need to analyze these opportunities in light of your company's mission, business plan, objectives, and resources.

As in problem analysis, your first step is to identify all opportunities, no matter how slight or improbable they may seem at first. State all opportunities in writing as specifically as you can.

When you are looking for opportunities, consider those that are associated with the following:

- Your specific company strengths and weaknesses
- Your financial capabilities and resource advantages
- Product innovation advantages
- Product servicing and product quality
- New applications of existing products and complementary products
- Product differentiation possibilities
- New technologies for new and current products
- Pricing advantage strategies
- Market expansion into new target markets
- Expansion into new target segments
- Promotional advantage and coverage
- Distribution structure
- Geographic coverage
- Changing consumer lifestyles
- Changing customer wants and needs

Analyzing Opportunities

The environmental analysis, which you have already completed, is an excellent data source for finding problems and opportunities both within and outside of the firm. The problems and opportunities identified are associated with the strengths and weaknesses of your firm. With this in mind, you should look at potential opportunities and utilize the firm's strengths in order to maximize the probability of success. In many cases, when you eliminate major weaknesses, the firm's problems will start to diminish and its assets prosper. This will lead to more potential opportunities for the firm to develop.

Opportunity analysis also involves a cost/benefit analysis. Here you compute the total cost of the opportunity, determine all the expected benefits, and subtract the total cost from the total benefits. If the answer is positive, the opportunity passes the initial economic screening phase. If hard numbers are available, this analysis is relatively straightforward and is sometimes called an *economic evaluation*.

The opportunity analysis then moves on to the capital budgeting techniques that the firm uses for the final go/no-go decision based on your firm's capital budgeting results criteria. If the opportunity meets those criteria and is determined to be a good fit within the company, it will be placed on a list of opportunities for possible implementation. Remember, since capital is a scarce resource, not all opportunities can or will be implemented unless your firm has the requisite cash or can obtain it from the capital markets. More than likely, if you need to go to the capital markets for funding, the discount rate used in your capital budgeting process will increase. This, in turn, may eliminate some of the opportunities from your list. (For a full explanation of how the discount rate is developed via the weighted-average cost of capital, you may wish to consult a good text on financial management.)

The cost/benefit analysis will allow you to rank the opportunities in terms of their value and attractiveness to your firm. Sometimes the variables involved in the cost/benefit analysis cannot be quantified. In this case, you may be able to assess the variables qualitatively and assign a number to that assessment. Qualitative data are not preferred, but in some instances, they are all that is available and will be part of the input into capital budgeting decisions.

Once you have developed your list, you will need to look carefully at each opportunity to determine which ones are worth pursuing. Your analysis will follow these steps:

1. Using Figure 5.4, first list all potential opportunities. An opportunity can be assessed in terms of two dimensions: its attractiveness to the firm and the firm's probability of successfully developing the opportunity. Next, determine a value from 1 to 10 for how attractive the opportunity is to the firm (where 1 is least attractive and 10 is most attractive). Finally, assess the probability of a successful development of the opportunity as being from 0 percent to 100 percent (where 0 percent is the least likelihood of a successful development and 100 percent is a certain development). Use the attractiveness values and the probability of success values to plot each opportunity on Figure 5.5, the Opportunity Matrix.

    As shown previously, Figure 5.5 illustrates an Opportunity Matrix with four cells. The Opportunity Matrix is interpreted as follows:
    •   Opportunities that fall in Cell 1 have the greatest attractiveness and the highest probability of success. To realize these, you would design specific strategies (action steps) and include those strategies in your marketing plan.
    •   Opportunities that fall in Cells 2 and 3 are worth monitoring, although you will not develop specific steps to achieve them at this point.
    •   Opportunities that fall in Cell 4 have little attractiveness and little chance of success; they should be dropped from consideration.

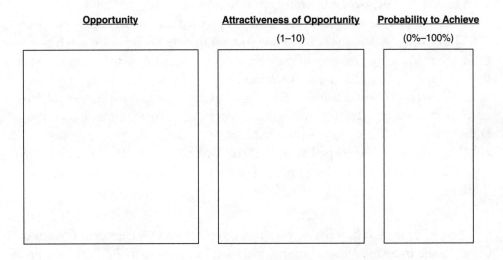

FIGURE 5.4
Opportunity Analysis

Assign a numerical value from 1 to 10 for each opportunity, where 10 is the most attractive to the firm.

Assign a probability of achievement for each opportunity (0 to 100 percent).

Opportunity	Attractiveness of Opportunity (1–10)	Probability to Achieve (0%–100%)

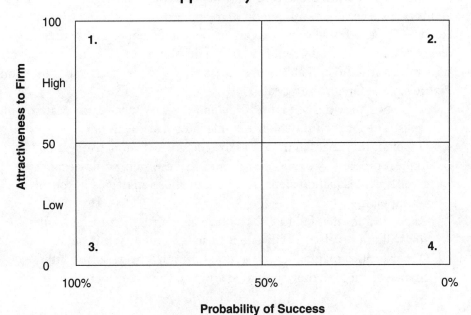

FIGURE 5.5
Opportunity Matrix

Attractiveness to Firm

100 — 1.   2.

High

50 —

Low

3.   4.

0 —

100%   50%   0%

Probability of Success

The sample case shows a list of value-weighted opportunities and a completed matrix.

2. Each firm has limited resources that restrict the number of opportunities it can pursue. Rank the opportunities you find in their order of importance or value to your firm. Opportunities can be external, such as purchasing new technology from an outside firm, or internal, such as having your firm's R&D department enhance a product to increase its market share and increase the firm's revenue.
3. Determine which opportunities are most compatible with your firm. Compatibility is judged on the basis of growth, market share, your business plan, and your vision/mission. In determining a good corporate fit, you should ask:
   - Does the firm want to capitalize on products that complement its current product line?
   - Does the firm want to diversify into totally new areas?
   - Does the firm want to become a market leader or merely to increase or maintain its market share?
   - Does the firm have the resources and skills necessary to pursue the opportunity?

   The opportunities that the firm finally selects should be completely in line with the direction and the vision/mission of the firm as stated in its business plan.
4. Develop action steps to realize potential opportunities. After each opportunity, list the action steps your firm must take to achieve it. Figure 5.6 will aid you in this process.

Identifying Resources

Once you have selected the opportunities that are worth developing, you must determine whether your firm has the resources needed to realize them. Resource analysis will help you to focus on practical results and to keep your planning realistic in terms of your company's strengths and limitations. Try to avoid asking, "What would we *like* to do?" Instead, ask the question, "What is *possible* for us to do?"

In identifying company resources, consider the following areas:

- Can the firm financially afford to exploit a new marketing opportunity?
- Do we have qualified personnel to manufacture, sell, and manage the new opportunity?

- Do we have enough capacity to produce the necessary quantities to meet projected demand?
- Can raw materials be acquired easily?
- Can the product be priced at different levels over time to get increased market share and still contribute a profit?
- Can an effective advertising program be developed to reach the target market as it changes and competition comes into play?
- Are current distribution channels adequate to transport the product to its dealers or end users in a timely fashion, or will we have to find different distribution channels because competition may clog up the current channels, dates, and usage?

FIGURE 5.6
Opportunity Action Steps

Opportunity	Action Steps

List specific reason(s) for your action steps.

If you find yourself answering no to most of these questions, then even an excellent opportunity may have to be discarded because your firm doesn't have the necessary resources to develop it. Conversely, if an opportunity is somewhat risky, but the firm has adequate resources, you may decide to take a calculated risk and pursue the opportunity. Some factors, such as available capacity and price structure, are difficult to estimate in a rough analysis. For this reason, they are not included on the Opportunity Analysis form.

The analysis in this chapter provides a survey of the problems and potential opportunities facing your firm. To handle them appropriately, you will need to do more detailed work to develop specific tactical plans.

Study the sample case and then fill out Form 5, "Problem Analysis," and Form 6, "Opportunity and Resource Analysis." Resource analysis examines the opportunities that a firm has discovered and lists the resources needed for successful development and implementation of a particular opportunity. Form 6's Resource section for the sample case may be different from yours, since it is developed in concert with the product and opportunities of the sample case. Usually, each opportunity will require a different set of strategies and resources for its optimal development.

Remember to keep an open mind when examining your data on problems or opportunities. Don't assume that you know what they are or where to find them. Pay particular attention to slight changes in product performance or market conditions. You may discover that even minor problems or opportunities can be turned into the competitive edge your firm needs.

Summary

- Problem and opportunity analysis is a practical means of identifying even minor problems and opportunities early in the marketing plan development process. Steps can be taken to minimize the problems and maximize the opportunities.
- A problem can be identified as a question or situation that presents uncertainty, perplexity, or difficulty to affirm. In practical terms, it is something that may prevent a company from achieving its goals and that requires attention and correction. The purpose of problem analysis is to go beyond symptoms to the core problem.
- To spot a problem in its early stages, start with the following: (1) identify any variances from previous plans, and (2) determine which obstacles are blocking any of your company's goals.

- Analyze problems using the following procedure: (1) rank the problems according to their importance to your firm; (2) determine whether the problems are internal or external; (3) plot the problems on the Problem Matrix; (4) separate the problems into those that can be solved and those that cannot;(5) list the problems with the associated action steps that can be taken to solve each problem; (6) determine whether the problems are industry- or company-related; (7) when choosing your action steps, determine whether two or more problems share a single cause; (8) determine whether solving the problem, will lead to a significant and positive change in your current position; and (9) determine which problems can be turned into opportunities.
- To analyze opportunities, follow these steps: (1) determine which opportunities are most compatible with your firm, (2) rank the opportunities in order of their importance or contribution value to your firm, (3) assign numerical values to opportunities (their attractiveness and probability of success), (4) plot opportunities on the Opportunity Matrix, (5) develop action steps to realize potential opportunities, and (6) determine whether your firm has the resources to fully develop the opportunities you have identified.

Sample Case, Phase 5

Harris discussed the portfolio view of Storage Extreme and Techna's other five products with all concerned managers. He gained additional information regarding why the products were behaving the way the product positioning and portfolio matrices projected. The managers seemed more genuinely involved in the process this time around, and some even expressed their appreciation for what they had learned from the product evaluations and portfolio analysis.

Harris then called his marketing team together to begin the problem analysis for Storage Extreme and Techna's other six products. "You can use a two-step, systematic approach to this process," Harris told the team. "First, determine whether any variances from previous plans, statistics, market share data, or sales figures has occurred. Second, determine what internal and external obstacles are preventing Techna from achieving its current goals."

Harris gave the marketing team Forms 5 and 6 to fill out for each product. He instructed them to analyze the problems they uncovered as follows:

- Rank the problems according to their importance to the firm.
- Determine whether they are industry or company problems.
- Examine each problem in detail to determine whether two or more problems share a single cause.

- Separate problems into those that are solvable and those that are unsolvable.
- List preliminary actions that can be taken to solve problems.
- Determine whether solving the problem will lead to a meaningful and favorable change in the product's market position.
- Determine financial options to meet our goals and objectives.
- Cover the four Ps in terms of the effect upon them
- Review the final list of problems and determine whether some of them can be turned into opportunities.

When the team turned in their analyses for each product, Harris was particularly interested in the completed Form 5 for Storage Extreme (shown at the end of the sample case). The marketing team had uncovered the following problems:

1. Storage Extreme's major competitor is entering a joint agreement with three large computer manufacturers to purchase the competitor's products and possibly produce its products under a private label. This agreement will provide the competitor with increased market share and an immediate national distribution system. In contrast, Storage Extreme's distribution system is still less than one year away from achieving national coverage unless it moves on the problem.
2. Sales staff training is a problem for Storage Extreme and its competitors alike. Storage Extreme has an adequate number of salespeople, but they need to be trained to sell Storage Extreme to the national target markets and global markets, and also through e-commerce. Developing and instituting the training program could take up to five months. A time lag that long might allow competitors to catch up on sales, installation, and service.
3. Storage Extreme does not have an alliance with a large computer manufacturer, a lack that may send customers and market share to its competitor. This will also limit financing, distribution channels, and pricing flexibility.

Once the problem analysis was completed, Harris instructed his staff members to take a similar look at the opportunities. In their analyses, they would do the following:

- Rank opportunities according to their importance and/or contribution value to the firm.
- Determine which opportunities are most compatible with the firm.

- Assign numerical values to opportunities, indicating their level of attractiveness to Techna and their probability of success. Plot these opportunities on the Opportunity Matrix.
- Determine which of the opportunities Techna has the resources to pursue.

The marketing team filled out Form 6 for all of Techna's products and turned in its findings to Harris. He saw that for Storage Extreme, the team had identified several important opportunities (Form 6 is shown at the end of the sample case):

1. Form an alliance with a major computer manufacturer to increase market share and gain wider and faster distribution for Storage Extreme and possible quicker national and global distribution.
2. Develop distribution channels more rapidly, either through the alliance just mentioned or through the potential acquisition of competitors.
3. Increase funds for training sales and service employees to educate them about Storage Extreme's features and specifications.
4. Be flexible in pricing structure. Although this is not the best way to increase market share, Storage Extreme may have to change its philosophy on pricing, particularly if the competitor offers a similar, lower-priced memory drive. However, the firm must give this approach careful consideration. Techna's reputation among customers for high quality may serve to counteract the competitor's pricing strategy. Customers may buy Storage Extreme even with a higher price tag because they know that they are also buying the company's service, installation skills, future complementary products, and technology.

Harris was satisfied with the team members' work and told them that they now had enough information to begin developing marketing objectives and strategies for the final marketing plan. He had one word of caution, however. "Keep in mind," he advised them, "that we need to consult the department heads, product managers, and their staffs at every step in the planning process. We want them involved as we go along, so that the final plan is their plan, not just ours."

The marketing team agreed, although Harris thought some of its members were a bit reluctant.

FORM 5
Problem Analysis

Product: <u>Storage Extreme</u>   Date: <u>xx/xx/xx</u>

Problem Analysis

Assign a numerical value from 1 to 10 for each problem, where 10 is the most serious for the firm.

Assign a probability of solution to each problem (0 to 100 percent).

Note: if the probability of solution is low (relative to your requirements), consider a strategy of dropping the product or a strategy of maintaining the product without its causing increased harm to the firm.

Problems	Potential Seriousness to the Firm	Probability to Solve
	(1–10)	(0–100%)
A competitor will have a similar product out in six months.	9	90%
It will take three to five months to fully train Techna's salesforce.	8	85%
A competitor is in negotiations with three large manufacturers for joint agreements.	10	50%
Consumers are not familiar with this new technology.	7	70%
High cost initially to consumers.	8	30%
Lack of national coverage.	7	45%

1.   List problems that share a single cause.

Problems   Cause

A competitor will have a similar product out in six months. A competitor is in negotiations with three large manufacturers for joint agreements. High cost initially to consumers.	We did not engage in negotiations with large manufacturers and distributors early enough, and as a result we cannot count on them for any type of financial consideration. Our marketing research did not confirm that as early as six months from now, one of our major competitors may have its prototype products completed.

2.   Industry-related problems:

Standards for protocol interfaces have not been established.

Very short product life before technologically superior products are developed. This translates into a need to position our product so that we have customer loyalty and can migrate customers to the next generation without losing any of them in the process.

3.   Company-related problems:

Pricing

Salesforce not being trained fast enough or in enough depth

Service

Distribution channels

Below-average strategic planning

4. What action steps can you take to solve these problems?

Industry-related: Make Storage Extreme compatible with large computer manufacturers and users.

Increase training funds to lower the learning curve for the salesforce.

Increase R&D for next-generation products and complementary products for Storage Extreme.

Pricing can be more flexible if agreements with computer manufacturers are established.

Develop a higher and more comprehensive business and strategic marketing planning process.

5. What problems can be turned into opportunities?

Industry standards: Make our equipment compatible with that of large computer manufacturers and form an alliance with them to increase our market share and improve our distribution network. Our product may actually set industry standards.

Distribution: Increase distribution structure by acquiring competitors and finding new users of products to increase market share and exposure of the firm to large customers.

Salesforce training: Increase the skill levels of account executives to increase distribution, sales, and revenue. Consider expanding the salesforce by including other sales techniques.

High initial prices: Try to decrease price and increase market share in the short run, since our firm is basically alone in offering this product at present.

FORM 6
Opportunity and Resource Analysis

Product: <u>Storage Extreme</u>   Date: <u>xx/xx/xx</u>

Opportunities

1. List all potential opportunities.

1. Be first in the market with new storage drive using all nonmechanical parts.   2. Develop alliances with manufacturers to set industry standards.   3. Increase R&D program to keep Techna a leader and not a follower.   4. Increase the skills of the salesforce from national to global and e-commerce.   5. Increase the distribution structure for national and global sales.   6. Increase pricing flexibility to increase market share and to compete effectively.

2. Determine which opportunities are compatible with your firm and rank-order them.

1, 3, 2, 5, 6

3. Assess the opportunities' attractiveness to your firm and their probability of success.

Opportunity	Attractiveness to Firm*	Probability of Success
1. First in market with Storage Extreme.	8	95%
2. Stay as leader via R&D.	8	75%
3. Develop alliances.	5	65%
4. Increase distribution structure.	6	70%
5. Increase pricing flexibility.	4	45%

*Scale is 1 to 10, with 10 indicating greatest attractiveness to the firm.

4. Plot opportunities on Opportunity Matrix.

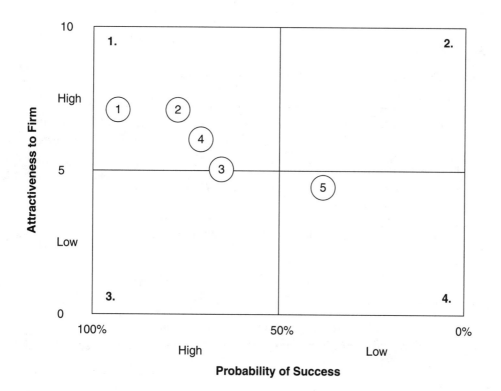

5.   Select action steps to develop strategies to obtain the opportunities selected.

Opportunities   Action Steps

Opportunities	Action Steps
1. First in market with Storage Extreme. 2. Increase distribution structure. 3. Develop alliances.	Develop relationships with other major manufacturing executives and set up mutual R&D agreements, financing for price strategies, and distribution structure enhancements. Expand capacity and put strategic emphasis on developing potential acquisitions to again aid in pricing flexibility.

Resources

1.   Personnel needed to obtain opportunities:
   a.   Management:

   > None at this time, but this will be reevaluated if the firm continues on its current path of moving away from being a marketing-oriented organization.

   b.   Research and Development:

   > Human Resources has determined that we need three experts in storage devices.

   c.   Manufacturing:

   > Capacity will have to increase by 22 percent if Storage Extreme and its complementary products meet or exceed their demand forecast.

d. Sales:

> Determine whether salesforce needs to be increased to achieve national and global coverage.

e. Marketing:

> Marketing personnel will need to be increased by 8 percent in various areas to develop marketing plans and for new product managers.

2. Financial resources available to develop opportunities:

Financial Resources

> Our firm has the financial resources to develop credit lines, sell bonds, secure private and institution dollars, and possibly go to other financial markets for cash. The only major consideration with these moves is that our weighted cost of capital will increase, and thus the discount rate used in our capital budgeting process will also increase.

3. Raw materials needed:

Raw Material	Difficult to Source	Moderately Difficult	Moderately Easy	Easy to Source
All electronic components.			X	

4.   Promotion/advertising effort needed to develop selected opportunities:

Opportunities

| Advertising Effort |

| 1. Distribution. |
| 2. First in market. |
| 3. Industry alliance. |

All three will depend on the target market segments. Each will require many, but not the same, advertising efforts and medium. The alliance agreement will depend on the actual agreement itself.

5.   Distribution channels:

Opportunities

Distribution Channels

| 1. Industry alliance. |
| 2. Pricing. |

This situation depends on the actual alliance agreement. We may be able to piggyback on the manufacturers' channels. This will also help us decrease cost and aid in pricing flexibility.

PART III

Developing the Marketing Plan

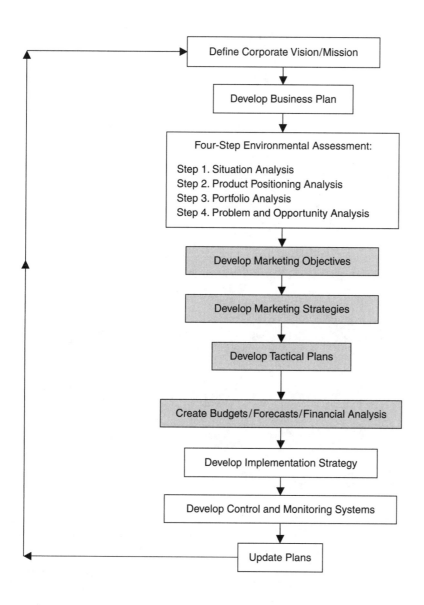

Define Corporate Vision/Mission

Develop Business Plan

Four-Step Environmental Assessment:

Step 1. Situation Analysis
Step 2. Product Positioning Analysis
Step 3. Portfolio Analysis
Step 4. Problem and Opportunity Analysis

Develop Marketing Objectives

Develop Marketing Strategies

Develop Tactical Plans

Create Budgets / Forecasts / Financial Analysis

Develop Implementation Strategy

Develop Control and Monitoring Systems

Update Plans

6

Strategic Marketing Objectives

Introduction

At the core of your marketing plan are your marketing objectives. All of the preceding steps were leading to them, and all succeeding steps are designed to achieve them. These steps are carried out within the context of the corporate vision/mission statement and the overall business plan. Objectives are considered the endpoints of your firm's vision/mission statement's goals. They are specific results that move the firm toward its vision/mission. It can be argued that strategies and/or tactics are more important than objectives because they get the job done, but objectives link the corporate level of planning to each department's plan. Sound marketing objectives will also enable you to select the best marketing strategies to position your products successfully. (Strategies will be reviewed in Chapter 7.)

Objectives also enable the organization to measure its performance. Corporate objectives may be established in any functional area, such as marketing, finance, production, operations, or human resources. A firm typically sets objectives for growth and market share increases, improvement of product quality, reduction of net returns caused by quality issues, new product innovations, return on investment, and earnings growth.

Many firms utilize both short- and long-term objectives. Short-term objectives are set for less than one year and are usually associated with a long-term objective, up to five years out. To meet that distant objective, short-term results are measured at specific points to be sure that they are on target. If the short-term effort lags in performance, then the root cause of the problem must be found and corrected.

In the first three sections of this chapter, how firms balance their objectives, list their underlying assumptions, and develop criteria for testing objectives are explained. The final two sections provide examples of good marketing objectives and examine the need for contingency plans.

Balancing Objectives

Objectives provide targets and guidance for the direction of marketing strategies. They should identify an actual result (benchmark or target) to be achieved within a specific period. Objectives should include specific quantitative benchmarks by which the firm measures its efforts toward meeting the objective. Remember, a goal without an objective is meaningless, since without objectives, it is not possible to measure your progress toward the goal.

Marketing requires a number of objectives if it is to fulfill the corporate vision/mission statement and the goals stated in the overall business plan. You will need objectives for the following:

- Existing products and services in current and future markets
- Promotion of products in target markets
- Disinvestment in unprofitable or out-of-date products or services
- Entrance into new markets
- New products and services in current markets
- Developing new market segments
- Pricing of new ventures in new target markets
- Design of new products and enhancements of current products
- The distribution structure
- The economic and pricing program
- Service and quality standards

The decision on how to balance these objectives always requires some risk. Management must weigh objectives in terms of the following:

1. *Attainable profitability.* What rate of return or profit margin can you achieve now versus in the future?
2. *Demands of the immediate period versus the more distant future.* What objectives can you delay attaining in order to achieve longer-range objectives?
3. *Other company objectives.* What trade-offs can be made between desired performance in one area and desired performance in another?

You will need to decide, for example, which is more important: an expansion in markets and sales volume or a higher rate of return. How much time, effort, and energy should be expended on improving manufacturing productivity? Each company must decide on its own balance of future goals and short-term objectives.

There are two types of objectives that often conflict: financial and strategic (marketing). The achievement of acceptable financial objectives is a necessity if a firm is to maintain its credit rating, grow its stock price, and garner investment dollars from the capital markets. The strategic marketing objectives include developing new ventures, gaining long-term market share, increasing target market segments, globalizing expansion, and, compared to competitors, lowering cost per unit, and optimizing distribution. These marketing objectives will, if successful, increase the value of the firm—but at a monetary cost.

A firm that is questioning whether it will achieve its financial goals and the associated objectives will consider holding back on long-term marketing strategies in order to meet its short-term financial objectives. Doing so may jeopardize its long-term growth in market share, and it may slow revenue increases. Obtaining short-term bottom-line objectives through a trade-off of long-term marketing objectives can be hazardous to the firm—especially in a very competitive environment.

Many people believe that marketing always enhances value. That is, retaining any type of marketing advantage over the long run involves pursuing marketing objectives that will ultimately, if successful, strengthen the firm's position relative to its competition and thus increase the firm's value. This result leads to meeting the firm's financial objectives by focusing first on certain marketing objectives. These objectives will, first, increase the firm's value; second, increase the firm's market share; and third, increase its competitive position for the long run of three to five years out. Whatever you believe, your firm will have to make wise trade-offs. The most important issue, at this point of the strategic marketing planning cycle, is that compromises have to be balanced between what objectives are essential and what objectives are practical, given the constraints the firm faces.

All objectives should be set within the framework of your environmental analysis in relation to what future product positioning you would like to achieve. As in other planning stages, make sure that all departments are involved in developing objectives. Department heads should feel that the plan is theirs; this attitude should help reduce conflicts and power struggles among departments when the team implements the marketing plan.

Assumptions of Objectives

No set of objectives in a marketing plan should be presented without first stating the assumptions upon which they depend. *Assumptions* are estimates of future operating conditions that will have an impact on your marketing plan. You may not be able to predict exactly what is going to happen, but clear assumptions will help the firm contend with a variety of possibilities.

In many instances, stated assumptions explain why certain objectives were developed. Those who read your plan can judge whether the assumptions are valid or reasonable. Any disagreements over basic assumptions should be resolved at this stage to prevent more serious conflicts from erupting later—conflicts that could prove costly to the firm.

In the marketing plan, typical assumptions could be related to the following conditions:

- Changes in gross domestic product (GDP)
- Future economic conditions
- Anticipated inflation rate
- Consumer disposable income
- Anticipated interest rates
- Market size
- New segments in the target market
- New entrants
- Technological innovations
- Status and projected objectives of key competitors
- Competitors' actions
- Availability and cost of raw materials
- Changes in distribution structure
- Government regulations
- Expected innovations

You should state your assumptions as specifically as possible; but first make sure that they are categorized.

Categorizing Assumptions

When categorizing assumptions, it is not necessary to cover the entire range of possible conditions. Develop only those assumptions that are likely to influence the achievement of your objectives. For example, you could categorize assumptions about the economy and your competition as follows:

1. With respect to general economic conditions, we assume that:
   - GDP will decrease from 3.7 to 3.2 percent per year over the next year.
   - The prime rate will decline from 8.4 percent to 7.9 percent over the next year.

2. With respect to our competitors, we assume that:
   - New, technologically superior products will be introduced in our target markets over the next three years, rendering two of our main products obsolete.
   - Several new competitors will enter our target market over the next three years.

Stating Assumptions Specifically

After you have categorized your assumptions, state them as specifically as you can. The degree to which you can quantify an assumption depends on the information available to you. You can define your assumptions at three levels of specificity: general, specific, and quantified. For example:

1. *General.* The market growth rate for Product A will decrease.
2. *Specific.* The market growth rate for Product A will decrease to 4 percent per year in the next 12 months.
3. *Quantified.* The market for Product A will decrease to a 4 percent annual rate of growth because we expect GDP to decline from 3.7 to 3.2 percent, and the trade deficit to increase by 5.1 percent.

The more information you have on hand, the more detailed your assumptions will be.

Developing accurate assumptions is a critical step toward establishing your marketing objectives. Through the assumptions, you have a chance to identify factors that will influence your objectives—factors that are somewhat unpredictable and uncontrollable. These factors will become even more important after the plan is implemented and you begin monitoring your progress.

This stage is also a good time to develop contingency or "what-if?" assumptions. What if your competition enters the market first? What if oil prices continue to fall? Develop alternative assumptions and objectives to the ones you put in your marketing plan. (Contingency objectives are discussed at the end of this chapter.) Once you have drawn up your list of assumptions, you must establish criteria for which of your balanced objectives you will select and develop.

Criteria for Objectives

Proactive planners use several primary criteria when developing sound objectives. They seek to establish objectives that are:

- *Measurable*—for example, to raise sales by a specific percentage or to increase production by a specific number of units.
- *Realistic*—based on a sound assessment of the company's resources and the conditions in the marketplace.
- *Attainable*—able to be reasonably attained within the time frame stipulated.
- *Defined time period*—for example, implement Product A's enhancements in four months.
- *Quantitatively measured outcomes*—for example, to increase sales by 11 percent by the end of the year.

In addition, you should strive to make your objectives results-oriented, flexible, and acceptable to all departments in the company. Avoid generalities such as *maximize profits, increase efficiency, increase sales*, and *decrease cost*; these cannot be measured, as they are not assigned a dollar value, percentage, volume, or market share.

While these criteria may seem somewhat excessive, they are not as constraining as they look. Remember that objectives are broader in scope than either strategies or tactics. If your objectives satisfy most or all of the criteria, you will have a clear idea of the desired results you are pursuing.

Using these criteria as a guide, ask yourself some basic questions as you formulate your marketing objectives. For example:

- Is this a realistic and attainable objective?
- Can we enhance any of our products?
- Can our products be differentiated?
- Is this objective consistent and compatible with the others we have developed?
- Are these objectives within our area of responsibility?
- Have we thoroughly assessed the needs and wants of our consumers?
- Can the market be segmented?
- Is the current market large enough to absorb the product quantity stated in our objectives?

- Can the firm's production facilities actually produce the product at a competitive price and in the estimated quantity?
- Can our current distribution channels handle the objective of increasing market share or starting new ventures?
- Are there any new regulations being considered that will affect our products?
- What reactions can we expect from competitors, and how will their reactions affect the achievement of our goals?
- How will attaining this objective affect our products, our departments, and our functions in the firm?
- Is the new venture we are proposing compatible with the company's long-term growth objectives?
- Are our product lines too far along in their life cycle to obtain the desired profit margins?

Such criteria can test your thinking before you select objectives and develop strategies to meet them. Be sure you have considered as many contingencies as possible and that your resulting objectives are based on sound research and analysis. Once you have completed balancing, assumptions, and criteria, you are ready to formulate your marketing objectives.

Marketing Objectives—Examples

The following are sample objectives for each major marketing-mix area. These lists are merely representative and cover only a few conditions for each area. You can adapt the lists to fit your company's particular situation.

Product-Related Objectives

1. Differentiate Products A and B and return them to the growth stage by the end of the year.
2. Reduce production cost by 6 percent over the next 12 months.
3. Increase market penetration in Target Market X by 8 percent during the next 12 months.
4. Expand into Target Market Y within the next eight months and obtain a 14 percent market share.
5. Study the effects on revenue of dropping products that have a gross margin of 6 percent or less.

Price-Related Objectives

1. Increase ROI by 1.8 percent for the next fiscal year.
2. Decrease the price of Product A by 6 percent to stimulate demand, assuming that Product A's price is elastic.
3. Decrease the average collection period from 52 days to 38 days by changing the current credit policy to 3/15/net 45.
4. Set competitive prices—within 9 percent of our major competitors—that produce a minimum unit contribution to profit of 14 percent.
5. Increase the profitability of personal sales calls by using telemarketing and the Internet to screen out uninterested customers, which will lower cost per sales call by 7 percent.
6. Decrease the price of Product B by 8 percent to compete directly in the low-income market segment.

Promotion Objectives

1. Increase buyer awareness of new-venture Products A and B by 13 percent by the end of the year.
2. Develop high-quality inquiries for the company's products at $7 per inquiry.
3. Decrease advertising of cash cow products by 11 percent and expend those dollars on products with a gross margin of 16 percent or better.

Distribution Objectives

1. Establish three new distributors in specific geographic regions by the end of the year.
2. Phase out all marginally profitable sales channels and centralize operations.

Other Objectives

You would also develop objectives for areas such as new venture development, budget and control, service programs, customer relations, profitability, market share, and any other areas that are essential to your firm. The more complete your list of objectives, the more clearly you will be able to monitor results as you implement the plan.

Contingency Objectives

Contingency objectives are one of the hallmarks of successful marketing planning. For any firm, the internal and external environments are constantly changing. For example, a major competitor may introduce a technologically superior product and have a very strong balance sheet to penetrate your target market segments. This competitor may lower prices to below breakeven, have a superior distribution network, and have promotional plans to gain market share and drive out competitors. Your firm will need to act quickly in order to survive.

Proactive planning means that you consider several courses of action based on "what-if?" questions. What if your major distributor experiences a labor strike that paralyzes deliveries? What if your promotional costs unexpectedly increase? What if one of your major products is now regulated by the state?

Successful firms spend a considerable amount of time developing contingency objectives when they identify their basic assumptions. Should conditions call for them, these contingency objectives then become the new marketing objectives.

Form 7, "Marketing Objectives," is designed to help you establish strategic marketing objectives for the marketing mix and other functional areas, such as training, sales, and production. By clarifying your objectives, you will be able to develop strategies to achieve them. A completed Form 7 is presented in the sample case.

Summary

- Marketing objectives are the core of the marketing plan. They are the link between the corporate level of planning and each department's plan, and they provide targets that let you direct and guide your marketing strategies.
- Objectives can be short-term and associated with a long-term objective; in those cases, you can measure performance of the short-term objective and take corrective action if it lags.
- Balancing near-term and longer-range objectives requires weighing objectives on the basis of (1) attainable profitability, (2) demands of the immediate term versus the more distant future, and (3) other competing objectives.
- Because of constraints on a firm, not all objectives are feasible to implement fully; thus, firms must compromise and channel the most resources to those objectives that maximize the value of the firm in the long run.
- No set of objectives should be presented without first stating the assumptions upon which the objectives depend. Assumptions are estimates of future operating conditions for your marketing plan. They explain why certain objectives were developed rather than others.
- When stating your assumptions, make sure that they are categorized and stated as specifically as possible. You can define your assumptions at three levels: general, specific, and quantified.
- Proactive planners seek to establish objectives that are measurable, realistic, and attainable.
- During this stage of strategic planning, you should also begin developing contingency objectives based on "what-if?" questions.

Sample Case, Phase 6

Now that the marketing team had completed work on the firm's basis view, product positions, portfolio analysis, and problem and opportunity analysis, it had the data to develop a set of basic assumptions and establish overall corporate marketing objectives.

Although Paul Harris preferred quantified assumptions, he realized that this time around, many of the firm's assumptions would have to be general or only somewhat specific. Because this was the first year that the planning process had been conducted in the firm, some of the data were still rough or based on managers' estimates or best judgments. As the process was repeated in the future, the data would become more complete and quantitative.

However, if too many of the assumptions for a certain product were general, Harris would know that the team was lacking in support for the objectives. The team could then focus on getting more information about that particular product for next year's planning process.

The members of the marketing team developed and categorized their basic assumptions. (These assumptions are abbreviated for purposes of the sample case. In fact, assumptions are often lengthy and more detailed.) The assumptions are as follows:

1. **Economic conditions**
   - The GDP will move up slightly, from 2.7 percent to 3.0 percent, over the next three years.
   - Increases in the Consumer Price Index will remain steady at 3.7 percent per year for the next two years and will rise to 4.6 percent by the end of the third year.

2. **Competition**
   - Direct foreign competition with our computer products will increase by 27 percent over the next three years.
   - Price cutting for office products (noncomputer) will continue, but will decrease in three years, as the market will be saturated and new technology will be developed.
   - The number of U.S. and non-U.S. entrants into the computer peripherals area is expected to increase 22 percent over the next 14 months.

3. **Raw materials**
   - Certain microchips will be in short supply over the next nine months until the suppliers can expand their capacity.

- Prices of electronic components will drop by 17 percent over the next two years as a result of increased foreign supplies.

4. **Government regulations**
   - Import quotas will be imposed on foreign electronics firms over the next 18 to 24 months; the amount of these quotas is not known.

5. **Market size**
   - Market size is not expected to increase substantially for Products 2 and 4.
   - Market size for Product 3 is expected to decrease by 47 percent in two years because of product obsolescence and new technology.
   - Market size will increase an average of 12 percent for Products 1, 5, and 6 over the next two to three years.

The marketing team was eager to begin setting corporate marketing objectives, but Harris reined in their enthusiasm.

"I want to be sure you understand the context for developing these objectives. First, you have to fulfill the requirements of the business plan and the corporate vision/mission statement. You all have copies of these documents? Good.

"Second, all objectives should be set within the framework of our environmental analysis and the future product positioning we want to achieve for each product. Remember that financial and marketing objectives can often be in conflict with each other—you will need to balance those objectives. Do not forget to be ready to present the assumptions underlying your objectives before you present your objectives. And finally, you will need contingency objectives for the internal, external, and set objectives so that we are not caught off guard but are ready to quickly offset these unforeseen changes.

"And third," Harris looked carefully around the table at each team member, "we have to involve all department heads and staff members in developing these objectives."

An immediate chorus of protests erupted. "We can't do that," one team member said. "If we have to involve them in this step, the process will take forever!"

"Just getting them to see me will take a week," another member said.

"Have you ever tried talking with some of the product managers?" a third staff member demanded. "You can't get five minutes without interruption."

Harris let the protest run on longer and then spoke up. "I'm going to say this over and over until everyone understands: the more we involve people in the planning process, the more ownership and investment in its success they'll have. Think about it. How would you feel if the production departments set the objectives for the marketing team without consulting you?"

The team fell silent.

"All right, how do you think the product managers are going to react when you present them with a finished plan, complete with objectives and strategies, that they had no part in developing?"

The team members exchanged glances.

"I'm a strong believer in a company where all employees are team players. It may be hard to work with at first, but in the long run it prevents many conflicts and power struggles among people. What we are doing in this planning process is more than simply gathering data and analyzing questionnaires. We're building a team that involves everyone from top management down to support staff who will work together to achieve the company's goals."

Harris softened his approach. "Don't worry about getting time to meet with managers or anyone else you need to see. I'll arrange that with the partners."

Harris then gave the team some guidelines to use when working with department heads and staff members on the objectives. "The criteria for all objectives are that they should be measurable, realistic, and attainable. They must be balanced in terms of attainable profitability, the demand of the immediate versus the long-term future, and other objectives that the managers may have. Any questions?"

"Yes. Suppose we cannot agree on a set of objectives? Who will arbitrate?"

"I will be available to help resolve any disputes, and so will the three partners. Keep in mind that you have top management support for this process, not just my backing. All right, let's get started. I'll set up the first meetings by the end of this week, and we'll set a target date of the first of next month to have all the corporate objectives set."

By the end of the month, despite some difficulties working with management and the department heads and staffs, the team had finished its task. The overall abbreviated corporate marketing objectives follow.

1.   **Overall Corporate Marketing Objectives**
   - Increase ROI by an average of 7.1 percent for the entire six products over the next 24 months.
   - Decrease service complaints by 80 percent by the end of the current fiscal year.
   - Establish sales and service training programs to train staff members in the characteristics of Product 6 (Storage Extreme). Introduce e-commerce in the sales department.

- Decrease production cost by 8.8 percent through automation over the next 12 to 16 months.
- Extend the collection period from 30 days to 45 days to stimulate dealer orders.

2. **Product Marketing Objectives—All Six Products**
    - Differentiate Product 4 back toward its growth stage in the next two years. If this is not feasible, R&D should develop replacement products to introduce in two years.
    - Decrease advertising expense for cash cow Product 1 by 42 percent and channel funds to the advertising budgets for Products 2, 5, and 6 (Storage Extreme).
    - Decrease the price of Product 2 to meet the competition's price and to minimize market share loss.
    - Enhance the features of Product 3 to appeal to new segments and to increase market share by 11 percent by the end of the third quarter.
    - Drop Product 4 from the portfolio. Stop expending any additional funds to market this product.
    - Expand Product 1 into the West Coast region through increased sales and service force; obtain an 18 percent market share within 12 months.
    - Increase buyer awareness of Product 6 by 32 percent over the next 12 months.
    - Open a new channel of distribution for Products 5 and 6 through a joint venture within 12 months.

Once the overall corporate marketing and product line objectives were set, the product managers' next step was to develop objectives for each line. Harris devised a form to help them set objectives for each of the marketing-mix elements and any additional goals that might be required.

He focused particular attention on Product 6, Storage Extreme, since the product's official entry into the national market was only a few months away. When the form was completed, Harris felt confident that the team had established a set of realistic objectives that would enable Techna to achieve the greatest return from the new product.

FORM 7
Marketing Objectives

Product: Storage Extreme   **Date:** xx/xx/xx

I. Overall Corporate Marketing Objectives

List and describe the overall marketing objectives.

> - Increase ROI by an average of 7.1 percent for the entire six products over the next 24 months.
> - Decrease service complaints by 80 percent by the end of the current fiscal year.
> - Establish sales and service training programs to train staff members in the characteristics of Product 6 (Storage Extreme). Introduce e-commerce in the sales department.
> - Decrease production cost by 8.8 percent through automation over the next 12 to 16 months.
> - Extend the collection period from 30 days to 45 days to stimulate dealer orders.

2. Product Marketing Objectives

List and describe marketing objectives for each major marketing criterion.

Profitability

> Minimum of 26 percent return on the product over its life span.

Pricing

> 1. Offer volume discounts of 22 percent to high-volume distributors.
> 2. Obtain ROI of 12 percent in the first and second years and increase to 28 percent by the end of the third year.
> 3. Market to early adopters when the price is highest and then lower prices to the next level of price-sensitive buyers as the target segment becomes saturated.

Market Share

1. Have 65 percent of the total market by the end of the third year.
2. Have 14 percent of the market by the end of the first year and increase to 42 percent by the third year.

Promotion/Advertising

1. Achieve maximum domestic and global market coverage.
2. Position Storage Extreme as a premium item to convince the market to pay an initial high price.
3. Use a quick skimming strategy.

Distribution

1. Offer longer collection periods to induce dealers to carry larger stocks of all six products and complementary products.
2. Establish a national distribution system over the next 12 to 18 months via acquisitions, alliances, or franchised dealers.

Product Development

1. Migrate current customers to Storage Extreme as old products are phased out.
2. Create customer awareness of Storage Extreme as a premier technological product.

Sales Volume

1. Increase sales volume by an average of 11 percent over the next three years.

Other (Training, Customer Relations, Service)

1. Introduce e-commerce.
2. Increase training of salesforce.
3. Decrease turnaround time for repairs by 75 percent.
4. Increase training of repair personnel.

7

Marketing Strategy Selection

Introduction

Developing marketing strategies begins the action part of your marketing plan—how to get the job done. While objectives establish the desired end results, strategies outline the specific marketing approaches to be taken to achieve those results.

The strategies you select should take into account the life-cycle stage of your products; the marketing mix of product, price, promotion, and place (distribution); and such concerns as customer service and packaging. The balancing and creative implementation of these strategies will determine the effectiveness of your marketing plan.

At the same time, you should consider alternative strategies and develop contingency plans for achieving your objectives. Every proactive marketing plan contains provisions for the unexpected. If circumstances change radically or if your primary plan proves ineffective, you need to have contingency strategies on which to base an alternative plan. Having them will give you added flexibility in responding to changes in market conditions.

This chapter provides a brief survey of product life-cycle and product mix strategies, then discusses several other strategies—market segmentation, market niche, product differentiation, and product regeneration—in the final sections.

Because each firm's circumstances are unique, only general guidelines about which strategy may be appropriate for you can be provided. However, one way to select the best strategy is to look at the current positions of your products or services and their projected positions, as analyzed in Chapters 3 and 4. Products that are in the introduction, growth, mature, and decline stages of their life cycle all require different strategies to manage them. The more you know about each product's performance within its life cycle and the impact of that product on your portfolio, the better your chances of choosing the optimum strategy for your firm.

Marketing Strategy

Although definitions for the term vary, this book defines *marketing strategy* as a consistent, appropriate, and feasible set of principles through which a particular company hopes to achieve its long-run customer and profit objectives in a particular competitive environment.

Factors in Marketing Strategy

Whatever strategy you ultimately choose must take into account several factors:

- The company's position in the market
- The company's mission, policies, objectives, and resources
- Your competitors' marketing strategies
- The buying behaviors of customers and your target markets
- Your products' current and projected life-cycle stage
- The general economic conditions in which you must do business

The attainment of your objectives is the sole purpose of each strategic program. Each strategy must be linked to an objective, and any objective without a supporting strategy will not be accomplished. For example, if your objective is to increase Product A's market share by 12 percent, your strategy might outline how to reposition the product, reach a greater number of buyers within the market segment, overhaul its pricing structure, and improve its distribution structure.

Requirements for Marketing Strategies

Each strategy you develop must meet six requirements:

1. It must have specific deadlines. (When is the objective to be accomplished?)
2. It must control performance. (Are the proper steps being taken to achieve the objective?)
3. It must allocate resources, both directly and indirectly. (Do you have sufficient resources to accomplish your objective?)
4. It must be carefully timed. (Have you taken seasonal factors, economic conditions, and the like into account?)
5. It must be directly associated with an objective.
6. It must not be in conflict with any other strategy.

As you finalize your strategies, they must be fully communicated to everyone who will be involved in carrying them out. Successful implementation depends on the coordinated efforts of all concerned.

FIGURE 7.1

Characteristics of Product Life-Cycle Stages

Marketing Elements	Introduction Stage	Growth Stage	Mature Stage	Decline Stage
Sales	Low	Fast increases	Little or no growth	Decline
Cash flow	Low to negative	Moderate	High	Low
Profits	Low to negative	Growing fast	Peak and decline	Very low
Competition	Little competition	Increasing in number and strength	Highly competitive	Declining in number
Customers/ buyers	Early adopters/ innovators/risk takers	Mass market/ target markets	Mass market/ replacement laggers	Replacement laggers
Marketing expenditures	High	Continued high but decreasing as a percentage of total sales	Declining	Very low

Product Life-Cycle Strategies

As discussed in Chapter 2, products go through a life cycle from their introduction into the market to their final demise. The four stages in the life cycle and their impact on various marketing elements are summarized in Figure 7.1.

Product life-cycle strategies have been developed for each life-cycle stage and for each of the four marketing elements: product, price, promotion, and place (distribution). These strategies have been implemented successfully by a wide range of firms, from small, entrepreneurial companies to major corporations. To use these strategies effectively, you will need to know the life-cycle stage for each of your products—information that you developed in Chapter 3. It is recommended that you consider life-cycle strategies before evaluating the other strategies discussed in the next sections.

Strategies Matrix

Since firms face a variety of situations and constraints in projecting product growth, it is not possible to list all the life-cycle strategy combinations that could be developed. As a result, a matrix of representative strategies for each life-cycle stage and marketing-mix element has been displayed in Figure 7.2.

FIGURE 7.2
Product Life-Cycle Strategies Matrix

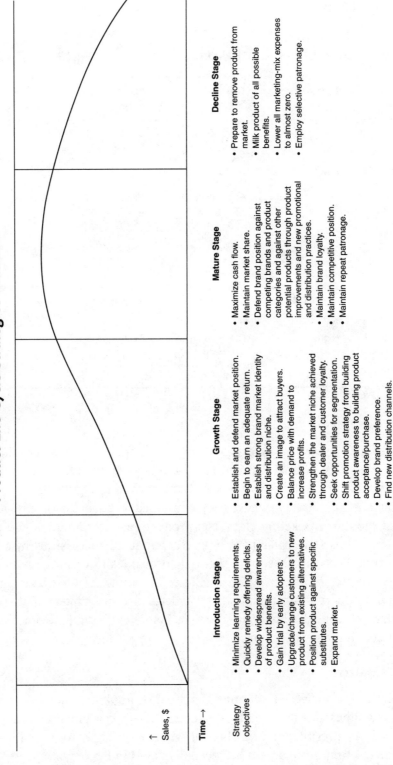

Sales, $ ↑

Time →

Strategy objectives

Introduction Stage
- Minimize learning requirements.
- Quickly remedy offering deficits.
- Develop widespread awareness of product benefits.
- Gain trial by early adopters.
- Upgrade/change customers to new product from existing alternatives.
- Position product against specific substitutes.
- Expand market.

Growth Stage
- Establish and defend market position.
- Begin to earn an adequate return.
- Establish strong brand market identity and distribution niche.
- Create an image to attract buyers.
- Balance price with demand to increase profits.
- Strengthen the market niche achieved through dealer and customer loyalty.
- Seek opportunities for segmentation.
- Shift promotion strategy from building product awareness to building product acceptance/purchase.
- Develop brand preference.
- Find new distribution channels.
- Lower prices to attract next level of price-sensitive buyers into the market.
- Increase market penetration to capture mass market.
- Build repeat patronage.

Mature Stage
- Maximize cash flow.
- Maintain market share.
- Defend brand position against competing brands and product categories and against other potential products through product improvements and new promotional and distribution practices.
- Maintain brand loyalty.
- Maintain competitive position.
- Maintain repeat patronage.

Decline Stage
- Prepare to remove product from market.
- Milk product of all possible benefits.
- Lower all marketing-mix expenses to almost zero.
- Employ selective patronage.

Product strategy	• Limited number of models. • Physical product and offering designs both focused on minimizing learning requirements. • Build association of brand name with product. • Product design and cost tailored to appeal to most receptive segment. • High attention to quality control. • Quick elimination of market-revealed defects in design. • Define product weaknesses.	• Maximize product quality. • Fit buyers' needs with product changes as needed. • Modular design to facilitate adding new features that appeal to different segments. • Eliminate unnecessary specialties with little market appeal. • Increase features.	• Pay close attention to possibilities for minor product improvement and cost cutting. • Pay close attention to opportunities through either bold cost and price penetration of new markets or through major product changes. • Consider introduction of new products.	• Eliminate any items not returning a direct profit.
Price strategy	• Set high to cover initial costs. • Establish pricing to impose the minimum value perception learning and to match the value reference perception of the most receptive segment. • Use high trade discounts.	• Use trade discounts. • Have different prices from low end to premium product. • Use aggressive promotional pricing, with prices cut as fast as costs decline as the result of accumulated production experience. • Intensify sampling. • Increase attraction to market-broadening and promotional pricing opportunities.	• Use defensive pricing to maintain market share and product category franchise. • Search for incremental pricing opportunities. • Increase private label contracts to boost volume and gain an experience advantage. • Reposition price whenever demand patterns and competitors' strategies permit.	• Decline to increase remaining volume. • Maintain or decline profit level pricing with total disregard of any offsets on market share.
Promotion strategy	• Create widespread awareness and understanding of benefits. • Gain trial by early adopters. • use publicity, personal sales, mass media. • Aim at needs and wants of innovators.	• Create and strengthen brand preference among trade and final users. • Stimulate general trial. • Use mass media, personal sales, sampling, publicity, dealer promotions. • Make mass market aware of products and services.	• Maintain consumer and trade loyalty. • Put strong emphasis on dealers and distributors. • Promote more frequent use. Use mass media, dealer-oriented promotions. • Use promotion to differentiate among major competitors.	• Phase out promotion of product. • Keep only enough to maintain profitable distribution. • Emphaize low price to increase volume.
Distribution strategy	• Use exclusive or selective strategy. • Have distributor margins high enough to justify heavy promotional spending. • Acquire high quality of distribution.	• Find new distribution channels. • Put strong emphasis on keeping dealers well supplied with minimum inventory cost. • Pay close attention to rapid resupply of distributor stocks.	• Strongly emphasize keeping dealers well supplied, but at minimum inventory cost.	• Phase out outlets as they become marginalized.

You should not be concerned with developing specific tactical budgets and plans at this point; instead, you should be establishing an overall strategic approach for your firm. Each firm will have its own methods of determining such tactical actions as budgets for promotion and advertising. As you study the matrix, you may wish to note for yourself which strategies seem appropriate for your marketing plan.

Life-Cycle Strategies

Introduction Stage

The introduction stage of the product life cycle begins when a product first appears in the marketplace. Sales are normally zero, and gross profits are usually negative or only marginally positive. In the introduction stage of a new product, the marketing managers can set high or low levels of expenditures for all marketing-mix variables. Since there is a strong relationship between the price and the promotion expenditures, the two can be used to set pricing strategies based on the promotional expenditures and the mix. Four possible strategic alternatives are available.

Using a low price with heavy promotion may result in very quick market penetration and a large market share. For this strategy to be successful, the following assumptions must apply:

- Economies of scale for the manufacturing process exist.
- Price elasticity exists in the market.
- Future competition is projected to be high.
- Consumer awareness of the product is very low.
- The target market is large enough for several competitors.

Using a high price and few promotion activities allows the maximum recovery of profit per unit from the high price, while the low promotion aids that effort by keeping expenses down. These assumptions apply to this strategy:

- Most customers are aware of the product.
- Consumers who want the product will pay the high price.
- The threat of new competition is low.
- The potential market is small.

Using a low-price and low-promotion approach should increase the market's acceptance of the product. Low promotional expenses mean greater profits on product sales. This strategy is based on the following assumptions:

- The target market is large.
- There is competition.
- Consumers are very aware of the product.
- The market is price-sensitive.

The purpose of using a high price and high promotional effort is to recover as much profit per unit as possible and to convince the market through promotional efforts that the product merits the high price. Thus, high promotion is expected to accelerate the rate of market penetration. The following assumptions must apply for this strategy to be successful:

- The majority of potential customers are initially unaware of the product.
- Customers who become aware of the product want it and will pay the high price to get it.
- The firm anticipates future competition and desires to build early brand preference and loyalty.

Growth Stage

The growth stage, which will result from the introduction stage strategies, may require some adjustments in those strategies to keep the product competitive and profitable. Remember that in using product life-cycle strategies, you must select strategies that correlate with your product's stage in the life cycle. If you do not, your strategies will not be compatible with your product and its environment, and will not lead to the fulfillment of your objectives.

During this stage, sales of your product will begin to accelerate quickly, which will provide you with high profit margins and market share—if your strategies are properly selected and implemented. This accelerated growth will begin to slow as more competition enters the market, target market saturation occurs, and substitute products become available.

Mature Stage

Three major strategies for the mature stage are product differentiation, product regeneration and market modification. One major objective in the mature stage is to find strategies that will increase or stimulate the mature product's sales.

1. *Product differentiation strategy.* This strategy seeks to attract new customers or increase current customers' usage by changing the product in some way.

2. *Product regeneration strategy.* This strategy attempts to extend the life cycle of a product by finding new uses for it and repositioning it back in the growth stage.
3. *Market modification strategy.* This strategy focuses on looking for opportunities to find new buyers for the product. These opportunities can include identifying new markets and new segments and increasing product usage by current customers.

Decline Stage

When a product enters the decline stage, it must be managed by exploring a variety of strategic alternatives. Since each of the possible strategies has a different purpose, the marketing-mix possibilities for each one can vary widely. Thus, the marketing-mix selection depends not only on the strategy chosen, but also on the environmental conditions in which the product operates.

Because of this factor, the marketing-mix alternatives have been omitted from the discussion of decline stage strategies (see Figure 7.2 for more detail). These alternatives will have to be formulated by the product manager according to each product's specific situation. These are the strategic alternatives:

1. *Product modification strategy.* Because in the decline stage, much of the market has shifted to substitute products, this strategy will be more difficult to apply. It should be used only if your product has some minor defect that can be easily identified and changed at a minimal cost. You should not commit any sizable amount of funds to product modifications unless market research clearly shows that the new product will be a strong competitor in a new market.

   If this strategy was not implemented during the mature stage of a product's life cycle, the decline stage represents your last opportunity to use it. Proceed cautiously, however.
2. *Product elimination strategy.* In this strategy, you increase a product's current profits by sharply reducing all expenses associated with its marketing program. This approach accelerates the rate of sales decline and quickly eliminates the product from your portfolio.
3. *Concentration strategy.* With this strategy, you concentrate your resources only on the strongest markets while phasing out the product elsewhere.

4. *Continuation strategy.* With this strategy, you continue to market the product in its present segments using the current marketing-mix variables until you decide to drop the product from the portfolio.

5. *Phase-out strategy.* You can take advantage of declining demand by phasing out the product gradually, since it may still contribute to company objectives, have some impact on sales, or support other products. You gradually decrease expenditures on the product, discontinue maintenance parts and systems, and so on.

   In using this strategy, you must assess the impact of phasing out the product on other offerings in the company's portfolio. If market research shows that it makes economic sense to continue offering the product despite its low or negative cash flow, you can use the phase-out strategy until a substitute product is developed.

6. *Product maintenance strategy.* With this strategy, you do not sell the product to new customers because superior products have already filled its target market. Instead, you offer only maintenance parts to current customers until a new substitute product fills the void.

Market Segmentation

Market segmentation begins not with identifying product possibilities but with determining target customer groups and their type of needs.

The power of this concept is easily apparent. In any environment that is intensely competitive for the customer dollar, a firm can prosper by developing products and services for specific market segments. A company can target particular groups rather than blanket the entire market, and it can achieve a higher rate of return on the dollars it has invested.

The question is how to identify and categorize the market and what criteria to use for developing segments within it.

Identifying and Categorizing the Market for Segmentation

For market segmentation to be effective, two general conditions must be met.

First, you must identify actual or potential customers and categorize them into relatively homogeneous segments according to their responses to marketing-mix variables.

Second, you must be able to identify characteristics of the segments or groups that can be used as a basis for special marketing efforts to reach them.

A practical approach for identifying and categorizing differences and preferences among customers is to ask the following questions.

Who:
- Are the members of segments that have been identified through the previous questions?
- Buys our product or service?

What:
- Benefits do customers seek from a product?
- Marketing-mix factors influence demand?
- Use does the product perform for the customer?
- Are customers' buying criteria?
- Risk does the customer perceive?
- Are their price points?

How:
- Do customers buy?
- Long does the buying process last in each life-cycle stage?
- Do customers use the product?
- Does the product fit into customers' lifestyles or operations?
- Much are customers willing to spend?
- Much do they buy?
- Many times on average is the product repurchased?

Where:
- Is the decision to buy made?
- Do customers seek information about products or services?
- Do customers buy the product or service?

When:
- Is the first decision to buy made?
- Is the product repurchased?

Answers to these questions can help you identify customer segments by categorizing customers' preferences. Figure 7.3 summarizes these categories as homogeneous, diffuse, and clustered.

In some markets, customers' preferences will be *homogeneous*; that is, all customers will prefer the same characteristics in a product or service. For example, if the product is a dirt bike, they may all prefer heavy tires, foot brakes, and a

FIGURE 7.3
Customer Preferences and Market Segments

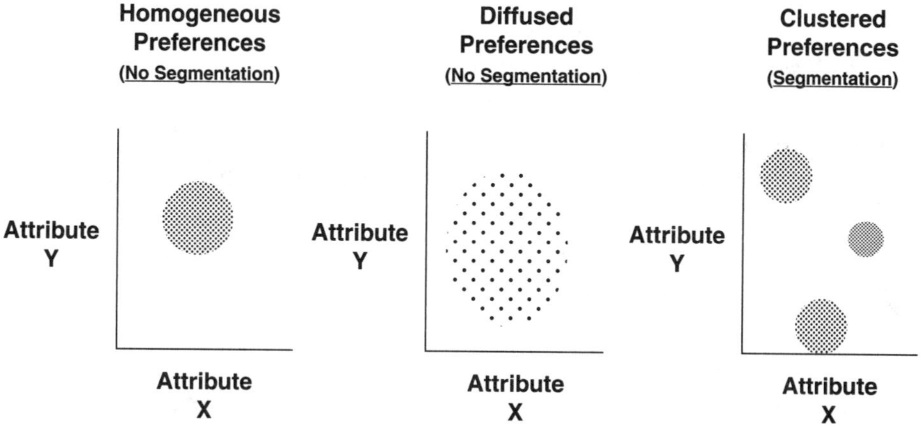

Homogeneous Preferences (No Segmentation)	Diffused Preferences (No Segmentation)	Clustered Preferences (Segmentation)

lightweight frame. In such a market, there is only one segment, and no market segmentation can occur.

In other markets, preferences will be *diffused*. There will be no clear-cut desires for various product or service characteristics. Suppose, for example, that everyone wanted a different type of dirt bike: some with hand brakes, others with 24-inch wheels, still others with 16-inch wheels, some with a heavy frame, and others with a light one. Since no concentration exists, there is a multitude of smaller markets. Again, segmentation cannot occur.

In the third type of market, customer preferences are *clustered* around various product or service characteristics. In our previous example, one group of customer wants a dirt bike with hand brakes, lighter wheels, and a heavier frame; another group wants foot brakes, dropped handlebars, and heavier wheels; and still another group wants foot brakes, raised handlebars, and a lightweight frame. These clusters of customer preferences identify natural market segments. You would then be able to develop marketing strategies to target the needs of each segment.

Segmenting Markets—Five Variables

Once you have identified the target market and determined that it can be segmented, you can use five variables as the basis for grouping consumers into target segments. These variables involve behavioristic, geographic, demographic, psychographic, and benefit factors.

Behaviorist segmentation focuses on customers' similar behavior in the market. Many marketers believe that behavioristic variables are the starting point in identifying segments. Behavior can be categorized in several ways:

- *Benefits sought:* customers' motivations for purchasing the product or service
- *Use status grouping:* customers who can be grouped as nonusers, users, first-time users, and regular users of a product or service
- *Usage rate:* customers who can be grouped as light, medium, or heavy users of a product or service
- *Purchase occasion:* customers who share a similar occasion (such as an anniversary or birthday) for purchasing a product or service

Geographic segmentation groups customers according to certain geographic features, such as region, county, city, population density, or climate. This method is easy to apply and is useful for many products, particularly where distribution is a key factor.

Demographic segmentation allows the marketing strategists to classify consumers in a direct and efficient manner. Demographic variables include sex, family size, age, race, and income. Relating buying patterns to one or more of these variables is useful in targeting the segment.

Psychographic segmentation focuses on using such variables as personality traits, lifestyle, and buyer motives to segment a market. Such information can increase a firm's understanding of buyer behavior, although data may be difficult to obtain. From a marketing perspective, psychographic information is useful in diagnosing markets and in deciding what actions to take.

Psychographic data may be particularly helpful in the beginning stages of developing marketing strategy because it can be used to determine why consumers buy. These data can then be correlated with demographic and geographic variables to fine-tune a strategy for a particular target market segment.

Benefits segmentation focuses on the benefits associated with a product or service. It is used to determine what benefits or problems exist and their importance in a purchase decision. Benefits may be related to such factors as economics, social status, convenience, savings, and performance.

Criteria for Effective Segmentation

Once you have chosen the method you will use to segment your market, you need to make sure that a segment is worth the time and effort it will take to market your products to it. Effective segments should have the following characteristics:

- *They must be substantial.* Segments should be large enough and profitable enough to be worth a separate marketing effort.
- *They must be measurable.* You should be able to measure the size and purchasing power of the segments. Minimum cutoff points can be established for segment size and buying power. If the number of consumers within a segment falls below this cutoff point, the segment can either be combined with other segments or be dropped.
- *They must be accessible.* You must be able to reach the segments through advertising, promotion, and distribution. You must be able to serve customers once you have reached them. Without accessibility, segmentation has little value.

Benefits of Segmentation

Given the limited resources of any size firm, targeting specific segments generally offers three major benefits.

First, your firm is in a better position to spot and compare market opportunities. Customers may be dissatisfied with their current suppliers and on the lookout for better products and services from another firm, or changes in customer demand may present new opportunities that you can exploit.

Second, your firm can develop marketing programs based on a clearer idea of how customers and specific segments will respond. You can focus your marketing efforts on the segments that are most likely to purchase your product or service.

Third, you can make finer adjustments in your products and marketing programs. You can tailor your offerings and programs to the needs of each segment and respond more quickly to changes in customer requirements.

Segmenting and targeting markets enable you to satisfy customer needs, capture a higher return on investment, increase profitability, and gain market share.

Product Differentiation

Product differentiation is defined as making changes in a product's characteristics that will attract new customers and/or increase usage among current customers. These changes include quality, feature, and style improvements. It is important to recognize, however, that product variations are not based on an analysis of natural market segments. Product differentiation is used to hold or capture more of a market that has already been defined and penetrated.

One of the best examples of product differentiation strategy can be seen in the famous "burger wars" among the top fast-food chains. McDonald's, Wendy's, and Burger King all sought to differentiate a basic product—the hamburger—in order to increase their share of the highly competitive fast-food market. Thus, consumers were treated to the flame-broiled hamburger, the gourmet burger, and the have-it-your-way burger.

Product differentiation is a particularly important concept when a product reaches its mature stage. Competition intensifies, prices drop, and sellers' earnings decline. At this stage, companies recognize the value of introducing different product features, quality, or style as a way of maintaining or capturing customers' attention and loyalty. This approach leads to a proliferation of sizes, models, options, packaging, discounts, and other variations for a product that is essentially the same among competitors.

Product Regeneration

In the late mature stage of a product, dollar sales have peaked and begun to decline. Firms can use *product regeneration* to extend the life cycle of a product by finding new uses, new markets, or new product characteristics or by updating the basic product. This approach repositions the product in the growth stage, as shown in Figure 7.4.

FIGURE 7.4
Product Regeneration

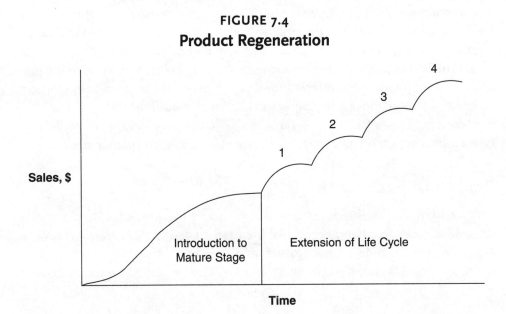

If product regeneration is not feasible, the product will continue to fall into the decline stage and will eventually be dropped from the company's portfolio.

Market Niche Strategy

Market niche strategy is a subset of segmentation and can be used in conjunction with a market segmentation strategy. Many companies use a niche strategy to avoid direct competition with the market leaders in an industry. Instead, these companies identify and serve a specific segment or niche of a large market. Firms can specialize in developing products and services for these niches, which are usually ignored or overlooked by the market leaders because of their small size or requirement for custom products.

Niche strategies are used by firms of all sizes across many industries. In fact, finding market niches is becoming the primary strategy of many successful firms. Most of these firms compete in areas where their particular strengths are highly valued; they specialize rather than diversify, and they emphasize profits over sales growth or market share.

The key to a market niche strategy is *specialization*. A company may specialize in the types of end users it services or in a particular customer group or geographic region. It may provide special products, services, quality features, or pricing structures. Whatever form specialization takes, it is essential to a firm's success.

In identifying market niches, you should look for the following characteristics:

- The niche is large enough in purchasing power to yield a profit.
- The niche has been overlooked or ignored by the market leader.
- The niche can be serviced efficiently and effectively by your company.
- You can defend the niche against a market leader and other competitors by using the goodwill you develop with customers.

Your major goal in using this strategy is to find specific market segments that your firm can serve to the best of its ability.

Contingency Strategy Development

Just as contingency objectives are needed in any successful marketing plan, so are contingency strategies. At some point, changes inside or outside the firm may prevent you from achieving your original goals. You will need to have an alternative course of action to fall back on. Also, developing contingency strategies will ensure that you have looked at several alternative plans and given yourself the opportunity to choose the best ones. You will be in a better position to counter your competitors' strategies as they change.

Contingency strategies need not be given in detail in your marketing plan. In fact, doing so may interfere with the smooth implementation of the strategies you select as your primary action program. You need give only a brief statement covering your contingency strategies and your readiness to implement them if necessary.

Evaluating the Selected Strategies

Once you have chosen the primary strategies to meet your company's objectives, evaluate these strategies for possible self-defeating conflicts before you set them in final form. The basic criteria for evaluation include the following:

- *Internal compatibility.* Is (are) the specific strategy or strategies you have chosen compatible with the assigned objective?
- *External compatibility.* Is each strategy compatible with external market conditions?
- *Resource availability.* Are all the resources you need to accomplish each strategy available?
- *Time frame.* Are the strategy deadlines compatible with the time frame outlined in the objective? Do you have enough time to complete the steps called for in each strategy? Have you mapped out the sequence and timing of various marketing efforts that will be needed to be implemented?
- *Risk factor.* How much of your total resources are committed to each strategy? If you begin to vary from a strategy significantly or if the strategy fails, will this mean failure to achieve the objective? Keep in mind that the risk of failure increases as the amount of time allotted to a specific strategy is extended.

Evaluating your selected strategies can help you spot weaknesses or contradictions before you implement your plan.

Form 8, "Marketing Strategies," contains a separate section for each of the marketing-mix elements. The form can help you to clarify your strategies and formulate contingency plans should your original strategies prove inadequate in the face of changing market conditions. The completed Form 8 for the sample case will give you some idea of the contingencies you may want to consider.

Summary

- Marketing strategy is a consistent, appropriate, and feasible set of principles through which a particular company hopes to achieve its long-run customer and profit objectives in a particular competitive environment. Strategies should take into account the life cycle of your products, the marketing mix, and such concerns as customer service and packaging.

- The sole purpose of the strategic program is to attain the company's objectives. Each strategy must be linked to an objective and must (1) meet specific deadlines, (2) control performance, (3) allocate resources directly and indirectly, and (4) be carefully timed.

- Product life-cycle strategies are developed based on the life-cycle stage of each product.

- Mature stage strategies include market modification, product differentiation, and product regeneration.

- Decline stage strategies include continuation, product maintenance, product modification, concentration, phase-out, and product elimination.

- Market segmentation is based on identifying customer groups and their needs. A firm must identify customers, categorize them into relatively homogeneous segments, and identify characteristics of these segments that can be used as a basis for special marketing efforts.

- Markets can be segmented on the basis of behavioristic, geographic, demographic, psychographic, or benefit characteristics. To be useful, segments must be substantial, measurable, and accessible.

- Market niche strategy is based on segmentation and is used to identify and serve a specific segment of a larger market. The key to a market niche strategy is specialization to avoid direct competition with market leaders.

- Product differentiation is defined as changes in a product's characteristics that will attract new customers or increase usage among current customers. This strategy is used to hold or capture a market that has already been defined and penetrated.

- Product regeneration can extend the life cycle of a product by finding new users, new markets, or new product characteristics, or by updating the product.

- Contingency strategies are an important part of your marketing plan. They will ensure that you have an alternative course of action to fall back on to counter competitors' strategies.

- Once you have chosen your primary strategies, evaluate them for internal and external compatibility, resource availability, appropriate time frame, and risk factor.

Sample Case, Phase 7

When it came time to select the best strategies for Techna, Harris made sure that his marketing team and all department heads and their staffs understood two important points.

"First, remember that the marketing strategies we choose for the firm serve as the objectives for each product plan. Second, always keep the portfolio view in mind. Product managers are not developing the plans in a vacuum. They must take into account the strategies for other products as well.

"For example, say that we're putting too much money into a cash cow item. The strategy to lower expenditures for that product must be coordinated with a strategy to raise expenditures for other products that need a cash infusion. Strategy development is a very interactive process; that's a key point I want you to remember."

Harris explained that the marketing team and time management would work on selecting the overall strategy to achieve the firm's objectives. Department heads and product managers would then develop their own strategic plans based on the company's overall marketing strategy. He gave the team and all management-level personnel some guidelines for selecting the strategies.

"Be sure to take into account the company's position in the market; our mission, policies, objectives, and resources; our knowledge of the competitors' strategies; the buying behaviors of our target customers; our products' current and projected life cycle stages; the general economic conditions in which we do business, and the results of our scenario runs.

"The attainment of objectives is the sole purpose of the strategic program. You must have a strategy linked to each objective. The strategy you develop must satisfy four criteria: it must be specific regarding deadlines, control performance, allocate resources directly and indirectly, and be carefully timed.

"We'll develop the corporate marketing strategy first and then help each department and product manager develop their own strategies. In my experience, it takes about a month to get the job done."

Harris and his team met with Bartly, Hamilton, and Farlin to choose the corporate strategies. After a week of discussion, they selected a life-cycle strategy for each product. The marketing team devised a matrix outlining general strategies for each of the four phases of a product's life cycle. The matrix was circulated to all department heads and product managers. The marketing team helped them to coordinate their strategies in light of the firm's portfolio view.

When all department and product plans were completed, the managers turned them into the marketing department. All strategies were evaluated by the marketing team for internal and external compatibility, resource availability, appropriate time frames, and risk factors.

The sample Form 8 has been completed for Storage Extreme and shows the development of individual product strategies. Each strategy has a contingency plan that can be put into effect should the primary strategy fail.

FORM 8
Marketing Strategies

Product: Storage Extreme   **Date:** xx/xx/xx

Product Objectives and Strategies

1.   Describe the product objectives.

> 1.   Create a perception of the product among customers as a premier technology item.
> 2.   Over the next 12 to 18 months, migrate our current customers and competitors' customers to our new products while phasing out old products.

2.   Describe the product strategies.

> 1.   Very high attention to service and quality control for both the product and customers.
> 2.   Fast elimination of defects revealed in the market or in the product itself.
> 3.   Designed and engineered to appeal to early adopters and introduction stage target markets; trying to produce in modular form for ease of developing complementary products.

Pricing Objectives and Strategies

1.   Describe the pricing objectives for the product.

> 1.   If the competition starts to equal Storage Extreme, then Techna will have to stress product quality, advanced technology, superior engineering, and very strong customer support.
> 2.   Differentiate Storage Extreme by enhancing currently stand-alone features with complementary products. This will be easy to do because of its modular design.

2.   Describe the pricing strategies for the product.

> 1.   Use the pricing strategy of going to the next level of price-sensitive buyer when a market segment is saturated.
> 2.   Offer dealers volume discounts to keep distribution channels open.
> 3.   Use a very rapid skimming strategy to increase target market share so that the economies of scale will result in higher profit margins.

3.   Briefly describe contingency strategies and the conditions under which they may be implemented.

> If the target market becomes saturated with competitors, we will change pricing strategies to match competitors' prices or go below them. This may allow the firm to gain market share and shed some of the competitors who do not have the financial resources to match them—as long as we are making a gross profit. The technology is changing so rapidly that the product may be in the mature stage in two years instead of the projected three years; therefore, the firm will have to shift to mature stage strategies. This situation will have an effect on most of the firm's strategies and would require a review of the corporate business and marketing plan.

Promotion/Advertising Objectives and Strategies

1.   Describe the promotion/advertising objectives for the product.

> 1.   Maximize U.S. and global market coverage.
> 2.   Utilize e-commerce.
> 3.   Position Storage Extreme as technologically superior and a premier product to convince the market to pay the initial high price.
> 4.   Change advertising and promotion to the next layer of price-sensitive buyers when early adopters have saturated the introductory life-cycle stage of the product.

2. Describe the promotion/advertising strategies for the product.

1. Make the mass market aware of the product and its services as superior to current technology.
2. Develop mass promotion; direct promotion to reach high-volume customers; and media, personal sales, and dealer promotions to show that the current product is a replacement for the old product to attract new users and migrate old users to the new product.
3. Develop and create brand preference among trade and private customers.
4. Develop and utilize mass market awareness of the new product, both domestic and global.
5. Utilize marketing research to find and develop mass market and global markets that are aware of the product and its services.

3. Briefly describe contingency strategies and the conditions under which they would be implemented.

If competition increases (as expected), emphasize product differentiation, focusing on product features, company reputation, new complementary products, and defensive advertising.

Distribution Objectives and Strategies

1. Describe the distribution objectives for the product:

1. National distribution and global distribution via alliances, buyouts, and/or franchise dealers.
2. Have longer collection periods initially, to induce dealers to carry larger amounts of stock and to carry the total product line.

2.   Describe the distribution strategies for the product.

> 1.   National and global distribution via alliances, buyouts, and franchised dealers.
> 2.   Offer longer collection periods to dealers in exchange for their carrying more products.

3.   Briefly describe contingency strategies and the conditions under which they would be implemented.

> 1.   Offer dealers and alliances higher discounts to induce them to carry Techna's lines.
> 2.   Develop alternative distribution channels that would be available if competition increases and begins to saturate our dealer channels.

Other Objectives and Strategies

1.   Describe other objectives for the product.

> Since the product has not yet been launched and data are not available, none at this time.

2. Describe other strategies for the product.

> Since the product has not been launched and all objectives and budgets are just preliminary, none at this time.

3. Briefly describe contingency strategies and the conditions under which they would be implemented.

> Currently, at this stage, none.

8

Budgeting, Forecasting, and Financial Analysis

Introduction

The marketing budget is directly related to the developed objectives, strategies, and planned tactical actions of the marketing plan. While strategies outline a plan of attack, the budget specifies how much it will cost.

It is important to remember that developing a budget is not the same thing as strategic planning. Budgets provide control, allowing you to monitor expenses and track revenue. However, if budgeting is used for overall planning or is the main focus of a plan, then the company's primary objectives may well shift to saving money rather than generating a profit through long-range strategic planning.

As a result, this chapter does not go into detail about how to prepare a budget. Each company has its own methods for accomplishing that task. Presented here are general guidelines on *how budgets fit into the development of strategic plans* and *how they affect the success of a marketing plan*. Once overall budget requirements are approved at the strategic level, detailed budget figures can be generated at the tactical level.

This approach follows up on the product and portfolio analysis discussed in Chapters 3 and 4, particularly when a product's contribution margin is examined later in this chapter. Although these methods are presented for purposes of strategic marketing at a superficial level, you will have to decide which ones you can utilize now and which will require further study.

Budget Organization

The first step in developing a budget at the strategic level is to identify your own department's area of fiscal responsibility. In many companies, total marketing costs are the sum of all costs required to manufacture the product and place it in the hands of the consumer. Many of these costs may be for functions or activities that are not necessarily part of your marketing plan or in your area of responsibility. Nevertheless, they must fit into the total allocation of resources available for marketing.

To isolate your area of responsibility, you will need to look at two broad categories of total marketing costs:

1. Order-getting costs: selling, advertising, promoting, receiving incentives, and packaging
2. Order-filling costs: shipping, warehousing, inventorying, order processing, and billing

Your marketing plan, including the objectives and strategies, is almost entirely concerned with the order-getting process. Creative deployment of the marketing mix is aimed at obtaining orders from customers. In addition, order-filling costs tend to be more fixed; the marketing manager has less control over these items than over order-getting costs. The more you control order-getting costs, the more your department can contribute to company profits.

The next step is to obtain budget estimates from each department in the firm that is associated with marketing activities. One person from each department should be responsible for providing budget information to the marketing department to aid in developing the marketing plan. Organize the budget into discrete categories, preferably by marketing-function responsibility:

- Sales
- Market research
- Advertising
- Production
- Personnel (salaries and benefits)
- Other

This approach makes it easier to agree on the measures and procedures that need to be followed to control expenses.

Make sure your budget format is compatible with the reporting procedures used in the accounting department. More and more corporations are using management information systems to control reporting and information that will help managers make decisions. If your format is compatible with these systems, it will be easy for you to obtain meaningful financial reports that will help you control costs and manage your area of responsibility.

Budget and Forecasting

The marketing department is responsible for preparing a budget statement that projects the costs of the marketing plan and also forecasts revenue and sales by product. This information is needed in order to implement the plan successfully. Budgets are developed at the corporate and individual-product levels. Forecasting techniques are discussed in a later section.

Profit and Loss Statements

A simplified *corporate* budget statement, shown in Figure 8.1, is essentially a projected profit and loss (P&L) statement, or a summation of all individual-product sales and expenses.

FIGURE 8.1
A Simplified Profit and Loss Statement

Revenues from sales			$208,000
Cost of goods sold			88,000
Gross margin			$296,000
Operating expenses			
Selling expenses			
Advertising	$11,000		
Marketing research	7,700		
Salaries	38,500		
Miscellaneous	2,200		
Total selling expenses		$59,400	
General and administrative expenses			
Rent	$12,000		
Insurance	5,000		
Supplies	4,000		
Depreciation	7,000		
Total G&A expenses		$28,000	
Total operating and G&A expenses			$ 87,400
Net profit (loss) before taxes			$208,600

FIGURE 8.2

Combined P and L Statement for Three Products

Products:	Memory	Flat Screens	Disk Drives
Revenues from sales	$161,000	$40,250	$103,500
Cost of goods sold	66,700	19,550	25,300
Gross margin	$ 94,300	$20,700	$ 78,200
Operating expenses			
Selling expenses			
Advertising	$ 4,830	$ 2,358	$ 7,360
Marketing research	9,200	4,600	16,100
Salaries	18,400	5,060	14,375
Distribution	16,100	4,140	10,695
Maintenance	7,130	679	2,415
Miscellaneous expenses	2,645	1,208	6,670
Total selling expenses	$ 58,305	$18,045	$ 57,615
General and administrative expenses			
Rent (prorated by product)	$ 9,143	$ 2,243	$ 5,865
Insurance (prorated by product)	1,524	374	978
Depreciation (prorated by product)	3,657	897	2,346
Total G&A expenses	$ 14,324	$ 3,514	$ 9,189
Total operating and G&A expenses	$ 72,629	$21,559	$ 66,804
Net profit (loss) before taxes	$ 21,671	$ (859)	$ 11,396

The *individual-product* budget statement is developed at the marketing department level and is illustrated in Figure 8.2, which shows a three-product profit and loss statement. The amount of detail in an individual-product P&L statement is up to the marketing department. Eventually all these statements are summed to produce the detailed pro forma P&L statement. These data can be used to define certain ratios, to be discussed later, not only at the corporate level, but also at the marketing level.

Forecasting

Forecasting is a way of predicting product demand and sales performance in the coming year or for a number of years. Once the product lines are well defined in the marketing plan, the marketing manager works with sales personnel to determine when, where, and how much of the product will be sold in each region or target market segment. They consider these factors:

- Market demand
- Product availability
- Competitive activity
- Customer brand acceptance
- Market saturation
- Life-cycle stage
- Product monitoring
- Other

You will notice that these factors were researched during product positioning analysis (Chapter 3) and portfolio analysis (Chapter 4). However, for forecasting purposes, you may need to quantify these data further. Techniques for forecasting demand and revenue, for example, vary from relatively simple to highly sophisticated econometric models. If your current forecasting methods are inadequate, you may want to consider changing them.

The forecast will need to be made on a product-by-product basis once you begin to develop budget figures at the tactical level. Budget categories at the product level are concerned solely with tactical issues. These categories are summed up as the budget moves up the planning ladder and the categories become broader and have more strategic applications.

During budget development, product managers must keep the positioning analysis in mind so that their budget requests reflect future product positioning strategies. For example, mature cash cow products would not necessarily require a high advertising budget to maintain their current product position.

These individual predictions provide next year's forecast for sales performance. Once the tactical budget and forecasts are made, they are summed and placed in a single pro forma statement for the final marketing plan. However, since this chapter is concerned with the strategic level of budget and forecasting, the tactical details will be omitted.

One word of caution: make sure that salespeople and product managers do not either overstate their expected sales to impress top management or understate them to avoid future criticism. Inaccurate forecasting is a common cause of ineffective market planning. Stress the need for accurate, reliable estimates in budget and forecast development. The next section, on forecasting sales demand, will survey current techniques used by marketing planners for developing their marketing plan.

Forecasting Sales Demand

A persistent dilemma for all firms is forecasting future sales. Sales forecasts can be short-term, such as for one year; medium-term, such as for two years; or long-term, such as for five years or more. It is clear that longer-term forecasts offer proportionally less accuracy and inspire less confidence. The objective of forecasting is to develop a systematic and quantitative statement of expected demand for a defined time period—a statement that will be the basis for planning and controlling by using variance analysis. Inputs into the forecasting process may include opinions, facts, and judgments. However, long-term forecasts are an important input for top management, as they provide a basis for deciding both the direction in which the organization should move and long-term capital-investment levels.

When developing a forecast for a specific product or service, it is usual to make a broad forecast of the general business or economic climate of your current target market segment. Different industries are often affected differently by changes in certain economic variables, so you may need to understand how these variables fit into the forecast for your particular industry. With that information, your company's sales forecast can be determined. At a minimum, that forecast should include these variables: your firm's own sales and those of its competitors for each target market segment; the increase or decrease in your firm's share of the market segment; the effect of potential population shifts that may affect disposable income for purchasing your products; changes in consumer tastes in your target market segment; your new product introductions, product enhancements, and new ventures (by your firm or by your top competitors) in your target market segment; and the possibility of selling in new market segments or discontinuing sales in existing segments.

In general, very few products or services are easy to forecast. One exception is forecasting for a monopoly, such as a public water company, where demand is either constant or growing or slowing at a predictable rate. But usually, as the forecasters look at the data, they find that the demand for the company's products or services is not stable, and shrewd forecasting becomes a very important task in the development and success of the company's marketing plan. In the discussion to follow, a few of the many methods of forecasting will be examined.

Expert Opinion

Expert opinion is a methodology that involves evaluating the opinions of top executives or those people in the firm who know best what future sales demand is likely to be. Expert opinion is one of the oldest forecasting methods and reflects a broadening of the base for predicting sales demand. Any firm operating under such a system brings together executives from various departments so that their experience can be pooled and refined into a forecast. The advantages of this method include the following: the forecast can be quickly and inexpensively prepared, it does not require statistics, and, in some cases, it may be the only means of forecasting, especially in the absence of appropriate data. The disadvantages include the following: this method is inferior to a more fact-based forecast, since it relies heavily on opinions rather than on historical or other data; it creates difficulties in making breakdowns by product, target market segment, and time intervals; the forecaster may be too optimistic or too pessimistic in the forecast; and the forecaster has only experience and not data as a guide for deciding what future demand will be.

Surveys

Surveys are a common technique used to forecast sales demand and define buyers' intentions. When no past data exist, surveys can also help define needed product improvements, test the success or failure of a new venture, and assess expansion into a new segment. Surveys also obtain information directly from users, whose buying actions will actually determine sales; they thus aid in determining changes in consumers' taste and offer a basis for forecasting in situations where other methods may be inadequate or impossible to use.

Surveys also have disadvantages: customers may not be able or willing to estimate their future purchases accurately, the survey participants may intend to buy a product but fail to follow through, and surveys consume a large amount of time, personnel, and money.

Salesforce Composite Method

The salesforce composite method consists of obtaining information primarily from salesforce personnel. Some forecasters believe that since the members of the salesforce are closest to the consumers, they will have an acute sense of those consumers' future demand. This method has major advantages: it taps the specialized knowledge of the product from the people who are closest to the market itself, places responsibility for the forecast on those who produce the results, provides results that have greater stability because of the larger sample base, and, finally, lends itself to the breakdown of data by product, territory, and salesperson. Some disadvantages include the following: salespeople usually are not good estimators, often being more optimistic or pessimistic than conditions warrant; they are inclined to underestimate demand to make their quotas easier to achieve; they are sometimes unaware of the broad economic conditions shaping future sales and are poor long-term forecasters; and the salesforce composite method is a time-consuming process for both executives and salesforce personnel.

Time Series Analysis

Time series analysis is a method that is frequently used when historical data are available. Time series analysis looks at past results and assumes that these results reflect a causal relationship between actions such as buying and trends in the environment that are likely to continue. The time series forecasts are usually affected by four factors: secular trends, seasonal variations, cyclical trends, and random or accidental residual fluctuations. To plan for changes in these factors, there are many statistical techniques for adjusting data. Fundamentally, however, the final forecasts are only as good as the data input into the analysis; thus, the quality of the past results used remains of critical importance.

Regression Analysis

Regression analysis requires the use of historical sales data. In regression analysis, the forecaster seeks to find a relationship between past sales (the dependent variable) and one or more independent variables, such as per capita income growth, GDP, population changes, and advertising response ratios. Simple regression uses one independent variable, whereas multiple regression analysis includes two or more independent variables. The main objective of a regression analysis of either type is to develop a mathematical model that describes the relationship between the firm's sales and one or more variables. Once an accurate formula has been established, the analyst inserts the necessary data to derive the sales forecast. Regression analysis is useful when a precise association can be established. The forecaster, however, seldom finds a perfect correlation. Furthermore, this method can be used only when historical sales data are extensive. Finally, no forecasting method that requires historical data can predict the sales of a new product or changes to a current product.

Market Test

The market test method entails making the product available to consumers in one or more geographic test areas and surveying how they respond to the product, its distribution, its promotion, its price, and the needs and desires it meets. A market test provides information not about intended but about actual purchases. In addition, purchase volume can be evaluated in relation to the intensity of other marketing activities, such as advertising, pricing, packaging, and distribution. Since it does not require historical sales data, market testing is effective for forecasting sales of new products or sales of existing products in new geographic segments. However, market tests are often time-consuming and can be expensive. In addition, a marketer cannot be certain that consumer response to a market test represents the total market response or that such a response will continue in the future. For a valid market test, the test area must actually mimic the target market segment into which you are going to be expanding or introducing a new product, or a new target market segment.

Depending on the type of product, it may be necessary for your firm to utilize two or three different methods for sales forecasting. For example, forecasting sales demand for a new venture or product enhancement would preclude the use of historical data. If a firm has substantial historical data, then it may use sophisticated mathematical or statistical techniques. In some instances, the forecaster will use several forecasting methods for the same product and compare them to determine that the results of each are within some type of acceptable variance range of one another; the forecaster will have to decide on the appropriate variance.

Product Contribution

When developing budget and forecast statements for individual products at the strategic level, the first item to consider is how much gross contribution the product generates and its level of contribution margin. To determine these factors, follow these steps:

1. Calculate the revenue or price that each product commands within each product line.
2. Determine the variable cost for each product.
3. Determine the overhead or fixed cost associated with each product.

An example of calculating gross product contribution and contribution margin is shown in Figure 8.3, which depicts, for a single product, the historical and projected revenue and cost. These calculations give you the number of contribution dollars being generated by each of the products. You will need to determine the gross and net contributions of every product in your portfolio. These calculations can be done fairly quickly on the computer, using appropriate software.

FIGURE 8.3

Three-Year Forecasted Sales and Projected Profit Data (Single Product)

	201X	201Y	201Z	Row Operations
A. Market—total units	3,220,000	3,450,000	3,910,000	
B. Market share percent	14	16	19	
C. Price per unit, $	6.90	7.60	8.16	
D. Variable cost per unit, $	4.15	4.50	4.83	
E. Gross contribution				
margin per unit, $	2.75	3.10	3.33	C − D
F. Sales volume in units	450,800	552,000	742,900	A × B
G. Sales, $	3,110,520	4,195,200	6,062,064	C × F
H. Gross contribution				
margin, $	1,239,700	1,711,200	2,473,857	E × F
I. Overhead $ to this product	44,000	50,600	57,500	
J. Net contribution margin	1,195,700	1,660,600	2,416,357	H − I
K. Advertising, $	276,000	381,800	432,960	
L. Computer, $	24,500	39,200	70,500	
M. Distribution, $	92,000	127,420	211,140	
N. Salaries, $	356,500	478,170	791,085	
O. E-commerce research, $	35,000	56,000	95,200	
P. Global research opportunities, $	24,000	49,200	83,640	
Q. Miscellaneous, $	22,000	37,500	43,125	
R. Total expenses, $*	$ 830,000	$1,169,290	$1,727,650	
S. Net operating profit/(loss)**†	$ 365,700	$ 491,310	$ 688,707	

*Sum of K. through Q.

†** Line J minus Line R.

At this point, it should be clear why it is appropriate to start with the product line as the basis for developing your marketing plan data. You should be able to analyze your company's past performance and determine how much of each product has been sold within a given time frame. With this information, you can quickly identify which products represent major sources of contribution and which do not.

Once the gross and net contributions have been calculated, the net contributions of all products can be entered on a form like the Product Line Matrix shown in Figure 8.4. After you have filled out this form, compare the contribution ratios with product positions on the Product Line Matrix and look for unusual patterns.

For example, you might assume that a high-priced, high-quality product will command a higher contribution margin than a low-priced, low-quality product. Generally, as a product's quality and price increase, the incremental costs do not rise as rapidly. Thus, you would expect to see the product's contribution margin increase along with its quality and price.

However, that assumption does not always hold true, since a number of variables can influence contribution margin. The benefit of viewing all products as a portfolio is that you are able to see each product's performance in relation to the others and analyze the product line(s) as a whole.

FIGURE 8.4
Product Line Matrix—Contribution Dollars (All Products)

Product Line:	Gross Contribution Margin	Net Contribution Margin
A		
1		
2		
3		
.		
.		
.		
B		
1		
2		
3		
.		
.		
.		
C		
1		
2		
3		
.		
.		
.		

Analyzing product contribution is a powerful factor in the success of any marketing plan. A product contribution margin of 30 to 40 percent is an appropriate range for a typical manufacturing and marketing effort.

A much higher contribution margin should be established if the business is extremely capital-intensive, with high, fixed manufacturing costs, or if the business spends a great deal on expense categories such as advertising and promotion (as many consumer products companies do). On the other hand, a business that is not capital-intensive would have contribution margins below the 30 to 40 percent range.

As a general rule, contribution margins below 15 percent make it difficult to generate a profit. Companies do not earn money on the basis of their contribution ratios or margins, but by generating contribution dollars that, when accumulated, are greater than the total fixed costs of the business.

Developing a Budget

In general, to establish a budget, firms tend to use one of three methods: mechanical, task, or group. The main appeal of the first two methods is that they require less work.

In the *mechanical method,* the budget is simply determined as a percentage of historical cost or through a simple computation of what is left after you account for all manufacturing costs, taxes, profits, and general and administrative (G&A) items.

In the *task method,* the budget is built from the bottom up, with lower levels of management estimating how much money they will need to perform their specific tasks. The budget is approved or rejected by upper management. However, in this method, upper management rarely understands how the budget was developed; it simply approves or rejects it.

These techniques are not in harmony with developing and using a proactive marketing plan. They simply reflect what has happened in the past. A proactive marketing plan needs a future-oriented approach that can help the firm meet objectives and strategies that have been developed through a close examination of the marketplace, market conditions, opportunities, voids, and interaction of products in the portfolio.

The *group method* is a more modern approach to establishing a budget, one that overcomes the pitfalls of the mechanical and task methods. It begins with top management sending down an overall budget estimate, based on corporate objectives, to be used as a planning guide for the allocation of marketing funds.

Within the limits of that estimate, the marketing manager develops strategies. However, the manager is also free to recommend exceptions that go beyond those limits, backed up by full details justifying all recommendations. In the end, top management reviews the marketing plan and the detailed marketing budget(s) and reaches a final approval figure.

The group method is more time-consuming than the other two and requires considerable communication between various department heads and top management. However, the benefits outweigh the costs. The group method of establishing a budget enables the developer of the marketing plan to communicate the established strategies to many areas, both inside and outside the marketing department. In addition, top management gains a clear idea of the costs required to implement the marketing strategies and reach the objectives described in the final plan.

Marketing Budget Allocation

Assigning specific budget figures to strategies and marketing activities can be a difficult task. For this step, firms may use mathematical models at various levels of sophistication.

As a general rule, start with the strategies and marketing activities for which you have the most reliable set of historical or projected data, such as historical personnel cost, cost per sales call, advertising expenses, and purchasing totals. This historical information gives you a base for predicting the future. However, be sure that budget allocations support the product portfolio strategies that you have designed to achieve your three-year objectives.

As you work through the budget process, you will come across new items or items with insufficient historical data to use as a base for estimating budget requirements. In these cases, you will have to rely on the judgment of a good, seasoned market planner.

As you develop a balanced and workable budget, the following questions should help. Among the questions you need to answer are:

- Is the amount of money requested sufficient to achieve a stated objective through the strategies you have developed?
- If more money is required to meet your objectives, from which activities can it be reallocated?
- Is the potential profit contribution of a given product congruent with the budget request?

- Does the potential for profit justify requesting additional funds from top management?
- Are there any alternative strategies that can achieve an equally favorable end result at a lower cost?
- Are the costs allocated realistic, given the product's life-cycle analysis?
- Does the budget adequately cover all the necessary elements of the marketing mix?

If the budget is not carefully prepared, is incomplete, has poor forecasts, and/or contains conflicting requests, top management may curtail certain budget items. Or top management may ask for a major revision, which drains time at both the departmental and top management levels.

Lack of budget planning can block objectives, frustrate marketing strategies, and even undermine the entire marketing plan. On the other hand, a well-prepared and well-supported budget can win the necessary allocations of money and resources from top management to implement the marketing plan to the fullest.

When those in upper management review the forecast and the budget, they may ask for modifications. Keep in mind that when you pare expenses, you must reevaluate the strategies that may be affected. You will need to reformulate those strategies to fit the new constraints and the budget.

Once top management approves the budget, it becomes part of the marketing plan. It serves as a basis for material procurement, production scheduling, personnel planning, and market operations.

Pitfalls to Avoid

Two major pitfalls to avoid in developing your budget and forecasting deserve mention. One has to do with inflating the budget, and the other with milking it dry.

In many companies today, there is an unfortunate trend to inflate the budget artificially when estimates are being developed. This happens for a simple reason: many planners know that when their budget is sent up for approval, it will be cut by a certain percentage. If an inflated budget is cut, the planner still ends up with the amount needed to implement the market plan successfully. This inflation game is likely to continue for some time to come, mainly because of planners who cannot estimate expenses correctly and cannot control their budgets.

One way to avoid playing this nonproductive game is to build a contingency fund into the budget to provide for unexpected expenses. The contingency fund is to be used only when necessary. Including these funds in the budget in this way provides a more accurate picture of the true budget needed to implement the plan.

The other pitfall arises when planners discover that they are running under budget. The temptation is to spend all the funds in the budget for fear that next year's allocations will automatically be lowered. However, keep in mind that the goal of each department is to save the firm expense dollars and add to the company's total profitability.

You can avoid this second pitfall if you explain to top management why you were running under budget. Perhaps a reduction in expenses was due to a one-time windfall, such as an unexpected surge in demand or the loss of a major competitor. This windfall may have enabled you to slash advertising costs and/or inflated sales, but it should not be treated as a precedent.

The past never guarantees the future. If you make sure that your projected budget requests are tied to future objectives and strategies, and not entirely to historical data projections, you are more likely to have your requests approved. The past may not be congruent with the new strategic path you are setting, particularly if you are changing the company's direction.

The group method of establishing budgets can help prevent managers from either artificially inflating or overrunning their budgets. By eliminating these two pitfalls, you can improve the firm's financial health and marketing success. The budget and forecasting process must show the firm where it is going, not simply where it has been.

In addition to the three methods mentioned here, some firms are introducing a *shared method* into their marketing departments. If one division is surpassing its objectives before the end of the fiscal year and another's product is doing poorly, then the successful division will subsidize price cuts and increased advertising for the other one. This shared budget method is very useful for increasing sales revenues. The next year could reverse the divisions' positions, but at least the firm's winners can help support its laggers. Ideally, shared budgeting could eliminate the two budget pitfalls.

Financial Assessment

The financial condition of a firm is often considered the best measure of its competitive position and attractiveness to investors, and is a prime tool in the development of the overall business plan and the strategic marketing plan. Determining an organization's financial strengths and weaknesses is essential if you are to formulate marketing strategies effectively. A firm's liquidity, leverage, working capital, profitability, asset utilization, cash flow, and equity can rule out certain strategies in their early stages. One of the major purposes of analyzing the firm's financial statements is to inform, disclose, and account for past and present conditions and provide a basis point for projecting future performance.

Financial ratio analysis is the most widely used methodology for determining an organization's strengths and weaknesses in both the investment and finance arenas. There are many different types of ratios that can be analyzed. Ratio analysis entails some problems, including comparability, industry characteristics, valuation problems, changes in accounting practices and principles, and changes in the nature of the business and/or industry itself.

In ratio analysis, comparability is problematic because a ratio by itself is basically just a number that has no meaning. In ratio analysis, the use of "rules of thumb" can be misleading. For example, many firms in the high-technology industry have virtually no debt, bank very large amounts of cash, and pay very low dividends. One argument is that if a firm does not have anything in which to invest its cash, it should pay out that cash as a dividend; and if management decides against such a dividend, then any ratio that has cash as an input variable will be distorted when it is compared to industry norms. So to understand such a ratio, the analyst must first determine how the firm's strategic planning works. A firm like the one just discussed may normally make very large investments and pay cash for them. Can you assess that firm's financial ratios via a simple rule of thumb? Just think about it logically: every industry is basically different, and different firms within an industry may have very aggressive or passive strategic plans. A good analyst should know the inner workings of the firm and adjust the ratios as needed. In most cases, before you assess a firm's ratios, you should compare those ratios with industry norms. These norms and firm-specific information are available via the Internet and other sources. They provide the deep background that will help you calculate the ratios and explain their meaning. It is also recommended that you compare your firm's ratios with those of your competitors. You want to know as much about your competitors as you do about your own firm. If your competitors are not comparing their firm's analysis to your firm's or if they are comparing it in an unorganized and sloppy manner, then you will have the competitive advantage.

There are literally hundreds of different ratios that can be developed and calculated, with relative ease, from the firm's balance sheet and income statement. The one major problem with ratio analysis is that there are several ways of calculating certain ratios. Either the firm's financial analyst or its marketing manager decides which ratios to use, for what purpose, and how those ratios will be calculated, making sure that each choice is explained fully in the marketing plan and is consistent with the other ratios. The next section will sketch a few of the ratios that are used for performance measurements that relate to the firm—especially those that have strong ties to the marketing function. I strongly recommend that you obtain a good basic *managerial finance text, investment book,* or *book on marketing ratios* for further reading and edification.

The first ratio to be examined is the *return on sales,* otherwise known as the *operating profit margin.* This ratio is calculated as earnings before interest and taxes (EBIT) divided by sales. The ratio shows profitability without any concern for taxes and interest. Many analysts like to use *net profit margin* or *net return on sales,* expressed as net income divided by sales. This ratio provides the after-tax profit per dollar of sales. For example, if you have $100 million in total sales as your denominator and net income of $10 million in the numerator, this would indicate a return of 10 percent, or $0.10 for each dollar of sales. Return on sales or net profit margin is a ratio that can help show whether the company is growing more efficiently, especially if that ratio is increasing. If the ratio is decreasing, that may be a signal of possible financial troubles and should be investigated to find the cause(s). Many times, when a firm is in the early to middle growth stage of its life cycle, its net profit margin will rise and continue rising. As the product moves into the mature stage and toward the decline stage, the net profit margin will be losing momentum and begin to decrease. At that point, you need to reassess where the product is positioned in relation to its target markets through careful analyses of markets, life cycles, and portfolios, as shown in prior chapters.

Return on investment ratios are those measurements developed to show, in terms of percentage return, how your investments are performing. These return ratios may also assess how profitably you are employing your firm's capital. Furthermore, return on investment ratios will help you gauge management's effectiveness: they relate net income to the investment dollars entrusted to management. The most frequently used of these measures of investment performance is *return on assets,* otherwise known as *return on investment.* It is simply net income divided by total assets, and it measures the after-tax profits per dollar of assets. If this ratio is high, that is normally considered good because you are earning a lot on your asset investments; if it is low, then you have to find the root cause of that problem. Again, check the ratio against your firm's industry norms before deciding what is a good or a bad ratio.

Some people believe that the major determinants of return on investment are market growth rate, life-cycle stage, marketing-expense-to-sales ratio, and market share. It has been shown, for example, that when your investments are increasing at a very fast rate, your return on investment will more than likely decrease until those investments start to generate large profits. Return on investment has been shown to grow as market share increases and the target market itself increases. Also, the same relationship has been shown in studies on increasing cash flow. As you continue learning and applying ratio analysis, you will start to see many other correlations among different variables.

Return issues come into play when you have a choice of calculating ratios on before- or after-tax net income. Many financial analysts suggest that you always use consistent methodologies unless you're trying to measure one ratio against the same ratio minus or plus certain components. This technique is usually used to discover which method presents a clearer picture of what you are trying to investigate. If possible, try to use historical data, current data, and even projected data for ratios, so that some type of simple trend can become evident for further analysis.

The most highly regarded ratio is *return on equity*, sometimes referred to as *return on stockholders' equity*. This ratio is calculated as net income divided by total stockholders' equity. It indicates after-tax profits per dollar of stockholders' investment in the firm. Return on equity is very important for stockholders, for the firm's ability to obtain external financing, and for the firm's ability to secure short-term financing for strategic marketing planning.

These are just a few of the ratios that are included in the profitability ratio category of ratio analysis. It is strongly suggested that you utilize other ratios to enhance your internal and external analysis, as this will help you develop your strategic marketing plan. Internal management will be looking at these measurements to aid it in deciding how the return on investors' dollars is performing relative to industry norms and competitors.

Another important calculation is that of your free cash flow. Free cash flow represents the financial performance calculated as operating cash flow minus capital expenditures. Or, in expanded form:

$$\text{EBIT} (1 - \text{tax rate}) + \text{depreciation and amortization} -$$
$$\text{change in net working capital} - \text{capital expenditures}$$

Free cash flow can also be calculated by taking operating cash flow and subtracting capital expenditures.

Free Cash Flow

Free cash flow represents the cash that a company generates after investing the money required to maintain or expand its asset base. Free cash flow is important because it allows a company to pursue opportunities that enhance shareholder value. Without cash, it is difficult to develop new products, make local and global acquisitions, pay dividends, and reduce debt.

Some people believe that financial analysis focuses too myopically on earnings while ignoring the "real" cash that a firm generates. For this reason, some investors believe that free cash flow gives a much clearer view of the firm's ability to generate cash and thus profits. It is important to note that a negative free cash flow is not bad in itself. If free cash flow is negative, it could be a sign that a company is making large investments. If these investments promise a high return, the strategy could greatly increase revenue in the long run.

In calculating margins, profit rates, and per-share data, it is important that you understand any external patterns, such as seasons or cycles, that govern performance. These patterns are crucial if you are predicting earnings. Some indication of likely patterns or fluctuations can be gained from industry background studies, and these patterns can be usefully compared to your own company's history. It is generally useful to derive a range of return ratios and other longitudinal data to gauge the risks of incurring debt or the general viability of the firm. Earnings patterns, growth trends, and declining conditions greatly influence future cash flows and will figure strongly in any lending arrangements that are being considered, which in turn will directly affect your chosen marketing strategies.

Price Elasticity of Demand

Elasticity is a measure of how a change in a variable affects demand. There are many types of elasticity, such as price elasticity of demand, cross-price elasticity of demand, arc elasticity, and income elasticity of demand. In practice, elasticities normally need to be estimated and are not considered to be constant. According to the law of demand, when prices for a good rise, the quantity demanded declines. What marketing managers need to understand is the extent to which the quantity demanded will fall as the price increases.

For marketing forecasters, price elasticity of demand is considered to be the most important elasticity. This value represents the percentage change in quantity demanded resulting from each 1 percent change in the price of a good. This relationship of product price to sales volume is of major interest to firms when they are establishing sales and pricing strategies, reaching objectives for market share and profit share, and setting marketing objectives and plans.

The price elasticity of demand coefficient is the percentage change in quantity demanded divided by the percentage change in price. By the law of demand, price elasticity of demand is always negative. If the price elasticity coefficient for a good is equal to -1, the good is considered to be neither price-elastic nor price-inelastic. This means that a percentage drop in price is offset by an equal percentage increase in quantity demanded, so that the revenue received is constant. A price elasticity coefficient greater than -1 is considered demand-elastic. This would indicate that a percentage increase in price generates a higher percentage decrease in quantity demanded. A price elasticity coefficient of zero indicates that demand is totally price-inelastic; this is usually called perfectly inelastic demand. In perfect inelasticity, demand will be the same no matter what changes in price occur. A price elasticity coefficient less than -1 would indicate that any price reductions would increase revenue growth. That is, a price elasticity coefficient between 0 and -1 indicates that as prices decrease, revenue will also decrease, but not at the same rate. This is called inelastic demand. (For those who need an update on elasticity, a basic economics text will refresh your memory on all the types and the ones you will need for developing your marketing plans.)

Many times the elasticity coefficient is not known; thus, the forecaster may have to rely on historical or causal data to estimate it.

Summary

- While strategies outline a firm's plan of attack, the budget specifies how much that plan will cost. It is important to remember, however, that drawing up a budget is not the same as strategic planning. Budgets simply provide control, allowing you to monitor expenses and track revenue.
- The first step in developing a budget at the strategic level is to identify your own department's area of fiscal responsibility, looking at two broad categories of total marketing costs: order getting and order filling. The marketing plan is almost entirely concerned with the order-getting process.
- The second step is to obtain budget estimates from each department in the firm associated with marketing activities, then organize the estimates into discrete categories, preferably by marketing function responsibility.

- The marketing department is responsible for preparing a budget statement that reflects the projected costs associated with the developed marketing plan as well as a revenue/sales forecast.
- A simplified corporate budget statement is essentially a projected profit and loss statement. An individual-product budget statement is developed at the marketing department level.
- Once the product lines are well defined in the marketing plan, the marketing manager works with sales personnel and company forecasters to predict product demand and sales performance.
- Forecasts are made on a product-by-product basis once you begin to develop budget figures at the tactical level. These forecasts are summed up as the budget moves up the corporate ladder.
- The objective of forecasting is to develop a systematic and quantitative statement of expected demand for a defined time period, a statement that will be the basis for planning and controlling via variance analysis.
- When you are developing budget and forecast statements for individual products at the strategic level, first consider how large a gross contribution the product generates and its contribution margin. Analyzing product contribution is a powerful tool in the successful implementation of any marketing plan.
- Firms tend to establish their budget using one of three methods: mechanical, task, or group. Although the group method requires more time, it enables the marketing plan to be communicated to many areas and gives top management a clear idea of the costs required to carry out proposed marketing strategies and reach the desired objectives.
- In assigning specific budget figures to strategies and marketing activities, start with the activities for which you have the most reliable historical or projected data.
- Two pitfalls to avoid in developing the budget and forecasting are artificially inflating the budget estimates and spending all unused funds before the end of the fiscal year. These two pitfalls distort budgeting. To avoid them, many managers are considering the shared group method.
- Free cash flow represents the cash that a company is able to generate after investing the money required to maintain or expand its asset base. Free cash flow is important because it allows a company to pursue opportunities that enhance shareholder value. Without cash, it is difficult to develop new products, make local and global acquisitions, pay dividends, or reduce debt.

- Elasticity is a measure of how a change in a variable affects demand. The many types of elasticity include price elasticity of demand, cross-price elasticity of demand, and income elasticity of demand. In practice, elasticity normally needs to be estimated and is not considered to be constant. According to the law of demand, when prices for a good rise, the quantity demanded declines. What marketing managers need to understand is the degree to which the quantity demanded will fall as the price of the good rises.

Sample Case, Phase 8

Harris had learned from his research on Techna that the budget was generally put together through the task method. Managers estimated their budget needs, and the finance department put the figures together. Upper management approved the budget but had little idea of how it was created. The budget was not future-oriented, but simply reflected what had been done in the past. In this type of budgeting, many firms just take last year's budget and increase it by some percentage that seems logical.

Harris called a meeting with top management to discuss the group method of developing the budget for the new marketing plan. He had to convince the three partners to become more involved in the budgeting process and to help create a budget estimate that was based on corporate objectives.

This estimate would be used as a planning guide for allocating marketing funds. All department heads and product managers, in turn, would develop their own budget estimates, using the top management estimate as a guide. Harris and his marketing team would work with the finance staff to coordinate all of these estimates and to create the final budget figures for the marketing plan.

Farlin agreed at once, much to Harris's surprise. "Financial categories are something tangible and solid. I can work with numbers better than I can work with objectives and strategies," Farlin stated.

But Bartly and Hamilton were less enthusiastic about the idea. They did not want to get involved in the details of developing budget estimates. To make the job easier, Harris suggested that they work with Farlin and the finance department just enough to have a basic understanding of how the numbers were being developed and why. Bartly and Hamilton agreed with this idea, since their strong points were in developing objectives and strategies for the future growth of the firm.

A draft copy of the corporate marketing objectives and strategies would be distributed to all department heads and managers to help them devise their budgets. Top management would have the business plan as well.

Harris said, "I'm also revising the budget format, since the current one does not show enough detail. The new format, with a finer breakdown of categories, will help in decision making and control procedures. We'll be able to track and analyze our financial statements more easily and identify variances more quickly."

Harris then outlined what the product managers would need to do to create their own budget estimates for each product.

They would have to provide a contribution analysis of each product and develop their own profit and loss statement. The marketing department would review the statements and then sum the individual budgets into an overall marketing budget that would be included in the final marketing plan.

"Forecasts of revenue by product will be done by the forecasting group in finance. The product managers will review these forecasts to make sure that all pertinent variables have been included and that the forecasts are reasonable. Just as the sum of all budgets by department equals the corporate budget, the total of all sales forecasts by product will equal the corporate revenue forecast.

"In a final step, top management will review and approve all budget items. I realize that this process will take more time than the prior method, but it involves everyone in creating estimates and budgets. People are much more willing to accept final budget allocations when they've had a hand in developing them," stated Harris.

Over the next two weeks, Harris and his team coordinated their efforts with the finance department to assist the department heads and product managers in their budget estimates. Harris wanted to make sure that no budget was inflated and that budget estimates truly reflected the new strategies and objectives, not simply last year's allocations.

An individual product estimate, the one for Storage Extreme, is reflected in the abbreviated forms that follow: the completed Projected Profit and Loss Statement (Form 9A) and the Three-Year Forecasted Sales and Projected Profit Data (Form 9B). Harris and his marketing team received similar data for all products. They aggregated all the estimates into a marketing budget. The final budget was included in the marketing plan.

FORM 9A

Product: Storage Extreme
Projected Profit and Loss Statement as of 12/31/201X

Revenues from sales			$9,090,750
Cost of goods sold			5,143,950
Gross margin			$3,946,800
Operating expenses			
Selling expenses			
Advertising	$ 727,950		
Distribution	545,100		
Marketing research	143,750		
Salaries	241,500		
Miscellaneous	34,500		
Total selling expenses		$1,692,800	
General and administrative expenses			
Rent	$ 16,675		
Office salaries	85,388		
Insurance	2,070		
Supplies	6,440		
Depreciation	15,928		
Total G&A expenses		$ 126,501	
Total operating expenses			$1,819,301
Net profit (loss) before taxes			$2,127,499

Note: All expenses have been directly identified with the product or allocated accordingly.

FORM 9B
Three-Year Forecasted Sales and Projected Profit Data

		201X	201Y	201Z	Row Operations
A.	Market—total units	97,750	107,525	118,275	
B.	Market share	0.11	0.22	0.33	
C.	Price per unit,	$ 892	834	725	
D.	Variable cost per unit	535	500	437	
E.	Gross contribution margin per unit,	$ 357	334	288	C - D
F.	Sales volume in units	10,753	23,655	39,030	A × B
G.	Sales,	$ 9,591,676	19,728,270	28,296,750	C × F
H.	Gross contribution margin,	$ 3,838,821	7,900,770	11,240,640	E × F
I.	Overhead $ to this product	126,500	132,250	138,000	
J.	Net contribution margin	3,712,321	7,768,520	11,102,640	H - I
K.	Advertising	$ 727,950	1,497,300	2,507,000	
L.	Computer	$ 48,300	72,000	111,600	
M.	Distribution	$ 545,100	1,255,800	1,926,250	
N.	Salaries	$ 241,500	276,000	207,000	
O.	E-commerce research	$ 65,000	97,500	146,250	
P.	Global research opportunities	$ 41,000	63,550	108,800	
Q.	Miscellaneous	$ 34,500	37,500	39,500	
R.	Total expenses*	$ 1,703,350	$ 3,299,650	$ 5,046,400	
S.	Net operating profit/(loss)†	$ 2,008,971	$ 4,468,870	$ 6,056,240	

* Sum of K through Q.
†Line J minus Line R.

PART IV

Implementation and Control

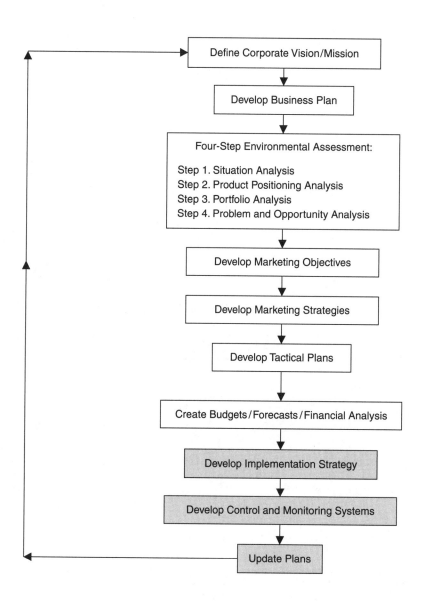

Define Corporate Vision/Mission

Develop Business Plan

Four-Step Environmental Assessment:

Step 1. Situation Analysis
Step 2. Product Positioning Analysis
Step 3. Portfolio Analysis
Step 4. Problem and Opportunity Analysis

Develop Marketing Objectives

Develop Marketing Strategies

Develop Tactical Plans

Create Budgets / Forecasts / Financial Analysis

Develop Implementation Strategy

Develop Control and Monitoring Systems

Update Plans

9

Marketing Plan Implementation

Introduction

Many strategists consider the implementation phase of new strategic plans the weakest link in the process. An excellent strategic marketing plan is basically worthless unless it can be successfully implemented. Therefore, implementing the finished marketing plan requires a strategy all its own. To be successful, implementation needs the support of top management, good communication among all managers and staff members, close coordination of all departments, a method for handling resistance to change, and potential changes in the firm's organizational structure and/or culture.

The goal of this chapter is to help you design an implementation strategy that will give your new marketing plan the best chance for success.

Implementation

Implementation is the part of market planning that is also a component of organizational change. It is a process that begins with the company's first ideas for a new marketing plan.

In a very real sense, then, implementation is the *art of introducing and managing change*. For example, does the plan call for entering a new market or developing a new venture? Is a new R&D group to be formed? Does the sales team need to be reorganized? Any changes described in the plan will require the company to adjust its procedures and personnel to fit the new direction.

Many companies believe that the implementation stage will take care of itself. This can be a fatal mistake. The best marketing plans can flounder on any one of a number of problems.

Implementation Problems

There are several reasons why completed marketing plans are not successfully implemented:

- *Lack of interest in the plan at top management levels.* Top management must take the lead in implementing and supporting the new plan. If top management fails to champion it, line managers and support personnel will not take it seriously either.
- *Poor communication with department heads and personnel.* If the users of a marketing plan see it only in final form, they may feel that it is unrealistic for their departments. Managers and their staffs should be consulted during the initial planning stages. Poor communication can breed not only planning errors but also determined resistance to the plan itself.
- *Faulty design of the plan.* For example, some marketing plans do not provide the information that management and staff members need if they are to implement the plan successfully. A well-designed plan includes appropriate strategies and tools for its various tasks.
- *Lack of resources to carry out the plan.* The resources required to carry out the plan must not be beyond the scope of the firm. Managers and support personnel cannot be asked to do too much too quickly. Your firm will need the skills to implement the strategic marketing plan and to evaluate and adjust the preliminary results. Faulty or myopic resource planning can sink a new marketing plan in the early stages of implementation.
- *Failure to subdivide the plan into tactical tasks.* Implementing a marketing plan is a gradual process. You will have to divide your marketing plan into small chunks that implementers can handle. Excellent implementation of the plan will depend heavily on how successfully your team can complete all the component tasks.

Most of these problems can be traced to poor communication between the planners and top management, department heads, and support staff. It is crucial to involve all levels of company personnel in the planning process from the very first stages. This process depends on planning from the bottom up as well as from the top down.

Implementation Strategy

Your new marketing plan represents two types of change: (1) organizational (new procedures, products, work routines, and areas of business, and matching structures and processes to the marketing strategies that are being developed and implemented), and (2) behavioral (changes in employee attitudes, skills, and routines). The marketing plan is the blueprint for what is going to happen over its stated time horizon, who is responsible for each task, how much it will cost, and the plan's expected results.

To introduce and manage these changes, you will need to establish a clear-cut implementation strategy. Although the situation will differ for each company, the following implementation outline should hold true across the board:

1. Gain top management approval and support for the final plan.
2. Have top management present the plan to managers and support staff as the company's blueprint for successful change.
3. Assign specific implementation tasks to department heads and managers.
4. Set schedules and target dates for the completion of implementation tasks (new procedures in place, new departments formed, new sales approaches in use, and so on).
5. Establish regular training and feedback sessions to train employees in new routines, resolve conflicts, and obtain feedback.
6. Develop a realistic operational budget for evaluating the cost and results of the plan to determine whether the implementation plan or the marketing plan itself is meeting its objectives, and to decide what action steps may be needed.

Each step is discussed more fully in the next sections.

Top Management Support

Of paramount importance is gaining top management approval of, and commitment to, the new marketing plan. That commitment is perhaps the key element in implementation strategy. Those in top management can perform five essential tasks:

1. Communicate the plan to their peers and to the entire company.
2. Describe why the plan's changes are necessary—including possible cultural changes—and explain both how these changes will affect individual departments and what results they will yield.

3. Allocate the necessary resources (money, staff, and materials) to carry out all implementation steps.
4. Be present at all major decision-making sessions.
5. Resolve conflicts among peers and mediate any power struggles. Without top management leadership, interdepartmental disputes can paralyze an implementation process. With top management commitment, it is much easier to resolve differences, deal with problem areas, and keep the strategic goals of the plan firmly in mind.

Ideally, this commitment from top managers supports the plan's design stages and can continue into the implementation phase.

Presenting the Marketing Plan to the Company

Top management should schedule a general meeting or series of meetings with department heads, at which top management presents the plan and explains how it will affect individual departments. Invite discussion and questions at these meetings. Make sure that every department head shares a common understanding of the plan.

The method of communicating the plan will vary depending on the size and organizational structure of the company. In some firms, top management may send a general memorandum to all department personnel, summarizing the new marketing plan and explaining its impact on each department. In others, department heads will be responsible for explaining to their staffs how the new plan will affect their areas.

Assigning Implementation Tasks

Avoid distributing a master copy of the plan to all managers. High-level strategic plans should be kept at top management level for security reasons. For example, if the entire plan is widely distributed, anyone leaving the company—from an executive to a sales rep—could carry the plan with him.

Each person who is involved in implementation should receive only the part of the plan that she needs if she is to perform her duties effectively. Everyone should know clearly what is expected of her and why. Each manager, in turn, can share appropriate parts of the plan with subordinates on a need-to-know basis. This approach also helps top management better coordinate and control the entire implementation process.

One of the most effective ways to implement a new plan is by forming committees. Committees may be set up within a department or among two or more departments to help coordinate the implementation steps. Reorganizing the sales force, for example, could involve the sales, marketing, and finance departments. A joint committee could help smooth the transition from the old procedures to the new ones.

Setting Schedules and Target Dates

Every implementation task should have a schedule and a target date for completion. These schedules and target dates should be coordinated by top management. If the salesforce is to be reorganized within nine months, then the new marketing materials must be ready and the new compensation system must be in place by that time.

Implementation committees can help to ensure open communication among departments and to resolve problems as they arise. Top management should be available to settle disputes that cannot be handled in committees or among staff members themselves.

Establishing Training and Feedback Sessions

If the change involves introducing new procedures, office equipment, or high-tech systems, make sure that staff members are given adequate training. Change is disturbing in itself, but it is particularly so when people must learn new skills. By giving employees the knowledge and practice time they need to become proficient, you can greatly ease the transition from one system to another and minimize the loss of productive time.

Also, schedule feedback sessions; these will keep all participants aware of how implementation is progressing, and they will celebrate accomplishments. Change is often easier to tolerate if people understand that they are making progress toward a specific goal and/or objective. These sessions can give employees an opportunity to offer suggestions or to point out problems in the early stages of the implementation process.

Behavioral Change Management

Your implementation strategy also should manage the behavioral aspects of change. How do you gain people's cooperation and compliance? What motivates people to accept change? How can you avoid some of the miscommunication that seems inevitable whenever change is introduced?

People resist change for many reasons. They fear losing what they have; they dislike disruptions in their routine; they fear being asked to learn new and seemingly complex skills; they fear losing their jobs, getting a pay cut, or being demoted. Those who introduce change can help to ease the transition by telling people what the change involves and how it will affect them.

While an in-depth study of human behavior and change is beyond the scope of this book, a few guidelines can be provided in three key areas: preventing resistance to change, identifying motivations, and meeting people's different communication needs. These guidelines can help you avoid or deal with some of the behavioral problems that often arise when companies introduce change into their organizations.

User Participation

Organizational psychologists have suggested that one of the most successful ways to approach change is through *user participation*—involving people in the process from its early stages. This technique has been tested in experiments and field studies. In each case, the results supported the importance of user participation in any implementation strategy. Some reasons include the following:

- Participation can be challenging and intrinsically satisfying to workers whose jobs are routine or fairly predictable. These workers are also likely to express positive attitudes toward change.
- Participating users learn more about the upcoming changes as the planning process moves from stage to stage. They become familiar with the plan's details and are usually better trained to implement the plan.
- Participation improves the overall quality of the results achieved through the change. Participants understand more clearly how and why the new plan is an improvement over the old one.
- Participants usually retain more control over their activities during the change. Research has shown that this sense of control is an important factor in developing positive attitudes toward change.
- Participation enhances the self-esteem of those who are included in the process. They feel important and tend to express more positive attitudes toward change.

If managers and workers are part of the planning process from the beginning and are consulted throughout the planning stages, they tend to feel greater ownership of the new plan and take more interest in seeing it implemented successfully.

Motivation

You are also more likely to persuade people to accept change if you know something about what motivates them. People will want to know how the new plan will benefit them. Some basic concerns that motivate people in a business environment include the following:

Loyalty: fidelity to others and oneself
Security: knowing what to expect
Prestige: position and pride
Profit: improving it
Comfort: a feeling of well-being
Curiosity: a sense of wonder and risk taking
Convenience: saving time and boosting efficiency
Saving: spending less
Health: maintaining or improving
Self-esteem: preserving a sense of self-worth
Productivity: increasing it

While people may be motivated by a combination of the concerns in this list, one will usually be dominant. Once you know the strongest motivator for the key people involved in implementation, you can pinpoint how the change satisfies that motivator. For example, a manager who is motivated primarily by productivity will want to know how the plan is going to save employee time, enable staff to work more efficiently, and streamline work steps.

People who feel that the new plan satisfies a primary motivator are usually more willing to endure the temporary upheaval that accompanies any change in company procedures, direction, or mission.

Communication Style Model

Many people resist change not primarily because it disrupts their routine, but largely because of miscommunication. Just as people are motivated by different concerns, so do they have different communication styles.

You can improve your chances of gaining people's cooperation if you communicate change to them in a way that they can understand, a way that satisfies their communication needs. For example, some people feel overwhelmed if they are told all the details of a new procedure at the beginning;

others need to know all the steps in advance before they attempt to learn the first one. By learning something about the various communication needs of key personnel in the company, you can tailor your presentation to meet those needs.

Psychologist Paul Mok, an expert in how people communicate in organizations, has developed a Communication Style Model that identifies four basic communication styles: emotive, directive, reflective, and supportive. According to Mok, people have various combinations of high and low *sociability* (how they interact with people) and high and low *dominance* (their need for control in a situation). By charting these variables, he has identified the basic characteristics of the four styles, as shown in Figure 9.1.

Emotive Style

People with an *emotive style* of communication have both high sociability and high dominance. They are emotional, vivid personalities who command attention and respect in any group. They are oriented toward action, like informality, and possess a natural persuasiveness. They do not necessarily need to know the details of a plan—only the action to be taken and the end results

FIGURE 9.1
Mok's Communication Style Model

High Dominance

	Emotive	Directive	
High Sociability	Supportive	Reflective	Low Sociability

Low Dominance

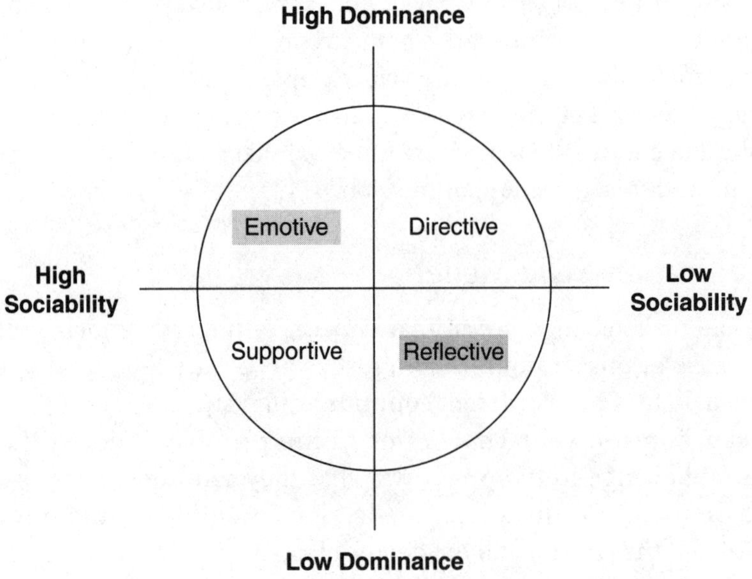

expected. They are likely to read the summary of the plan and leave the details to others.

Directive Style

Those with a *directive style* of communication have high dominance combined with low sociability. They are generally frank, demanding, aggressive, and determined. Sentiment plays little part in their thinking. They generally project a serious attitude, express strong opinions, and may seem aloof or distant to their staff. They will want to know what data you have to support the strategies in the new plan and the rationale for any changes or new directions.

Reflective Style

People with a *reflective style* are characterized by low sociability and low dominance. Reflective communicators are usually quiet, enjoy working on their own, and make decisions only after considerable deliberation. They tend to want detailed explanations of any new procedures and enjoy scrutinizing the fine print. They prefer orderliness, often seem preoccupied, and express their opinions in a formal, deliberate manner. In many instances, people with a reflective communication style are in the more technical fields, where their attention to detail is a strong suit.

Supportive Style

Those with a *supportive style* are low in dominance and high in sociability. They are people-oriented, sensitive, and patient; they are generally good listeners. They tend to avoid the overt use of power and rely on friendly persuasion in dealing with people. Their decisions are made and expressed in a thoughtful, deliberate manner. Supportive communicators tend to be concerned with the impact of a new plan on their staff or on the company's employees in addition to the more technical aspects of the proposed changes.

By identifying people's basic communication styles, you can present the new marketing plan in ways that satisfy their communication needs. If the marketing plan calls for developing a new product line, the directive communicator will want to know what facts and figures justify the risk. On the other hand, an emotive communicator may want to know the potential rewards for taking that risk. The reflective communicator will want details about research and development, timelines, raw materials, and production schedules. The supportive communicator may be concerned about extra demands on the workers.

It can be well worth your time to learn something about the primary motivations and basic communication styles of the people who must implement the new marketing plan. Introducing and managing change is not easy under the best of circumstances. Some background work on your part can help give the new marketing plan the best chance for success.

Measuring Implementation Success

How do you know when you have implemented a plan successfully? Researchers have not really agreed on any one indicator of successful implementation. However, two methods for judging whether the process is accomplishing your implementation goals are suggested: *cost/benefit* and *users' level of satisfaction*.

A cost/benefit study can be used to measure tangible costs and benefits. In this evaluation, you total the costs of developing the plan and compare the result with the dollar benefits resulting from implementing the plan. Data for a cost/benefit analysis can be obtained from monthly sales and cost reports, cash flows, and monthly pro forma statements.

But a cost/benefit approach is not very useful in evaluating the *intangible* costs and benefits of a new marketing plan. Your plan may be highly proactive and contain procedures that the firm has never used before. You may be looking three to five years into the future, with no immediate, measurable results for several months. For example, a plan for improving customer relations may initially cost the company more than it reaps in increased orders. But in the long run, the plan will achieve the goals of improving customer relations and, hopefully, increasing sales.

In such cases, you note may be able to evaluate your implementation strategy by determining the *users' level of satisfaction* in implementing the plan. High levels of satisfaction with new procedures, systems, and policies generally indicate high levels of use. Ask managers and support staff for specific comments on the implementation process. Is the plan meeting the strategies and objectives of each department? Are people accepting the changes or trying to go back to their old ways? Has the plan facilitated decision making? Are employees positive about the firm's new direction?

Answers to these questions will suggest how the initial implementation process is going. This approach can help detect problems early, whether in procedures or in behavior, before they become serious enough to threaten the success of the entire plan.

Form 10 in the sample case, "Implementation Strategy," will help you identify key steps that you need to take in implementing your new marketing plan. This outline can also help you to anticipate potential organizational and behavioral problems that may arise during implementation and to develop suggested strategies for avoiding or dealing with them.

The next chapter discusses how to set up control and monitoring procedures for longer-term evaluation of the new marketing plan.

Summary

- Implementation is the part of marketing planning that is also a component of organizational change. To be successful, implementation requires the support of top management, good communication among managers and staff members, close coordination of all departments, and some methods for handling resistance to change.
- Problem areas in implementation include faulty design of the plan, poor communication with department heads and personnel, apathy on the part of top management, and lack of resources to carry out the plan.
- In general, the strategy for implementing the marketing plan includes (1) gaining top management approval and support, (2) having top management present the plan to managers and staff, (3) assigning specific implementation tasks, (4) setting schedules and target dates for implementation tasks, and (5) establishing training and feedback sessions.
- To manage many of the problems that arise when change is introduced into an organization, it is wise to involve managers and staff members early in the planning process, know something about what motivates them, and gain some understanding of their individual communication styles.
- Mok's Communication Style Model identifies four distinct styles: emotive, directive, reflective, and supportive. Each style has different needs for sociability and dominance, and thus different communication needs.
- Two methods can help you monitor implementation: a cost/benefit study and determining how satisfying the changes are to the users.

Sample Case, Phase 9

The final marketing plan had been printed and bound, and the marketing team breathed a sigh of relief. Harris, however, reminded them that only half the job had been done. Now they needed to develop an implementation strategy for the plan, to optimize its chance of succeeding. Harris had learned from experience that this step was one of the most critical and the most frequently overlooked in the entire planning process.

"You need to understand," Harris told his team, "that designing a marketing plan means asking people to change organizational procedures and their own behavior."

"How are we going to plan implementation steps for so many different departments?" one member asked.

Harris outlined how their previous work would help ensure that the marketing plan would be implemented successfully:

- The design of the plan revolved around the mission statement and the business plan, which made it compatible from the onset with the direction and purpose of the company in the future.
- Top management had been involved from the beginning and had supported Harris and the marketing team.
- All department heads, product managers, and their staffs had been included in planning meetings and had reviewed and revised the draft plans before the final plan was developed.
- Early on, Harris had obtained the necessary resources to carry out the plan.

"As a result," Harris said, "the impact of organizational and behavioral changes should be minimal. Top management will support the plan and present it as the blueprint for the company. However, there's always some resistance to change, so we need to consider who's likely to give us trouble and how to handle their objections or resistance. Any ideas?"

"Yes," one team member replied. "We're going to be introducing global marketing and e-commerce to the sales department. The clerical staff will be doing the communication between customers and the salesforce. In my experience, unless the change is handled carefully, there is usually friction between the clerical staff and the field salesforce. Paul Sandler, the assistant sales manager, will be in charge of the training sessions, and he's pretty much of a by-the-book guy. I'm not sure he's going to see the potential conflicts in the changes."

"All right, let's do a little strategizing on this. How would you characterize Paul's communication style?"

"Definitely directive with some reflective thrown in. He's very thorough when he develops a program, and he often teaches it himself. I've heard that he's a hard taskmaster."

"How can we present the potential conflicts we see in his department so that he'll hear them?" Harris asked.

"Well... I think the best approach is to put it in terms of efficiency. If a training program can be designed that will prevent clashes between the clerical staff and the field salesforce, the global and e-commerce initiatives will be implemented faster, with a shorter learning curve and fewer problems on the job."

"What about the clerical staff and the salesforce; what are the basic conflicts that come up between them?" Harris asked.

"The people on the clerical staff usually haven't done any selling, so they don't understand how much time it takes to sell different clients. They often load too many calls on the salesforce. The people in the salesforce, on the other hand, feel that they've lost some of their autonomy and prestige by taking orders from clerks. They tend to see their new responsibilities as a step down."

"So how can we handle these problems?" Harris wanted to know.

"We can tell them that when the clerical staff screen leads, their chances of closing a sale goes up. They do not have to make nearly as many calls or go after questionable prospects," one team member suggested.

"We can introduce a new incentive system, maybe one based on clerical/salesforce teamwork as well as on individual sales efforts," another contributed.

"Good ideas," Harris said. "Once the plan is approved, we can set up a meeting with the sales manager and Sandler. Any other problem areas?"

"I know a big one," another team member said. "Hamilton and Bartly are not going to like the fact that engineering won't be driving the company as much. Even though they have backed us all the way, when it gets down to implementing the changes that this plan advocates, I think they are going to resist following some of the marketing objectives. They have always had control over the product lines, and we're taking over some of that function."

"Good point," Harris said. "This is a delicate issue. We want to prevent conflict between ourselves and top management and at the same time stand by the marketing objectives and strategies that have been developed mostly by them. That means we may have to be in the hot seat at times."

"Do you think there will be any infighting among the three partners?"

Harris replied, "Part of our job will be to help prevent a breakdown of communication among the partners."

"How do we do that?" one of the team members asked.

"By keeping them all involved in the implementation process as much as possible. They will have a chance to air any objections or problems before the issues get too big to handle. Remember, we have one fact working in our favor: it was their old way of operating that got the company in trouble to begin with. If they try to go back to that way, the same problems will crop up. The changes in the marketing plan will correct those problems and help the company grow. It will be hard for them to dispute that fact, but we need to present this point of view in a way that respects their concerns and interests."

"I know one thing; Hamilton has a reflective communication style, while Farlin is more directive. She'll want to know the details of why we need to follow the marketing objectives, while he'll just want to know the end results."

"We can prepare for both each time we meet with them," Harris said. "Any more problem areas we need to cover?"

The team suggested a few more in the production and finance departments, and Harris helped them to develop strategies to handle these potential problems.

"All right, we have to develop a list of top management personnel who need to approve the plan, a timetable for presentations, and a list of potential problems along with the strategies we've brainstormed for each one. At this point, it's important to keep the problems and strategies confidential. We do not want people feeling that we're singling them out as potential troublemakers.

"Once the marketing plan is officially launched, we'll help each department set implementation goals to coordinate the process on a companywide basis. The marketing department is the official liaison and communications link among all departments and management levels."

Harris and his team completed Form 10, "Implementation Strategy," and submitted only the implementation schedule to the three partners for approval. While only two problem areas are presented on the form for purposes of illustration, the list would actually include all potential problems and the strategies developed to handle them.

FORM 10
Implementation Strategy

Product: <u>Storage Extreme</u>   Date: <u>XX/XX/XX</u>

1. Members of top management who must approve and endorse the new marketing plan:

    > 1. Ted Bartly
    > 2. Abby Hamilton
    > 3. Will Farlin
    > 4. Paul Harris

2. How will top management present the plan to all levels of managers?

    > Through the use of direct meetings with all who will be affected by the new marketing plan. The meetings are scheduled as follows:
    >
    > | | | |
    > |---|---|---|
    > | 1. | Top management | May 2 |
    > | 2. | Product managers | May 4–6 |
    > | 3. | Sales managers | May 7 |
    > | 4. | Other department reps | May 8–9 |
    > | 5. | All support staffs | May 10 |

3. Potential organizational and behavioral problems that may arise during implementation:

    > 1. Mr. Loyde, the director of the salesforce, may have problems with training schedules being shortened, global operations training, and new e-commerce tools being used to increase our firm's salesforce productivity.
    > 2. Hamilton and Bartly may have difficulties moving the firm from one dominated by engineering to a much more market-oriented one. They may perceive this as a loss of power and control at their level in the firm.

4. Strategies for preventing or handling problems:

> 1. Meet with the director of sales and the sales managers to describe the benefits of faster training for domestic, global, and e-commerce. Listen to their feedback and try to make any changes possible without disruption of the marketing plan.
> 2. Involve all three partners throughout the implementation process, constantly listen to their concerns, and try to work out a congenial solution. Demonstrate the future effectiveness of the marketing objectives and strategies, tailoring the presentations and private talks to reflect the communication style of each partner.

Control and Monitoring of the Strategic Marketing Plan

Introduction

Since strategic marketing planning is a continuous process, marketing managers should have a system for monitoring, controlling, and evaluating implementation outcomes on an ongoing basis. Marketing control is the process of monitoring the strategic marketing plan as it proceeds through the implementation phase while making any adjustments needed to keep it on course. If an objective states when and where you want to be, and the strategic marketing plan sets out on a path toward that destination, then marketing controls will tell you whether you are approaching the objective or deviating from your plan. These controls are essential if the company is to abort problems and also to measure outcomes. The controls include the budget—the costs of everything in the plan.

Controls can be defined as the actions taken to keep the firm directed toward its objectives and to bring performance closer to the desired results. Control activities involve two types of actions:

1. Monitoring departmental and individual actions to determine progress toward goals and outcomes
2. Taking steps to ensure that performance matches the desired results or to adjust your objectives to match attainable performance levels

In establishing controls, you set standards and a schedule. Standards determine when variances exceed your stated range, and getting behind in your

274 The Ultimate Guide to Strategic Marketing

schedule can be costly. To monitor these variables, you can use a simple Gantt chart, use Program Evaluation and Review Technique, or use the critical path method. If activities begin to fall behind schedule or if cost overruns occur, you need to adapt your plan accordingly.

From a macro perspective, one critical issue during the control phase is coordination among functional areas concerning the use of scarce resources. Scarce resources are costly, so it is important to control their use in the marketing plan by setting standards. To measure these standards, the marketing manager will compare the actual results with the plan to verify whether the variance is acceptable. If it is not, you can take corrective action, if needed. If corrective action is required, you will need to determine why the variance occurred.

Control can be conducted at the *strategic level* (reshaping the programs to implement in the future) or at the *tactical level* (taking specific actions to keep the current plan on course). Both levels are included in each section of the following discussion.

The Marketing Controller Concept

The managerial responsibility for control and monitoring is generally assigned to the person who is responsible for developing the marketing plan. This person oversees the entire implementation and control process, maintaining communication among departments and coordinating data to determine how deviation from the plan in one area may affect other areas.

Some companies, however, are also establishing job positions known as *marketing controllers* to monitor marketing expenses and activities. Marketing controllers perform a function similar to that of the accounting department controller. In the accounting office, controllers conduct audits, fill out tax forms, monitor expenses and budgets, make sure all financial records are timely and correct, and so on.

Marketing controllers are trained in both the finance and marketing areas. They are usually on the same level as the marketing manager, and their duties include the following:

- Analyze the impact of sales and other promotions.
- Monitor the adherence to the profit plan.
- Evaluate geographic profitability.
- Determine the best timing for marketing strategies.
- Evaluate product financial reports.

Other duties may include:

- Ratio analysis
- Market share analysis
- Marketing information systems
- Analyzing feedback from customer-satisfaction surveys
- Preparing cash flow statements
- Overseeing customer relationship management (CRM) systems
- Monitoring market reaction to pricing policies (elasticity)
- Budgets
- Determining how competitors are reacting to aspects of your plan

Whichever methods the controller decides to use, these methods must fit with your type of firm, your industry, your environment, and any other criteria by which your firm performs the environmental assessments discussed in Chapter 2.

The marketing controller concept is an intriguing one, particularly in organizations in which marketing is still practiced with a primary eye toward sales rather than profits. The marketing controller contributes by analyzing how and where the company is making its money as the marketing plan is carried out. This analysis also includes monitoring actual strategies to make sure that they are being implemented as written. It is the marketing controller's job to inform management about any deviations from the plan.

Elements in a Control System

An effective control system enables the marketing controller to do the following:

- Detect when and where results deviate from what the plans predict.
- Determine the cause of any such deviations.
- Suggest ways to correct the situation, if possible, and bring activities back in line with the plan. Doing so may require creating an interdepartmental task force to handle complex situations.

In order to achieve those aims, the controller or planner needs yardsticks and comparative standards, a feedback or performance information system, diagnostic ability, an analytical system, and contingency plans and methods.

Yardsticks and Comparative Standards

Yardsticks are individual goals taken from the marketing plan that serve as the basis for product and personnel performance evaluation. Yardsticks are set at the tactical level to indicate what should happen when the plan is being met.

For example, a company may aim to increase market share by 9 percent by the end of the third quarter. If market share is up only 4 percent by the end of the second quarter, the original 9 percent serves as a yardstick for the manager, indicating that the company may be off course.

Financial data will determine whether you are making a profit or a loss, but they do not monitor the implementation of your strategic marketing plan or signal any nonfinancial variances.

The final marketing plan should contain clearly stated yardsticks so that deviations or problems can be detected early and timely actions can be taken through the use of contingency plans.

Feedback or Performance Information System

The feedback or performance information system should report results frequently. This system is based on various financial and other reporting forms, market research data, and personnel feedback.

The financial assessment of the strategic marketing plan is an important component of evaluation and control. Financial projections will be sharpened if you can estimate costs and revenues. Such budgetary considerations play a key role in the identification of alternative strategies and contingency plans. The financials of the firm must be monitored and controlled at all times to keep the strategic marketing plan on track. Remember that a mere analysis of the firm's financials, while important, needs to be broadened: you must also consider the factors used in your environmental assessment and/or those being utilized by the marketing controller.

Diagnostic Ability and an Analytical System

The controller and individual managers must be able to diagnose problems and develop a system to analyze each situation and determine the problem's underlying cause or causes. This system depends not only on the managers' personal insights, experience, and problem-solving abilities, but also on the availability of information regarding external and internal marketing activities.

While individual managers will diagnose problems in their own functional areas, the controller keeps the lines of communication among various departments open at all times. This process is much easier if the organizational culture of the firm is both internally and externally customer-focused. The marketing controller consults with managers to determine the impact of a problem, both departmentally and companywide. An increase in the price of raw materials, for example, will raise production costs and affect product pricing strategies. Individual managers are responsible for notifying the controller immediately when they detect problems so that corrective action can be taken. Thus, functional managers must see the interconnectedness among all departments when business decisions are determined.

Contingency Plans and Methods

When the company cannot achieve its goals, it must be able to fall back on contingency objectives and strategies. The market controller and individual managers must be able to make tactical changes to correct the diagnosed problems and to get the company back on track.

Control Guidelines

For control purposes, many questions must be addressed during the planning and implementation periods. And they must be addressed immediately so that problems can be corrected. These questions include the following:

- Is the market share increasing or decreasing as expected? If not, how does this affect the projected portfolio positioning?
- Are sales on track? If not, what are the dollar and percentage variances between planned and actual sales?
- Is the marketplace changing? If so, where, how, and why?
- Are the returns on assets and net worth meeting the firm's objectives?
- From a profitability perspective, which products should be added, deleted, or repositioned to keep the plan on track?
- Are expenses *ahead* of estimates? If so, why?
- Have assumptions changed?
- Should the objectives be modified?
  - Have the correct strategies been selected?
  - Is competition increasing, thus lowering profits?
  - Should budget cuts be considered?
  - Are unforeseen outside influences causing the variances?
  - Are there more effective ways to manage the salesforce, advertising, or distribution?
- Are expenses *behind* estimates? If so, why?
  - Are the strategies being properly carried out as planned?

> ○　Are the variances indicating new or expanding opportunities that were not considered or seen previously?
> ○　If the strategy is more effective than anticipated, should funds be added to accelerate profits further?

For example, when budget variances occur, either up or down, it is wise to reexamine your original assumptions. You may be able to pinpoint the cause of any variance and to use contingency plans and strategies to correct the situation. The budget should be flexible enough to adjust readily to changes in operating or marketing conditions (profit, cash flow, economic shifts, sales variances, expanded opportunities, seasonal factors, and competition). A thorough review of the budget should be scheduled at least monthly.

A Monitoring System

Once the basic elements of a control system are established, the company can begin monitoring the execution of the strategic marketing plan.

A monitoring system has two main parts. The first is a control and performance information system that informs management about the internal and external factors affecting the implementation and outcomes of the plan. The second is a set of standards to interpret that information. In monitoring the plan, you need to know the following:

- The extent to which the desired actions were actually implemented
- The effectiveness of those actions

It is relatively easy to measure the *extent* to which actions were implemented. For example, has the accounting department installed the new accounting system? Has the production manager begun manufacturing the new product line? Is the outside consulting firm completing its market survey?

The *effectiveness* of these actions is harder to determine. The marketing program is vulnerable to many factors in the external environment—factors over which the company has little, if any, control. However, it can be valuable to isolate the marketing plan's effectiveness or outcomes, even if that effort encompasses only one or two major elements of the plan.

Control and Performance Information System

The marketing controller or product manager depends heavily on obtaining information. It would be difficult to describe all the kinds of data that this person might find valuable. It can only be stated that a regular and systematic flow of information is essential to control and monitoring, a flow that can be called the control and performance information system. The position of this system in the total cycle of strategic planning is illustrated in Figure 10.1.

Notice that information flows both ways between the control and performance information system and the actual monitoring and correction stages. What you learn when you monitor performance or correct problems is fed back into the

FIGURE 10.1
Control and Monitoring System

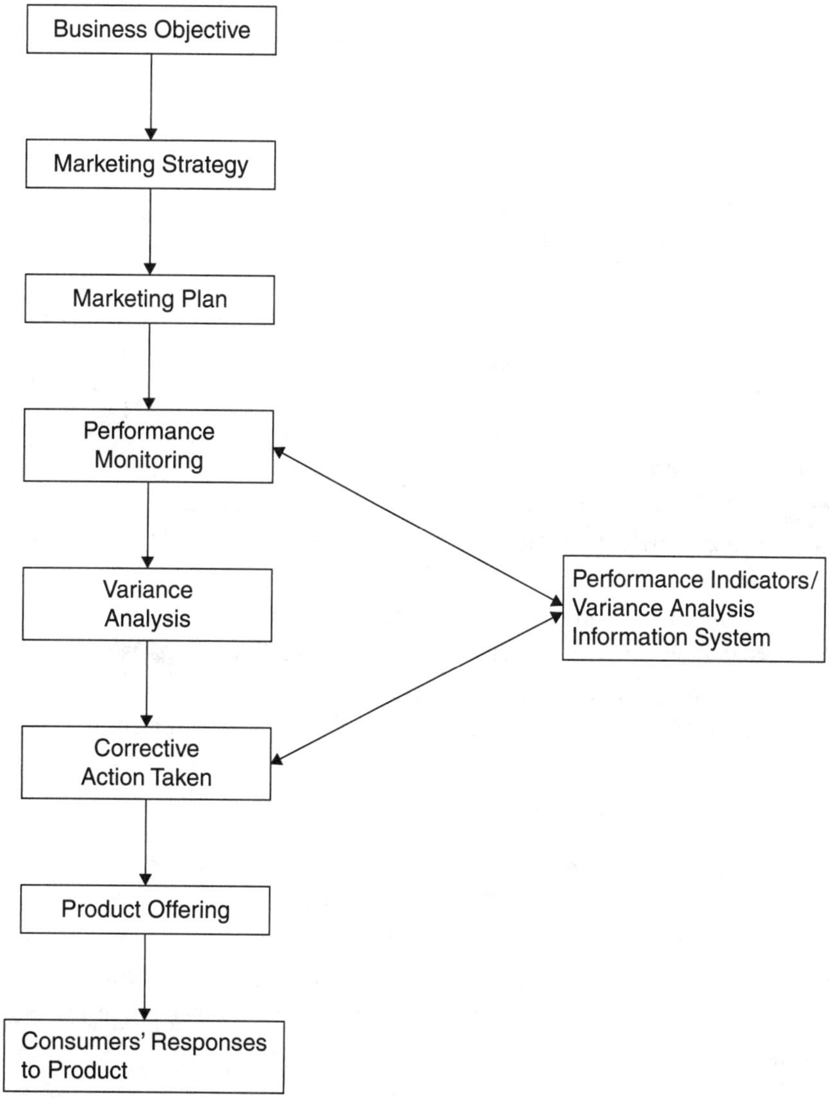

system. That system is also influenced by feedback from end users, and it affects the development of future marketing strategies.

Figure 10.1 is somewhat simplified to show the basic concept of how the system works. In reality, information does not come solely from end users. It also comes from monitoring the flow of products through distribution channels and from data obtained about distributors, competitors, environmental changes, and the internal activities of the firm itself. Some data are reported regularly through the accounting and marketing activities. Other data are gathered as needed and could include conducting market research to solve a product problem, defining particular market characteristics, or determining market position.

Control Standards and Criteria

It is impractical, if not impossible, to measure all the actions taken to implement a plan and measure all relevant environmental changes. You must select the key marketing and environmental variables that are to be measured and monitored for your firm.

Also, to establish control, you must set standards and criteria for evaluating results based on your marketing objectives. For example, what constitutes a deviation from budget? A 5 percent variance over or under the planned figures? A 10 percent variance? How far does market share have to decline before it is considered a problem?

The standards and criteria chosen should reflect the uniqueness of your firm and its resources and should flow from the marketing plan. If you compare the selected variables with the marketing plan yardsticks frequently, you can help to keep the organization on course to reach its objectives.

An approach for setting key variables and standards for control is outlined briefly in Figure 10.2. The standards indicated in the figure are merely averages, but you can set various standards for categories of variables or establish a sliding scale.

Determining Corrective Action

Once a marketing controller has adequate information on performance relative to standards, this person should determine whether any corrective action is needed. The first step in this process is *performance analysis*, in which the data are broken down to facilitate their interpretation. This step is followed by *diagnosis* of the situation and its impact on the firm, and finally by the *corrective action*, if any, that should be taken.

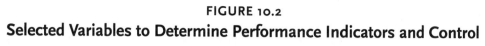

FIGURE 10.2
Selected Variables to Determine Performance Indicators and Control

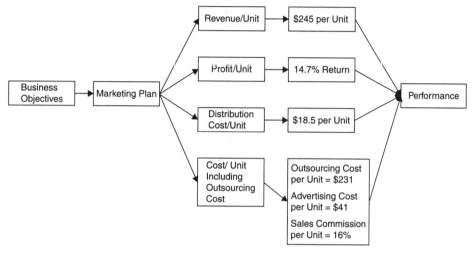

Performance Analysis

Performance analysis integrates the concepts of marketing strategy and plans with the concepts of managerial and cost accounting. As a result, it takes into consideration such planning variances as those found in sales, costs, and contribution margin. These calculations have been shown in prior chapters.

This approach analyzes the differences between actual and planned performance. While it has limited potential for diagnosing the cause of problems, its major benefit lies in identifying areas where problems exist.

Diagnosis

In diagnosis, individual product managers examine the analyzed data, seeking to explain a given problem and to determine its causes. Is the cause a sudden decline in consumer demand? Is it a rise in the cost of raw materials? Has a merger between two competitors blocked your firm from certain segments of the market? Is a promotional campaign having more or less impact than anticipated?

Once the cause or causes of a problem have been diagnosed, you need to assess their significance carefully. Does the firm need to take any action, or will the problem solve itself given time? How much of an impact will it have on operations, profitability, earnings, advertising, and so on? Careful diagnosis of a problem can help you decide not only what action may be appropriate, but also whether any action needs to be taken at all.

Corrective Action

Corrective action to solve the problems you have diagnosed may range from minor adjustments in the plan to a major overhaul of assumptions and strategies that requires you to fall back on contingency plans. Contingency planning, developed in the early stages of the marketing planning process, can be invaluable in the control and monitoring stages.

For example, if a sudden drop in consumer demand is the cause of declining sales, you may want to adopt a contingency plan of lowering prices and increasing promotion as a corrective action. Or you may want to phase out the product and reexamine your major strategic plan for the product line.

When you are evaluating corrective actions, use these guidelines:

- Can the firm control the factors that caused the problem?
- If so, what action would be effective?
- Is the action worth taking, given the time, cost, and risks involved?
- If the factors cannot be controlled, how can the firm adjust to the situation?

Control and Future Marketing Planning

The information gained during the control and monitoring process brings us full circle to the beginning of a new strategic marketing plan cycle. At the end of the current cycle, the company will have learned a great deal about the soundness of its strategies and objectives, the external and internal environments in which it operates, how well it adapts to unexpected problems or changes, and where it needs to be in the future if it is to maintain or increase its market share. This information can be used as the starting point for developing the next strategic marketing plan.

Well-planned and well-executed control and monitoring activities can also increase the knowledge and planning skills of the firm's strategists. They will be more experienced in using the plan and in responding to deviations from strategic goals and tactical action plans. The more active and imaginative the control measures, the more the firm's strategists will learn.

The two forms shown in the sample case will help you to establish a proactive control system to evaluate how well the company is meeting its marketing objectives.

Form 11, "Control and Monitoring," is designed to help you establish goals, standards or criteria, and tracking devices for your control and monitoring system. You should fill out a form for each of the key strategic objectives in your marketing plan.

Form 12, "Budget Deviation Analysis," can be used for monthly, quarterly, or yearly analysis to determine whether your budget is deviating from the plan.

Summary

- Many companies tend to limit their control and monitoring efforts to tracking financial reports. You should have control yardsticks for every strategic objective in your plan, a standard for evaluating progress toward that objective, and tracking devices to monitor progress and help you to determine the causes of any deviations.

- Control can be defined as the action steps taken to keep the firm directed toward its objectives and to bring its performance and its desired results closer together. Control activities involve monitoring departmental and individual actions and taking steps either to match performance with the desired results or to adjust the objectives to match attainable performance levels.

- Some companies are establishing a marketing controller position. This individual monitors marketing expenses and activities and informs management of any deviations from plan.

- An effective control system enables the marketing controller to detect when and where deviations from plan are occurring, determine the cause, and suggest corrective action.

- To achieve these aims, the controller needs yardsticks and comparative standards, a feedback or performance information system, diagnostic ability, an analytical system, and contingency plans and methods.

- A monitoring system can help a company know the extent to which the desired actions were actually implemented and how effective those actions were. The monitoring system has two main parts: a control and performance information system and a set of standards to interpret the information received.

- Corrective action involves these steps: (1) performance analysis to determine the difference between actual and planned performance, (2) diagnosis of any problems and their impact on the firm, and (3) action steps to correct problems.

- Information gained in the control and monitoring process is used as a starting point for the next strategic marketing planning cycle. Well-planned and well-executed control and monitoring activities can increase the knowledge and planning skills of the firm's strategists.

Sample Case, Phase 10

While the marketing team worked with the department heads and managers on their implementation steps, Harris formed a special four-member task force with the objective of developing a monitoring and control system.

He discovered in his research on Techna that the company had no formal system for checking on its progress toward its goals or for detecting deviations from planned strategies.

Harris outlined what an effective control system would enable the task force to do.

"First, it should allow you to detect when and where deviations from planned results are occurring. For instance, if the salesforce is making fewer sales after the e-commerce system is implemented, we need to take a look at what may be going wrong.

"Second, the system should enable you to determine the cause of the deviations from plan. Maybe communication lines between engineering and marketing have broken down.

"Third, you should be able to suggest ways to correct the situation and to bring activities back into line with the plan. If the problem involves more than one department—say, operations and finance—we may need to create an interdepartmental task force to handle the situation."

Harris explained to the members of the task force that they would develop yardsticks, standards, and tracking devices to monitor the firm's progress toward its marketing objectives and strategies. To establish these elements, the task force would work closely with department heads and product managers, creating a regular and systematic flow of information from the various departments to the control and monitoring task force. If the task force detected any deviation from plan, it would then alert the appropriate department or manager, determine the cause, and identify corrective action.

These procedures would build an ongoing performance information system for the firm that could be used to monitor all future marketing plans. The task force could ensure that yardsticks other than purely financial information would be used to monitor and control the company's progress.

Form 11 shows the yardsticks, control standards, and tracking devices that the task force and the product manager developed for Storage Extreme. Harris wanted the group to monitor this product carefully, since Storage Extreme was to be launched nationwide and globally.

Storage Extreme introduced its hard-disk drive amid a flurry of national advertising and promotional campaigns. By the time the new e-commerce system was in place, the company fully expected to realize its marketing objective of 11 percent market share per year.

The first three quarterly reports confirmed the most optimistic sales projections; the target consumer group was adopting the new product quickly, and the projected 11 percent market share figure was easily within reach. Early in the fourth quarter, however, the members of the monitoring task force noticed a small but significant drop in sales.

They checked with a few of Techna's customers who had yet to buy Storage Extreme and discovered that one of its major competitors was about to enter the market with its own version. The product was comparable to Storage Extreme, but would be priced $325 lower.

This development was a rude shock, as market research had predicted that this competitor would not be able to launch a comparable product until the second year of Techna's marketing campaign. By that time, Techna would have achieved at least a 22 percent share of the market.

Over the next few weeks, as the competitor's product penetrated the market, Techna management watched the company's market share slowly but steadily erode. The competing solid-state disk drive was similar enough to Techna's offering that many customers could not see the value of paying a higher price. Unless something was done quickly, Techna would fall far short of its projected 11 percent market share by the end of the year.

The task force recommended abandoning the original high-price, high-promotion strategy and adopting a lower-price, high-promotion approach. Management agreed, reduced Storage Extreme's price by $125, and shifted to the contingency strategy of product differentiation. The company emphasized Storage Extreme's quality features and superior engineering, made certain add-on features standard, designed a few changes in the product's appearance, and underscored Techna's strong customer service and support.

The new marketing campaign was designed to convince consumers that Techna's slightly higher price included far more value than the competition could offer. The lower price also meant that Techna could broaden its target markets and go after a wider range of customers.

The new strategy was clearly reflected in the budget, pushing up operating, G&A, and R&D expenses. Techna had to conduct additional market research, launch a new advertising campaign, broaden its e-commerce effort to reach the larger market, and seek out additional distribution channels to reach new customer segments. Techna was also seriously considering cutting back on its plans for global operations. The deviation from planned budget figures is shown in Form 12, "Budget Deviation Analysis."

Techna's control and monitoring system and its proactive strategic marketing plan enabled the company to detect and respond quickly to a sudden change in the external environment. Harris and his marketing team had devised an alternative strategy that took advantage of the company's reputation for quality and its high level of consumer acceptance to stop the decline in market share.

FORM 11
Control and Monitoring

Product: <u>Storage Extreme</u>   Date: <u>XX/XX/XX</u>

1. Goal/yardstick derived from marketing plan:

    1. Obtain a 17 percent market share within 18 months.
    2. Migrate 60 percent of current storage products to Storage Extreme within 18 months in order to keep or increase market share to our next level of product.
    3. Obtain a return on investment of 16 percent by the end of the first fiscal year.
    4. Have e-commerce in place in no later than 12 months.

2. Standards of control:

    1. Return on investment.
    2. View current customers instead of new customers to check whether they are migrating to Storage Extreme.
    3. Financial statement (both actual and pro forma) and current market share data.
    4. Sales to direct end users.

3. Tracking tools:

    1. EBITDA by product if possible or net income before interest and taxes by product
    2. Number of production runs on Storage Extreme
    3. Listing data on users of current products moving to Storage Extreme and listing data on new customers and segments of new customers
    4. Financial statements and actual sales results
    5. Marketing research

FORM 12
Budget Deviation Analysis

Product: <u>Storage Extreme</u>   Date: XX/XX/XX

<u>Profit or Loss as of 12/31/201X</u>

	Actual (A)	Budget (B)	Deviation (B − A)
Sales	$ 7,273,750	$ 9,090,750	$ 1,817,000
Cost of goods sold	4,364,250	5,454,450	1,090,200
Gross margin	$ 2,909,500	$ 3,636,300	$ 726,800
Operating expenses			
Advertising	$ 971,750	$ 727,950	$ (243,800)
Distribution	603,750	545,100	(58,650)
Market research	189,750	143,750	(46,000)
Salaries	201,250	241,500	40,250
Supplies	11,000	12,650	1,650
Computer	39,000	44,850	5,850
Miscellaneous	17,250	34,500	17,250
Total operating expenses	$ 2,033,750	$ 1,750,300	$ (283,450)
General and administrative expenses			
Rent	$ 19,838	$ 16,675	$ (3,163)
Salaries	112,125	85,388	(26,737)
Insurance	1,840	2,070	230
Depreciation	18,688	15,928	(2,760)
Computer supplies	3,400	3,913	513
General supplies	4,945	6,440	1,495
Miscellaneous	2,875	3,307	432
Total G&A expenses	$ 163,711	$ 133,721	$ (29,990)
Total expenses (operating & G&A)	$ 2,197,461	$ 1,884,021	$ (313,440)
Net profit (loss) before interest and taxes	$ 712,039	$ 1,752,279	$ 1,040,240

Index

About the Author

Robert J. Hamper worked for AT&T for more than 11 years in such areas as market analysis, marketing plan development, economic evaluation, marketing management, strategic planning, and financial management. He designed and implemented practical applications of portfolio theory and optimization modeling of resource allocation in the strategic marketing/planning process as well as developing the company's initial marketing plans.

Prior to working at AT&T, Robert worked at Bell Laboratories, where he developed several intricate financial/marketing models and applications. He also wrote testimonies to the Illinois Commerce Commission, the Federal Communications Commission, and the U.S. Justice Department. Robert is president of his own consulting firm, which specializes in strategic planning, and has been a consultant to Fortune 500 and midsized corporations for more than 19 years. He has been on several boards of directors and has also been court-appointed as a provisional director to oversee the restructuring of firms that are on the verge of bankruptcy.

He has been a full-time and adjunct professor in the Graduate School of Business at Dominican University and Loyola University of Chicago. He has presented papers in the fields of finance, marketing, and strategic planning to professional organizations. Robert has refereed marketing, economics, finance, and statistics texts for several major U.S. publishers. He holds a BSBA and an MBA degree from Illinois State University and is ABD at Northern Illinois University.